Housing Policy

An International
Bibliography

Housing Policy

An International Bibliography

Tony Newson

Mansell Publishing Limited

London and New York

First published 1986 by
Mansell Publishing Limited
(A subsidiary of The H. W. Wilson Company)
6 All Saints Street, London N1 9RL, England
950 University Avenue, Bronx, New York 10452, U.S.A.

British Library Cataloguing in Publication Data

Newson, Tony
    Housing policy: an international bibliography.
    1. Housing policy — Bibliography
    I. Title
    016.3635'8   Z7164.H8

    ISBN 0-7201-1785-2

Library of Congress Cataloging in Publication Data

Newson, Tony.
    Housing policy.

    Includes indexes.
    1. Housing policy — Bibliography.   I. Title.
Z7164.H8N48   1986   [HD7287]   016.3635'8   85-15598
ISBN 0-7201-1785-2

Printed in Great Britain by
Butler & Tanner Ltd, Frome and London

To my parents

Contents

Introduction

There are few people in the world for whom housing is not one of the basic necessities of life, reflecting man's aspiration to provide himself and his family with shelter, security, stability and a place to call 'home'. For centuries the means by which housing was acquired was left very much to the fortunes or initiative of individual people. In the past 100 years or so, however, responsibility for the provision of housing has increasingly been accepted by governments to such an extent that today virtually all housing activities are determined and controlled by government agencies. Increased government intervention in the housing market has provoked widespread debate on the policy alternatives which are available.

In the industrialized world, housing policies in different countries have developed in a variety of directions. The housing policy profile of one country may be completely different to those of its immediate neighbours. Much recent housing policy research has concentrated on identifying and describing basic underlying trends in housing provision which cross international boundaries, in addition to detailed research on the determinants of housing policy in individual countries. In the developing world, major international conferences such as the United Nations Conference on Human Settlements (Habitat) in 1976, have focussed attention on the problems of inadequate housing and uncontrolled settlements and the need for education and training in the management of human settlements. Concern with the plight of the homeless has prompted the United Nations to declare 1987 the International Year of the Homeless.

In this context there has inevitably been an increase in the quantity of published material on housing issues, which, especially since the early 1970s, has grown out of all proportion to the previous situation. This increase reflects the growing concern of governments, international organizations, research and academic institutions, pressure groups and the general public with housing policy issues. This bibliography, by selecting, classifying and listing over 3,000 of the more important contributions to the housing policy debate, attempts to provide an introduction to the literature of international housing polices. The literature of housing policy is diffuse and eclectic, emanating from a variety of sources and embracing a variety of disciplines. Although the study of housing policy draws on the disciplines of, for instance, architecture, town planning, construction, sociology and urban economics, housing policy here is defined in relatively narrow terms as the study of the formulation, implementation, monitoring and physical expression of housing decision making by organizations in ultimate control of the housing process. Where reference is made to related disciplines such as construction, it is only where they have immediate influence on, or are the immediate expression of, housing policy.

The bibliography thus represents, as far as the compiler is aware, the first attempt to draw together in one volume the most significant sources of information on international housing policies. Previous bibliographies tend to have concentrated on particular housing issues or geographical entities. This is a pioneering work in that it covers both international and comparative issues and detailed investigation of the circumstances of several individual countries. It includes references to other bibliographies and sources of information which will enable the user to identify further reading on topics of particular interest. In this way it should be of interest and value to housing professionals, academics, students, libraries and the interested layman in many parts of the world.

This bibliography does not claim to be totally comprehensive. Given the enormous quantity of published information available, such an aim would be impossible to achieve. Rather it is a selection of the most important and influential works on housing policy published in this century. Selection of items for inclusion has been based on the following criteria. Firstly, material must have been published in the English language or translated into

English. Secondly, material included must have been published and be easily accessible either in book form or in periodicals which are of sufficiently large circulation to be available in libraries internationally. Thirdly, material included is of major importance in its field in that it puts forward new arguments or ideas or consolidates existing material to provide an important review of a particular topic. Finally, although the bibliography is international in scope, approximately half the references refer exclusively to the British housing policy experience. For references to British housing issues, the bibliography is up to date to April 1985. For overseas housing issues the cut-off date is December 1984.

The bibliography is divided into 25 sections, each of which represents a major area of housing policy. Each section begins with a definition of the topic concerned, a brief discussion of its content and references to related sections. With each section the arrangement of entries is firstly by geographical areas; thus for each section there are usually subdivisions for international and comparative works, Europe, United Kingdom, North America, Australasia, and finally, Africa, Asia and Latin America. Within geographical areas the arrangement is by the name of author, or, where more than two authors are responsible for a work, it will be listed only under the first named author. Edited works follow a similar pattern. Where the work has no obvious author it will be listed under the title. Corporate author entries have been used for works with no personal author for which an organization or society has been responsible. Where this corporate author is an official department of government, the country name appears first. For example, publications from the Department of the Environment in the United Kingdom will appear under the author statement 'United Kingdom, Department of the Environment'.

Each entry contains full bibliographical information on the work cited. Where it is unclear from the title of the work what its content or format is, a brief annotation has been added to indicate its relevance, contents or conclusions. Such annotations appear for between one-third and one-half of the total number of entries. Each entry is preceded by a unique number, which enables the item to be isolated in the author and subject indexes appearing at the end of the bibliography.

To find entries in the bibliography the following procedure

should be followed. To find references on a particular subject the reader should refer either to the contents list at the beginning of the bibliography for a general outline of contents, or to the more specific subject index at the end, which will indicate the section under which a subject will appear. References to related topics can be found in the introduction to each section. To find an item by a particular author, reference should be made to the author index and thence to the main part of the bibliography. The number in the author index will refer to the unique number for the entry in the main text.

I am indebted to many people for their help in the preparation of this bibliography. I would like to thank former colleagues at the Centre for Urban and Regional Studies and the Institute of Local Government Studies at the University of Birmingham, especially Andy Thomas, for their advice and suggestions. To Philip Potter for his suggestions of European sources, to Jim Kemeny for Swedish references and to Peter Williams for references from Australia, I am also grateful. Thanks are also due to the Joint Centre Library and the Main Library at the University of Birmingham for the use of their resources and facilities. I would also like to thank Colin Hutchens of Mansell Publishing for his guidance and suggestions for improvement. Last but not least, my final thanks and gratitude go to Chris Jones for her patience, good humour and understanding in converting over 3,000 scrappy index cards into a workable manuscript.

Abbreviations

ACIR	Advisory Commission on Intergovernmental Relations
ACT	Australian Capital Territory
AIUS	Australian Institute of Urban Studies
ASCE	American Society of Civil Engineers
BC	British Columbia
BMRB	British Market Research Bureau
BNA	Bureau of National Affairs
BSA	Building Societies Association
Cd.	Command paper
CDP	Community Development Project
CES	Centre for Environmental Studies
CIB	International Council for Building Research Studies and Documentation
CIPFA	Chartered Institute of Public Finance and Accountancy
Cmd.	Command paper
CMHC	Canada Mortgage and Housing Corporation
Cmnd.	Command paper
CPL	Council of Planning Librarians
CRE	Commission for Racial Equality
CSE	Conference of Socialist Economists
CURS	Centre for Urban and Regional Studies
DHSS	Department of Health and Social Security
DOE	Department of the Environment
DTp	Department of Transport
EC	European Community
EEC	European Economic Community
ESRC	Economic and Social Research Council
FES	Family Expenditure Survey
FHA	Federal Housing Administration

GLC	Greater London Council
HC	House of Commons paper
HDD	Housing Development Directorate
HIP	Housing Investment Programme
HMSO	Her Majesty's Stationery Office
HUD	United States Department of Housing and Urban Development
IAHS	International Association of Housing Science
IFHP	International Federation of Housing and Planning
INLOGOV	Institute of Local Government Studies
ITCC	International Technical Co-operation Centre
LA	Local Authority
LCC	London County Council
MIT	Massachusetts Institute of Technology
NACRO	National Association for the Care and Resettlement of Offenders
NAHRO	National Association of Housing and Redevelopment Officials
NDHS	National Dwelling and Housing Survey
NEDA	National Economic Development Authority, Philippines
NFHA	National Federation of Housing Associations
NHIC	National Home Improvement Council
OECD	Organisation for Economic Co-operation and Development
OPCS	Office of Population Censuses and Surveys
RIBA	Royal Institute of British Architects
SDD	Scottish Development Department
SHAC	Shelter Housing Aid Centre
SS	Social Survey
SSRC	Social Science Research Council
UK	United Kingdom
UN	United Nations
UNECE	United Nations Economic Commission for Europe
US/USA	United States of America
USGPO	United States Government Printing Office
USSR	Union of Soviet Socialist Republics
WHO	World Health Organization

1

Housing policy: general works

This section includes works on general housing policy and collected works on various aspects of housing policy published together which defy classification in any of the more specialized following sections.

1.1 International and comparative

1   Abrams, C. *Housing in the modern world*. London, Faber, 1964.

2   Andersson, R. and Samartin, A. *Interdependence among housing, heating and transportation in cities*. Stockholm, Swedish Council for Building Research, 1979.

3   Bourne, L. S. *The geography of housing*. London, Edward Arnold, 1981.

4   Bryant, C. and White, L. G. 'Housing policies and comparative urban politics: Britain and the United States'. In J. Walton and L. H. Masotti (eds.) *The city in comparative perspective*. New York, Wiley, 1976. pp. 81–95.

5   Burns, L. S. et al. *Housing: symbol and shelter*. Los Angeles, University of California Press, 1970.
   Report prepared for the US Agency for International Development.

6   Burns, L. S. and Grebler, L. *The housing of nations: analysis and policy in a comparative framework*. London, Macmillan, 1977.

1

Attempts to link national housing strategies with policies for economic and social development. Wide ranging but eclectic.

7   Coppa, F. J. *Housing: a bibliographical overview.* Monticello, Vance Bibliographies, 1979. (Public administration series bibliography no. P-239).

8   Cox, K. R. and Johnston, R. J. (eds.) *Conflicts, politics and the urban scene.* Harlow, Longman, 1982.
Includes chapters by H. A. Morrow-Jones on the evolution of the US programme for subsidizing home ownership, and by Taylor and Hadfield on the popularity of different parts of the housing stock in Newcastle upon Tyne.

9   Deacon, B. *Social policy and socialism: the struggle for socialist relations of welfare.* London, Pluto Press, 1983.
Ch. 6 features comparative study of housing policies in socialist countries: USSR, China, Cuba, Hungary.

10   Engels, F. *Housing question.* Moscow, Progress Publications, 1979.
Nineteenth century prescriptions for the solution of housing problems.

11   Ettinger, J. V. 'Housing is the starting point'. *Ekistics* vol. 44 no. 261 (Aug. 1977) pp. 109–12.
Need for a world housing strategy to remedy future housing shortage.

12   Groak, S. and Koenigsberger, O. *Housing.* Oxford, Pergamon, 1980.

13   Gunlicks, A. (ed.) *Local government reform and reorganization.* Port Washington, NY, Kennikat Press, 1981.
Comparative international study of local government reform.

14   Hall, P. *The world's cities.* 3rd ed. London, Weidenfeld and Nicolson, 1984.
Discusses housing as an aspect of each city covered.

15   Headey, B. *Housing policy in the developed economy: the UK, Sweden and the US.* London, Croom Helm, 1978.

16   Heidenheimer, A. J. et al. *Comparative public policy: the politics of social choice in Europe and America.* London, Macmillan, 1983. Ch. 4 'Housing policy' (pp. 88–121) reviews UK and US housing policy.

17   Hill, D. M. *The planning and management of human settlements.* The Hague, International Union of Local Authorities, 1975.

18   'Home, house and shelter: quantities and qualities'. *Ekistics* vol. 51 no. 307 (July–Aug. 1984) pp. 284–390.
Special issue on housing and the homeless for UN International Year of Shelter for the Homeless 1987.

19   Kafandaris, S. 'Unanimous theories and consensus strategies: an assemblage of United Nations views on the housing question'. *Habitat International* vol. 4 no. 3 (1979) pp. 237–51.

20   Krapfenbauer, R. and Ural, 0. (eds.) *Housing: the impact of economy and technology: proceedings of the International Congress on Housing, Vienna, Austria, November 15–19, 1981.* New York, Pergamon, 1981. (Pergamon policy studies on urban and regional affairs).

21   Logie, G. *Glossary of population and housing.* Amsterdam, Elsevier, 1978. (International planning glossary no. 1).
Six-language glossary of housing terms containing over 800 entries.

22   McGuire, C. C. *International housing policies: a comparative analysis.* Lexington, Mass., Lexington Books, 1981.
Comparative but at times shallow study of institutional arrangements and housing finance in mainly western countries.

23   McLeay, E. M. 'Housing as a political issue: a comparative study'. *Comparative Politics* vol. 17 no. 1 (Oct. 1984) pp. 85–105.
Similarities and differences between the housing systems of Britain and New Zealand.

24   Macsai, J. *Housing.* 2nd ed. Chichester, Wiley, 1982.
Reference book on the design, building, financing and management of housing, including housing for the elderly and handicapped, with case studies.

25 Marcuse, P. 'The determinants of "housing policy"'. *Columbia University, Graduate School of Architecture and Planning, Papers in Planning* 22, 1980.
Role of housing in the political, economic and social structure, the conflicts and resultant determinants of policies affecting housing.

26 Marcuse, P. 'Determinants of state housing policies: West Germany and the United States'. In S. Fainstein and N. Fainstein (eds.) *Urban policy under capitalism.* Beverly Hills, Sage, 1982. pp. 83–115.

27 Mittelbach, F. G. *Housing policies and programs: international comparative dimensions.* Los Angeles, University of California, Graduate School of Management, 1974. (Housing, real estate and urban land studies reprint no. 64).

28 Muller, F. (ed.) *Inhabiting the earth as a finite world: an examination of the prospects of providing housing in a finite world in which prosperity is fairly shared, natural resources are not depleted, and the environment is protected.* Leiden, Nijhoff, 1979.
Results of the research group on living and surviving from the Academy of Architecture in Rotterdam, the National Higher Institute for Architecture and Town Planning in Antwerp, and the Erasmus University in Rotterdam.

29 Paulus, V. (ed.) *Housing: a bibliography 1960–72.* New York, AMS Press, 1980.

30 Pugh, C. *Housing in capitalist societies.* Aldershot, Gower, 1980.
Wide ranging and well referenced international and historical review of housing in the western world.

31 Rad, P. F. (ed.) *International Association for Housing Science International Symposium on Housing Problems: proceedings 1976.* 2 vols. Oxford, Pergamon, 1977.

32 Roistacher, E. A. 'A tale of two Conservatives: housing policy under Reagan and Thatcher'. *Journal of the American Planning Association* vol. 50 no. 4 (Autumn 1984) pp. 485–92.

Gains in efficiency are small when compared with increases in inequities in low income housing.

33   Rowat, D. C. (ed.) *International handbook on local government reorganisation: contemporary developments.* London, Aldwych Press, 1980.
Political context for housing policies in wide cross section of countries.

34   Smith, L. B. et al. 'The demand for housing, household headship rates, and household formation: an international analysis'. *Urban Studies* vol. 21 no. 4 (Nov. 1984) pp. 407–14.
Basic trends in household formation and headship rates in Canada, France, US and Britain examined.

35   Soules, G. *The housing crisis: causes, effects, solutions: long term solutions to the housing crisis in the western world.* Gordon Soules Economic and Marketing Research, 1976.

36   Stave, B. M. (ed.) *Modern industrial cities: history, policy and survival.* Beverly Hills, Sage, 1982. (Sage focus editions vol. 44).
Includes chapters on US housing policy 1918–68 and nineteenth century European housing reform.

37   Temby, W. *Housing policy in Australia and the United States.* Washington, DC, Department of Housing and Urban Development, 1983.

38   United Kingdom, Department of the Environment. *Housing policy.* London, HMSO, 1977. (Cmnd. 6851).
Technical vol. part III, chapter 11 'A review of foreign housing policies' (pp. 161–210). Studies of Australia, Canada, Denmark, Federal Republic of Germany, France, Netherlands, Sweden, US.

39   United Nations, Department of Economic and Social Affairs. *World housing conditions and estimated housing requirements.* New York, United Nations, 1965.

40   United Nations, Department of Economic and Social Affairs. *World housing survey 1974: an overview of the state of housing,*

5

building and planning within human settlements. New York, United Nations, 1976.

41   United Nations, Economic Commission for Europe. *Major trends in housing policy in ECE countries.* New York, United Nations, 1980.
Report by A. Andrzjewski and M. Lujanen. Comprehensive review of current housing problems and policies in Europe and North America; includes useful statistics.

42   Ural, O. (ed.) *Housing, planning, financing, construction: proceedings of the International Conference on Housing, Planning, Financing and Construction, December 2–7, 1979, Miami Beach, Florida.* 2 vols. New York, Pergamon, 1980.
Organized by Florida International University and the International Association for Housing Science. Study of North and South American housing issues.

43   Wendt, P. F. *Housing policy — the search for solutions: a comparison of the United Kingdom, Sweden, West Germany and the United States since World War II.* University of California, Institute of Business and Economic Research, 1962. Reprinted Westport, Conn., Greenwood Press, 1983.

44   Wheeler, M. (ed.) *The right to housing.* Montreal, Harvest House, 1969.

45   Wolman, H. L. *Housing and housing policy in the United States and the United Kingdom.* Lexington, Mass., Lexington Books, 1975.
Housing as a social service, public and private rental sector and role of local government.

46   Woltemade, U. J. 'Gimme shelter: the provision of housing'. *Public Management* vol. 58 (July 1976) pp. 7–12.
Compares housing policies in US and Western Europe.

1.2   Europe

47   Andrusz, G. D. *Housing and urban development in the USSR.* London, Macmillan in association with the Centre for Russian

and East European Studies, University of Birmingham, 1984.

48   Angotti, T. *Housing in Italy — urban development and political change*. New York, Praeger, 1977. (Praeger special studies).

49   Baker, T. J. and O'Brien, L. M. *The Irish housing system: a critical overview*. Dublin, Economic and Social Research Instutute, 1979. (Broadsheet no. 17).

50   Ball, M. et al (eds.) *Land rent, housing and urban planning: a European perspective*. London, Croom Helm, 1985.

51   Ball, M. and Harloe, M. *Housing policy in a socialist country: the case of Poland*. London, Centre for Environmental Studies, 1974.

52   Barlow, J. and Dickens, P. *Housing alliances and housing provision in Western Europe*. Brighton, University of Sussex, 1984. (Urban and regional studies working paper 42).

53   Barnes, K. 'Ireland's national housing programmes: a lesson in effective policy implementation'. *Journal of Housing* vol. 38 no. 8 (Aug.–Sept. 1981) pp. 444–51.
Public and private sector housing policy.

54   Barry, D. D. 'Housing in the USSR'. *Problems of Communism* vol. 18 (1969) pp. 1–11.

55   Blundell, C. 'Soviet housing: some impressions of its philosophy, standards and financing'. *Housing Review* vol. 28 no. 6 (Nov.–Dec. 1979) pp. 162–4.

56   Bullock, N. 'Housing in Frankfurt 1925 to 1931 and the new Wohnkultur'. *Architectural Review* vol. 163 no. 976 (June 1978) pp. 335–42.

57   Bullock, N. and Read, J. *The movement for housing reform in Germany and France: 1840–1914*. Cambridge University Press, 1985. (Cambridge urban and architectural studies 9).

58   Burtenshaw, D. et al. *The city in Western Europe*. Chichester, Wiley, 1981.

Includes chapter on housing.

59   Conroy, M. *Housing in the Republic of Ireland: a bibliography.* Dublin, National Institute for Physical Planning and Construction Research, 1979.
Includes some 200 entries, unfortunately not annotated.

60   Dandri, G. 'The evolution of the Italian housing situation from 1951 to 1978'. *Review of Economic Conditions in Italy* vol. 32 (Mar.–May 1978) pp. 137–52.

61   Del Nord, R. 'Housing policies USSR'. *Industrialization Forum* vol. 7 no. 4 (1976).
Housing shortage in the USSR: outline of finance and construction.

62   Dimaio, A. J. *Soviet urban housing: problems and policies.* New York, Praeger, 1974.

63   Duclaud-Williams, P. *The politics of housing in Britain and France.* London, Heinemann Educational, 1978.
Political science study examining the institutions and processes involved in housing policy making.

64   Einem, E. V. 'National urban policy: the case of West Germany'. *Journal of the American Planning Association* vol. 48 no. 1 (Winter 1982) pp. 9–23.

65   French, R. A. and Hamilton, F. I. (eds.) *The socialist city.* Chichester, Wiley, 1979.

66   Gallagher, P. 'Housing in Bulgaria'. *Housing Review* vol. 31 no. 4 (July–Aug. 1982) pp. 124–6.
Housing in a socialist republic where over eighty per cent of housing is owner occupied.

67   Gaspar, T. 'Housing in Hungary'. In J. S. Fuerst (ed.) *Public housing in Europe and America.* London, Croom Helm, 1974. pp. 126–33.

68   Giertz, A. 'Housing policy in Poland: its social and economic problems'. In United Nations, Economic Commission for

Europe. *Management, maintenance and modernization of housing.*
New York, United Nations, 1969.

69 Ginatempo, N. and Cammarota, A. 'Land and social conflict
in the cities of Southern Italy: an analysis of the housing question
in Messina'. In M. Harloe (ed.) *Captive cities: studies in the political
economy of cities and regions.* Chichester, Wiley, 1977. pp. 111–22.

70 Goldfield, D. R. 'National urban policy in Sweden'. *Journal of
the American Planning Association* vol. 48 no. 1 (Winter 1982) pp.
24–38.
The context for housing policy.

71 Grant, S. A. (ed.) *Soviet housing and urban design.* Washington,
DC, Department of Housing and Urban Development, 1980.

72 Greater London Council, Library. *Urban housing in Western
Europe.* London, GLC Research Library, 1978. (Research bibliography 102).

73 Grinberg, D. *Housing in the Netherlands 1900–40.* Delft
University Press, 1982.

74 Hallett, G. *Housing and land policies in West Germany and
Britain: a record of success and failure.* London, Macmillan, 1977.
Very good study on the housing policies of the Federal
Republic, but less useful on Britain.

75 Harloe, M. 'Current trends in housing policy: some European comparisons'. *Royal Society of Health Journal* vol. 100 no. 6
(Dec. 1980) pp. 207–13.

76 Hass-Klau, C. H. M. 'The housing shortage in Germany's
major cities'. *Built Environment* vol. 8 no. 1 (1982) pp. 60–70.

77 *Housing in the Nordic countries.* 2nd ed. Copenhagen, 1968.
Prepared by the ministries responsible for housing policy in
Denmark, Finland, Norway, Sweden and Iceland.

78 Ireland, Department of the Environment. *Current trends and
policies in the fields of housing, building and planning.* Dublin, The
Department, 1979.

79   Johannsson, I. V. and Sveinsson, J. R. 'Housing in Iceland: inflation helps those who help themselves?' *Acta Sociologica* vol. 24 no. 4 (1981) pp. 223–37.
Urbanization, housing market and finance.

80   King, J. C. 'Housing in Spain'. *Town Planning Review* vol. 42 no. 4 (Oct. 1971) pp. 381–403.

81   League of Nations, Economic Intelligence Unit. *Urban and rural housing*. Geneva, The League, 1939.

82   Louie, F. *Housing in Western Europe*. Monticello, Vance Bibliographies, 1978. (Public administration series bibliography no. P140).

83   Mandelker, D. R. 'Planning and housing in the Yugoslav Republic of Slovenia'. *Urban Law and Policy* vol. 4 no. 4 (Dec. 1981) pp. 357–72.
Workings of the decentralized Yugoslav federal system.

84   Marmot, A. F. 'Polish housing'. *Housing Review* vol. 30 no. 6 (Nov.–Dec. 1981) pp. 180–2.
Various reasons for Poland's housing crisis.

85   Mingione, E. *Social conflict and the city*. Oxford, Blackwell, 1981.
Includes discussion of the housing problems of large cities in Europe.

86   Morton, H. W. 'Who gets what, when and how? Housing in the Soviet Union'. *Soviet Studies* vol. 32 (Apr. 1980) pp. 235–59.

87   Morton, H. W. 'What have the Soviet leaders done about the housing crisis?' In H. W. Morton and R. L. Tokes (eds.) *Soviet politics and society in the 1970s*. New York, Free Press, 1974. pp. 163–99.

88   Musgrave, S. 'Housing in Czechoslovakia'. *Housing Review* vol. 33 no. 3 (May–June 1984) pp. 91–3.

89   Musil, J. 'The housing situation and problems in Czechoslo-

vakia'. In A. A. Nevitt (ed.) *The economic problems of housing.* New York, St. Martins Press, 1967. pp. 176–88.

90   Power, A. 'France, Holland, Belgium and Germany, a look at their housing problems and policies'. *Habitat* vol. 1 no. 1 (June 1976) pp. 81–103.

91   Rapoport, A. 'Housing and housing densities in France'. *Town Planning Review* vol. 40 no. 1 (Jan. 1969) pp. 341–54.

92   Sanne, C. 'Alternative scenarios for the future of housing in the Nordic countries'. *Ekistics* vol. 51 no. 307 (July–Aug. 1984) pp. 302–8.

93   Sawicki, S. J. *Soviet land and housing law: a historical and comparative study.* New York, Praeger, 1977. (Praeger special studies in international politics and government).

94   Searing, H. 'Amsterdam south: social democracy's elusive housing ideal'. *Via* vol. 4 (1980) pp. 58–77.
Early twentieth century housing schemes in Amsterdam.

95   Smith, W. S. 'Housing in the Soviet Union — big plans, little action'. In *Soviet economic prospects for the seventies.* Washington, DC, Government Printing Office, 1973. pp. 404–27.

96   Stratmann, M. 'Housing policies in the Weimar Republic'. *Architectural Association Quarterly* vol. 11 no. 1 (1979) pp. 16–23.

97   Suzuki, P. T. 'Urban planning and housing policies in the Netherlands'. *Habitat* vol. 6 no. 3 (1982) pp. 387–93.

98   Svenson, G. 'Origins and development of housing policy in Sweden'. *Habitat International* vol. 4 no. 3 (1979) pp. 363–71.

99   Sweden, Ministry of Housing and Physical Planning. *Swedish experiences of self-building, co-operation, consumer research, participation.* Stockholm, The Ministry, 1976.
Contribution to the Habitat Conference, Vancouver, 1976.

100   Szelenyi, I. *Urban inequalities under state socialism.* Oxford University Press, 1983. (Library of political economy).
Part 1 'Housing and social structure' (pp. 19–95) includes

discussion of the Hungarian housing system and housing policies in Eastern Europe.

101   United Nations, Economic Commission for Europe. *Human settlements in Europe: post-war trends and policies*. New York, United Nations, 1976.
Prepared as a contribution to the Habitat Conference, Vancouver, 1976.

102   Weesep, J. Van. 'Intervention in the Netherlands: urban housing policy and market response'. *Urban Affairs Quarterly* vol. 19 no. 3 (Mar. 1984) pp. 329–53.

103   White, P. M. *Soviet urban and regional planning: a bibliography with abstracts*. London, Mansell, 1979.
Contains section on housing.

104   Wild, T. (ed.) *Urban and rural change in West Germany*. London, Croom Helm, 1983.
Includes discussion of residential environments in German cities.

105   Winter, G. 'Housing in West Germany: legal instruments and economic structure'. In M. Partington and J. Jowell (eds.) *Welfare law and policy: studies in teaching, practice and research*. London, Pinter, 1979.

106   Wynn, M. (ed.) *Housing in Europe*. London, Croom Helm, 1983.

107   Zetter, R. *Housing policy and social change in Cyprus 1960–1980*. Oxford Polytechnic, Department of Town Planning, 1981. (Working paper 56).

108   Zetter, R. 'Housing policy in Cyprus: a review'. *Habitat International* vol. 6 no. 4 (1982) pp. 471–86.

1.3   United Kingdom

109   Aldridge, T. *The Housing Act 1980: as amended by the Housing and Building Control Act 1984*. London, Oyez Longman, 1984.

110   Aldridge, T. M. *The Housing Act 1980: a practical guide.* London, Oyez, 1980.

111   Arden, A. *The Housing Act 1980.* London, Sweet and Maxwell, 1980. (Current law statutes reprints).

112   Arden, A. *Manual of housing law.* 2nd ed. London, Sweet and Maxwell, 1983.

113   Arden, A. and Cross, C. *The Housing and Building Control Act 1984.* London, Sweet and Maxwell, 1984.

114   Arden, A. and Partington, M. *Housing law.* London, Sweet and Maxwell, 1983.

115   Association of Metropolitan Authorities. *Housing in the eighties: an analysis of prospects in the public and private sectors.* London, The Association, 1980.

116   Balchin, P. N. *Housing policy: an introduction.* London, Croom Helm, 1984.

117   Balchin, P. N. *Housing policy and housing needs.* London, Macmillan, 1981.
More on policy than needs; intended as an undergraduate text.

118   Becker, A. P. 'Housing in England and Wales during the business depression of the 1930s'. *Economic History Review.* 2nd series vol. 3 no. 3 (1951) pp. 321–41.

119   Berry, F. *Housing: the great British failure.* Croydon, Knight, 1974.

120   Bowley, M. *Housing and the state 1919–1944.* London, Allen and Unwin, 1945.
Remains a classic account of inter-war government housing policies.

121   Burnett, D. 'Housing: social service or market good'. In H. Elcock (ed.) *What sort of society: economic and social policy in modern Britain.* Oxford, Martin Robertson, 1982. pp. 116–34.

Policy alternatives for British housing.

122   Clarke, J. J. *The housing problem: its history, growth, legislation and procedure.* London, Pitman, 1920.

123   Clements, J. *Polls, politics and populism.* Aldershot, Gower, 1983.
Ch. 9 (pp. 71–6) reviews opinion polls on housing and assesses housing as an issue in the 1983 British General Election.

124   Cochrane, R. G. A. *Law of housing in Scotland.* Glasgow, Hodge, 1977.

125   Conway, J. *Capital decay.* London, SHAC, 1984. (Research report 37).
Analysis of London's housing crisis.

126   Cramond, R. D. *Housing policy in Scotland 1919–1964: a study in state assistance.* Edinburgh, Oliver and Boyd, 1966. (Glasgow University social and economic studies research paper no. 1).

127   Cullingworth, J. B. *Essays on housing policy: the British scene.* London, Allen and Unwin, 1979.
Collection of essays on various aspects of British housing policy.

128   Cullingworth, J. B. *Housing and local government in England and Wales.* London, Allen and Unwin, 1966.
Useful now as an account of housing policy in Britain during the 1960s.

129   Cullingworth, J. B. 'Housing policy: the conundrums of implementation'. *Urban Law and Policy* vol. 1 no. 3 (July 1978) pp. 197–228.
Problems of construction and implementation of national housing policies with particular reference to Britain.

130   Ditch, N. 'Northern Ireland'. *Roof* vol. 6 no. 2 (Mar.–Apr. 1981) pp. 16–18.

Background to Northern Ireland's housing problems.

131   Donnison, D. V. *The government of housing*. London, Pelican, 1967.
Classic introduction to housing as an area of study in its time, now largely superseded by no. 134.

132   Donnison, D. and Eversley, D. C. (eds.) *London: urban patterns, problems and policies*. London, Heinemann, 1973.
Includes several essays on London's housing problems.

133   Donnison, D. and Maclennan, D. 'What should we do about housing?' *New Society* vol. 72 no. 1163 (11 Apr. 1985) pp. 43–6.
Discusses, in the context of reductions in public expenditure and increases in owner occupation in the UK, what a fair housing policy should consist of.

134   Donnison, D. and Ungerson, C. *Housing policy*. London, Penguin, 1982.
Revised and updated version of Donnison's widely used student text (no. 131). Useful sections on international issues but concentrates mainly on the UK.

135   Douglas-Mann, B. 'Select scrutiny of housing policy'. *Roof* vol. 5 no. 4 (July–Aug. 1980) p. 128.
Review of the role of the House of Commons Environment Committee by its then chairman.

136   Draper, P. *Creation of the DOE*. London, HMSO, 1977. (Civil Service studies 4).
Interesting account of the foundation of the British department of government responsible for housing.

137   Ellender, P. *Housing in Britain: a select list relating to housing in Britain based on the material contained in the DOE/DTp Bulletin (1976–78)*. London, Department of the Environment, 1979. (Bibliography series 132).
Forms a supplement to no. 198. Represents a comprehensive, annotated introduction.

138   Elsas, M. J. *Housing before the war and after*. London, Staples Press, 1942.

Looks back to the progress made between 1918 and 1939, reviews the damage caused during the war and anticipates the problems of the post-war period.

139 *Encyclopaedia of housing law and practice.* London, Sweet and Maxwell.
Continuous, regularly updated, looseleaf reference source for the law of housing.

140 Ermisch, J. 'Housing in the eighties: demographic impetus and policy response'. *Policy Studies* vol. 2 no. 1 (July 1981) pp. 34–48.

141 Fleming, M. and Nellis, J. 'A new housing crisis?' *Lloyds Bank Review* no. 144 (Apr. 1982) pp. 38–53.
Development of housing policy up to the mid-1970s and work on demand and need following the Housing Policy Review.

142 Foster, C. D. 'Housing in the conurbations'. In G. C. Cameron (ed.) *The future of the British conurbations: policies and prescriptions for change.* Harlow, Longman, 1980. pp. 125–45.

143 Fox, D. 'Central control and local capacity in the housing field'. In K. Young (ed.) *National interests and local government.* London, Heinemann,1983. pp. 82–104.
Includes comment by A. Murie (pp. 101–4).

144 Fraser, D. and Sutcliffe, A. (eds.) *The pursuit of urban history.* London, Edward Arnold, 1983.
Historical perspectives on housing.

145 Goldsmith, M. *Politics, planning and the city.* London, Hutchinson, 1980.
Ch. 6 'Policy arena 1: housing' (pp. 109–25) analyses the ways in which government policies affect local service provision.

146 Gray, P. G. and Russell, R. *The housing situation in 1960.* London, HMSO, 1962.
Government social survey into housing and structural conditions in England and Wales.

147 Hall, P. 'Housing, planning, land and local finance: the British experience'. *Urban Law and Policy* vol. 6 no. 1 (June 1983) pp. 75–86.
Assesses the extent of policy changes under the Thatcher government.

148 Harloe, M. et al. *The organisation of housing: public and private enterprise in London.* London, Heinemann, 1974. (Centre for Environmental Studies series).

149 Hoath, D. C. and Brown, A. A. *Main changes in housing law 1977–1980.* London, Housing Centre Trust, 1981.
Supplement to no. 191.

150 Hoppé, M. et al. *Home truths.* London, Social Affairs Unit, 1983. (Agenda for debate no. 3).
Right-wing prescriptions for solving housing problems.

151 Houlihan, B. 'The professionalisation of housing policy making: the impact of housing investment programmes and professionals'. *Public Administration Bulletin* no. 41 (Mar. 1983) pp. 14–31.

152 Houlihan, B. 'The regional offices of the DOE — policemen or mediators? A study of local housing policy'. *Public Administration* vol. 62 (Winter 1984) pp. 401–21.
Within the framework of the regional state, discusses DOE local involvement in housing investment programmes.

153 *Housing Year Book.* Harlow, Longman, annual.
Invaluable reference work for British housing policy. First published 1983.

154 Institute of Housing. *Yearbook.* London, annual.
Useful source of information on British housing from the foremost British education and training organization.

155 Johnston, A. 'Metropolitan housing policy and strategic planning in the West Midlands'. *Town Planning Review* vol. 53 no. 2 (Apr. 1982) pp. 179–99.

156   Keating, M. and Midwinter, A. *The government of Scotland.*
Edinburgh, Mainstream Publishing, 1983.
Ch. 8 'Housing policy making' (pp. 157–68).

157   Kirby, D. A. 'Housing'. In M. Pacione (ed.) *Progress in human geography.* London, Croom Helm, 1983. pp. 7–44.

158   Lambert, J. et al. *Housing policy and the state: allocation, access and control.* London, Macmillan, 1978.
Includes a case study of allocation policy in Birmingham from the perspective of applicants.

159   Lansley, S. *Housing and public policy.* London, Croom Helm, 1979.

160   Leather, P. 'Housing and public policy: a review article'. *Policy and Politics* vol. 9 no. 2 (1981) pp. 227–33.

161   Lomnicki, A. J. *Housing, tenancy and planning law made simple.* London, Heinemann, 1981.
Concise review and introductory student text of law applied to housing, incorporating changes made in the Housing Act 1980.

162   Lundqvist, L. J. and Wiktorin, M. *Current trends in British housing: proceedings of a British–Swedish workshop on current housing policy research.* Gavle, National Swedish Institute for Building Research, 1983.

163   McKay, D. H. and Cox, A. W. *The politics of urban change.* London, Croom Helm, 1979.
Ch. 4 (pp. 107–58) considers housing and slum clearance.

164   Maclennan, D. and Wood, G. A. *Housing policy and research in Scotland.* Aberdeen University Press, 1978.

165   Malpass, P. and Murie, A. *Housing policy and practice.* London, Macmillan, 1982. (Public policy and politics).
Analyses the relationship between the central and local state in housing policy with local case studies.

166   Maxwell, K. *Joint initiatives in housing between the public and private sectors.* Glasgow, Planning Exchange, 1983. (Occasional paper no. 10).

167   Melling, J. (ed.) *Housing, social policy and the state.* London, Croom Helm, 1980.
Collection of essays on housing policy on the inter-war period from a Marxist perspective.

168   Midwinter, A. et al. 'The politics of Scottish housing plans'. *Policy and Politics* vol. 12 no. 2 (Apr. 1984) pp. 145–66.

169   Murie, A. *Housing policy and the inner city.* University of Bristol, School for Advanced Urban Studies, 1981. (Working paper no. 12).

170   Murie, A. 'Not so much a policy ...?' In P. M. Jackson (ed.) *Government policy initiatives 1979–80: some case studies in public administration.* London, Royal Institute of Public Administration, 1981. pp. 144–60.

171   Murie, A. et al. *Housing policy and the housing system.* London, Allen and Unwin, 1976.
Standard text which analyses the housing system as inter-relationships between various tenures.

172   National Federation of Housing Associations. *Inquiry into British housing: the evidence.* London, The Federation, 1985.
First report of the Committee chaired by the Duke of Edinburgh.

173   Nevitt, A. 'British housing policy'. *Journal of Social Policy* vol. 7 no. 3 (July 1978) pp. 329–34.
Critical review of no. 201.

174   Nevitt, A. A. 'Housing in a welfare state'. *Urban Studies* vol. 14 no. 1 (Feb. 1977) pp. 33–40.
Incrementalist housing policies have not always been consistent with welfare policies in the UK.

175   Newson, T. *A housing bibliography.* University of Birm-

ingham, Centre for Urban and Regional Studies, 1982. (Research memorandum 92).
Updates no. 195 to middle of 1982.

176 Newson, T. and Potter, P. *Housing policy in Britain: an information sourcebook.* London, Mansell, 1985.

177 Niner, P. and Watson, C. J. 'Housing in British cities'. In D. T. Herbert and R. J. Johnston (eds.) *Urban geography: prospect and retrospect.* Chichester, Wiley, 1978. (Geography and the urban environment vol. 1).

178 Niven, D. *The development of housing in Scotland.* London, Croom Helm, 1979.

179 Norton, M. *Housing.* London, Wildwood House, 1981. (Directory of social change vol. 4).
Alternative guide to housing information sources.

180 Pacione, M. 'Housing policies in Glasgow since 1880'. *Geographical Review* vol. 69 no. 4 (Oct. 1979) pp. 395–412.

181 Paris, C. and Lambert, J. 'Housing problems and the state: the case of Birmingham, England'. In D. T. Herbert and R. J. Johnston (eds.) *Geography and the urban environment: progress in research and applications 2.* Chichester, Wiley, 1979. pp. 227–58.

182 Prentice, R. 'Housing in the Isle of Man'. *Housing Review* vol. 33 no. 6 (Nov.–Dec. 1984) pp. 242–6.
Comparison with the UK.

183 Rollett, C. 'Housing'. In A. H. Halsey (ed.) *Trends in British society since 1900: a guide to the changing social structure of Britain.* London, Macmillan, 1972. pp. 284–320.
Contains valuable statistical information.

184 Royal Institute of British Architects. *Homes old and new: a housing strategy for the eighties.* London, The Institute, 1983.

185 Russell, J. L. *Housing amidst civil unrest.* London, Centre for Environmental Studies, 1980. (Research series no. 41).

Investigates Northern Ireland's housing problems against the background of disorder.

186 Seyd, P. 'Shelter'. *Political Quarterly* vol. 46 no. 4 (Oct.–Dec. 1975) pp. 418–31.
Assesses Shelter's aims, objects and organization as a housing pressure group.

187 Shelter. *Build homes, build hope: a report on Britain's mounting housing crisis.* London, 1981.

188 Short, J. R. *Housing in Britain: the post-war experience.* London, Methuen, 1982.
Concise and clear account of housing policy, unfortunately poorly referenced.

189 Short, J. R. and Bassett, K. A. 'Housing policy and the inner city in the 1970s'. *Institute of British Geographers Transactions* vol. 6 no. 3 (1981) pp. 293–312.

190 Sills, A. et al. *Housing and the inner city.* 2 vols. University of Leicester, Centre for Mass Communication Research, 1982.
Study of housing conditions in Leicester.

191 Smith, M. *A guide to housing.* 2nd ed. London, Housing Centre Trust, 1977.
Leading single volume introduction to British housing policy.

192 Smith, P. F. *Housing Act 1980.* London, Butterworths, 1981.

193 Stafford, D. C. 'Housing policy: efficiency and equity'. *Social Policy and Administration* vol. 13 no. 1 (Spring 1979) pp. 37–52.
General review of UK housing policy.

194 Stafford, D. C. 'Housing policy: objectives and strategies'. In R. A. B. Leaper (ed.) *Health, wealth and housing.* Oxford, Blackwell, 1980. pp. 71–94.

195 Stewart, J. M. et al. *A housing bibliography.* University of Birmingham, Centre for Urban and Regional Studies, 1980. (Research memorandum 84).

Bibliography containing 2,000 entries of significant British housing material up to 1980.

196 Taylor, G. H. *A review of housing in London 1966–1976.* Greater London Council, 1978. (Research memorandum 534). Summarizes the development of GLC housing policy, its administration and the recommendations of various committees.

197 Thomas, R. 'Housing trends and urban growth'. In P. Hall et al. *The containment of urban England vol. 2.* London, Allen and Unwin, 1973. pp. 246–94.

198 Thompson, M. *Housing.* London, Department of the Environment Library, 1975. (Bibliography series 132). Covers material published up to 1975 and is updated by no. 137.

199 United Kingdom, Department of the Environment. *Change or decay.* London, HMSO, 1977. Final report of the Liverpool Inner Area Study.

200 United Kingdom, Department of the Environment. *Fair deal for housing.* London, HMSO, 1971. (Cmnd. 4728).

201 United Kingdom, Department of the Environment. *Housing policy: a consultative document.* London, HMSO, 1977. (Cmnd. 6851). Conclusions of the Housing Policy Review accompanied by three technical volumes.

202 United Kingdom, Department of the Environment. *Inner London: policies for dispersal and balance.* London, HMSO, 1977. Final report of the Lambeth Inner Area Study.

203 United Kingdom, Department of the Environment. *Policy for the inner cities.* London, HMSO, 1977. (Cmnd. 6845). Resources to be concentrated on inner cities at the expense of new towns.

204 United Kingdom, Department of the Environment. *Unequal city.* London, HMSO, 1977.

Final report of the Birmingham Inner Area Study.

205   United Kingdom, Department of the Environment. *Widening the choice: the next step in housing.* London, HMSO, 1973. (Cmnd. 5280).

206   United Kingdom, Departments of the Environment and Transport Library. *Housing publications 1971–81.* London, 1983. Useful listing of publications of government department responsible for housing policy in England and Wales.

207   United Kingdom, Departments of the Environment and Transport Library. *Sources of information on housing.* London, 1979. (Information series).
Useful guide to sources, unfortunately never updated.

208   United Kingdom, Ministry of Housing and Local Government. *Houses — the next step.* London, HMSO, 1953. (Cmd. 8996).

209   United Kingdom, Ministry of Housing and Local Government. *Housing.* London, HMSO, 1963. (Cmnd. 2050).

210   United Kingdom, Ministry of Housing and Local Government. *Housing in England and Wales.* London, HMSO, 1961. (Cmnd. 1290).

211   United Kingdom, Ministry of Housing and Local Government. *The housing programme 1965 to 1970.* London, HMSO, 1965. (Cmnd. 2838).
Includes useful housing statistics and recommends the establishment of house condition surveys.

212   United Kingdom, National Economic Development Office. *Housing for all: a document for discussion.* London, HMSO, 1977.

213   United Kingdom, Northern Ireland Housing Executive. *Housing problems.* Belfast, HMSO, 1974.

214   United Kingdom, Scottish Development Department. *Homes for people: Scottish housing policy in the 1970s.* Edinburgh, HMSO, 1973. (Cmnd. 5272).

215   United Kingdom, Scottish Development Department. *Scot-*

tish housing: a consultative document. Edinburgh, HMSO, 1977.
(Cmnd. 6852).
Scottish equivalent of the Housing Policy Review.

216   United Kingdom, Scottish Development Department. *The Scottish housing programme 1965 to 1970.* Edinburgh, HMSO, 1965. (Cmnd. 2837).

217   Ward, C. *Housing is theft, housing is freedom.* Nottingham, Old Hammond Press, 1984.

218   Watson, C. J. 'The housing question'. In G. E. Cherry (ed.) *Urban planning problems.* London, Leonard Hill, 1974.

219   Weir, S. 'Housing'. In R. Delbridge and M. Smith (eds.) *Consuming secrets: how official secrecy affects everyday life in Britain.* London, Burnett Books, 1982. pp. 42–67.
Reviews three case histories (1977 Housing Policy Review, 1979 public expenditure white paper, and council house sales) to assess the limitations of access to official information.

220   Whitehead, C. 'Housing under the Conservatives: a policy assessment'. *Public Money* vol. 3 no. 1 (June 1983) pp. 15–21.

221   Woolf, M. *The housing survey in England and Wales 1964.* London, HMSO, 1967.
Government social survey report.

222   Yates, D. 'The English housing experience: an overview'. *Urban Law and Policy* vol. 5 no. 3 (Sept. 1982) pp. 203–33.

223   Young, K. and Kramer, J. *Strategy and conflict in metropolitan housing.* London, Heinemann, 1978.
Party political and professional struggles between the GLC and the inner and outer London boroughs, including housing issues in the period 1964–77.

1.4   North America

224   Adams, J. S. 'The meaning of housing in America'. *Annals of the Association of American Geographers* vol. 74 no. 4 (Dec. 1984)

pp. 515–26.
Presidential address.

225 'An analysis and review of housing and community development legislation'. *Journal of Housing* vol. 38 (Dec. 1981) pp. 589–600.
Review of housing legislation in the US.

226 Bleakly, K. D. *A case study of local control over housing development: the Neighborhood Area Strategy Demonstration.* Washington, DC, Department of Housing and Urban Development, 1983.

227 Bradbury, K. L. et al. *Urban decline and the future of American cities.* Washington, DC, Brookings Institution, 1982.

228 Canada Mortgage and Housing Corporation. *The performance of housing: Canadian experience in studying it and putting the results into effect.* Ottawa, The Corporation, 1981.
Prepared for the Canada – Japan Housing Committee, Tokyo, June 1981.

229 Carver, H. *Houses for Canadians: a study of housing problems in the Toronto area.* University of Toronto Press, 1948.

230 Casper, D. E. *Housing and community development: recent writings 1980–1983.* Monticello, Vance Bibliographies, 1985. (Architecture series bibliography A1347).

231 Checkoway, B. 'Large builders, federal housing programmes and post war suburbanization'. *International Journal of Urban and Regional Research* vol. 4 no. 1 (1980) pp. 21–45.

232 Connolly, E. 'Refugee influx highlights emergency housing problems'. *Journal of Housing* vol. 38 no. 1 (Jan. 1981) pp. 21–4.

233 De Hancock, T. M. 'Foreign urban experiences are traced by HUD to spot ideas that can be adapted to the United States'. *Journal of Housing* vol. 35 (Dec. 1978) pp. 578–81.

234 Devito, A. P. 'Fantasia on familiar housing themes'. *Urban Law and Policy* vol. 5 no. 4 (Dec. 1982) pp. 333–46.

Basic objectives of US housing policy.

235   Dumouchel, J. R. *Dictionary of development terminology: the technical language of builders, lenders, architects and planners, investors, real estate brokers and attorneys, appraisers, land taxing and zoning authorities, government officials, community organisers, housing managers, urban renewal specialists.* New York, McGraw-Hill, 1975.

236   Duncan, B. and Hauser, P. M. *Housing a metropolis — Chicago.* Glencoe, Free Press, 1960.

237   Egan, J. J. et al. *Housing and public policy: a role for mediating structures.* Cambridge, Mass., Ballinger, 1981. (American Enterprise Institute book).

238   Ellickson, R. C. 'Suburban growth controls: an economic and legal analysis'. *Yale Law Journal* vol. 86 (Jan. 1977) pp. 385–511.
Legal rights of housing consumers in US suburbia.

239   Epstein, A. K. 'Multifamily dwellings and the search for respectability: origins of the New York apartment house'. *Urbanism Past and Present* vol. 5 no. 2 (Summer 1980) pp. 29–39.

240   Everett, R. O. and Johnston, J. D. *Housing.* Dobbs Ferry, NY, Oceana Publications, 1968. (Library of law and contemporary problems).
US housing: Part 1 'Perspective and problems'; Part 2 'The federal role'.

241   Fernsler, J. P. et al. 'Historical perspectives, current trends and future roles in housing and community development'. *Urban Lawyer* vol. 16 no. 4 (Autumn 1984) pp. 683–700.

242   Fishman, R. P. (ed.) *Housing for all: new directions in housing, land use and planning law.* Cambridge, Mass., Ballinger, 1978.
Federal state and local measures to promote neighbourhood improvement in US cities.

243   Frej, W. and Specht, H. 'The Housing and Community Development Act of 1974: implications for policy and planning'. *Social Service Review* vol. 50 (June 1976) pp. 275–92.

244   Fried, J. P. *Housing crisis USA.* New York, Praeger, 1971.

245   Frieden, B. and Solomon, A. P. *The nation's housing 1975–85.* Cambridge, Mass., MIT Joint Centre for Urban Studies and Harvard University, 1977.

246   Fuerst, J. S. and Petty, R. 'Bleak housing in Chicago'. *Public Interest* no. 52 (Summer 1978) pp. 103–10.
Housing problems in Chicago: lack of public housing construction and opening up of suburbs to blacks.

247   Goetze, R. *Rescuing the American dream: public policies and the crisis in housing.* New York, Holmes and Meier, 1983.

248   Goldberg, M. A. and Mark, J. H. 'The roles of government in housing policy: a Canadian perspective and overview'. *Journal of the American Planning Association* vol. 51 no. 1 (Winter 1985) pp. 34–42.
Roles of four levels of government in the housing sector in Canada and a comparison with the US system.

249   Gray, C. *The St. Lawrence neighbourhood in Toronto: an analysis of municipal housing policy.* University of Toronto, Department of Urban and Regional Planning, 1979. (Papers on planning and design no. 22).

250   Grigsby, W. G. et al. *Re-thinking housing and community development.* Philadelphia, University of Pennsylvania, Department of City and Regional Planning, 1977.

251   Grigsby, W. G. and Rosenburg, L. *Urban housing policy.* New Brunswick, Rutgers University, Centre for Urban Policy Research, 1975.
Includes analysis of data from Baltimore.

252   Handlin, D. P. 'Housing and city planning in the United States 1910–1945'. *Martin Centre for Architectural and Urban Studies Transactions* vol. 1 (1976) pp. 317–44.

253   Hartman, C. W. (ed.) *America's housing crisis: what is to be done?* Boston, Routledge and Kegan Paul, 1983. (Alternative policies for America).

254 Hartman, C. W. *Housing and social policy.* Englewood Cliffs, Prentice-Hall, 1975. (Prentice-Hall series in social policy). Introduction to American housing policy issues.

255 Hartman, C. and Stone, M. 'Housing: a radical alternative'. In M. Raskin (ed.) *The federal budget and social reconstruction.* New Brunswick, Transaction Books, 1978. pp. 205–48.

256 Hartman, C. and Stone, M. E. 'A socialist housing program for the United States'. In P. Claval (ed.) *Urban and regional planning in an age of austerity.* New York, Pergamon, 1980. pp. 219–41.

257 Hayden, D. *Redesigning the American dream: the future of housing, work and family life.* New York, Norton, 1984. Architectural history, feminist housing issues and future housing policies.

258 Heung, R. *The dos and don'ts of housing policy: the case of British Columbia.* Vancouver, Fraser Institute, 1976.

259 Horowitz, C. F. *Housing indicators and housing policy.* Monticello, Vance Bibliographies, 1980. (Public administration series bibliography no. P-487).

260 Howe, E. 'Code enforcement in three cities: an organizational analysis'. *Urban Lawyer* vol. 13 no. 1 (Winter 1981) pp. 65–87. Housing code enforcement in New York, Boston and Baltimore.

261 Jacobs, B. G. et al. *Guide to federal housing programs.* Washington, DC, Bureau of Federal Housing Program, 1982.

262 Johnson, M. B. (ed.) *Resolving the housing crisis: government policy, decontrol and the public interest.* Cambridge, Mass., Ballinger, 1982. Collection of papers on the housing crisis in the US.

263 Kain, J. 'America's persistent housing crisis: errors in analysis and policy'. *Annals of the American Academy of Political and Social Science* vol. 465 (1983) pp. 136–48.

264 Keith, N. S. *Politics and the housing crisis since 1930.* New York, Universe Books, 1973.

265 Kingman, W. 'The challenge at HUD: getting housing programs to work'. *Institute of Socioeconomic Studies Journal* vol. 2 (Spring 1977) pp. 39–49.

266 Kirwan, R. M. *The inner city in the United States.* London, Social Science Research Council, 1980. (Inner city in context 8).

267 Kremer, P. C. and Oliver, H.P. 'The emerging California shelter crisis'. *Urban Land* vol. 40 no. 7 (July–Aug. 1981) pp. 3–8.

268 Levine, M. D. *Federal housing policy: current programs and recurring issues.* Washington, DC, Government Printing Office, 1978. (Congressional Budget Office background paper).

269 Loewenstein, L. K. 'The New York State Urban Development Corporation: a forgotten failure or a precursor of the future?' *American Institute of Planners Journal* vol. 44 no. 3 (July 1978) pp. 261–73.
Study of the NYSUDC, which built over 30,000 new housing units and 3 new communities and then went bankrupt.

270 Lowry, I. S. et al. *California's housing: adequacy, availability and affordability.* Santa Monica, Rand Corporation, 1983.
Generally good state of housing.

271 McFarland, M. C. *Federal government and urban problems.* Boulder, Westview Press, 1978.
History of US Department of Housing and Urban Development and discussion of its housing policies.

272 McGurk, P. 'Public sector under threat?' *Housing* vol. 21 no. 1 (Jan. 1985) pp. 18–19.
Housing problems in the US.

273 Mandelker, D. R. et al. *Housing and community development.* Rochester, Michie, 1981. (Contemporary legal education series).

274 Mandelker, D. *The zoning dilemma.* Indianapolis, Bobbs-Merrill, 1971.

275   Marcuse, P. 'Housing policy and the myth of the benevolent state'. *Social Policy* vol. 8 no. 4 (Jan.–Feb. 1978) pp. 21–6.
History of housing legislation in the US, and factors influencing government policy.

276   Mason, J. B. *History of housing in the United States 1930–80*. Houston, Gulf Publishing Co., 1982.

277   Montgomery, R. and Marshall, D. R. (eds.) *Housing policy for the 1980s*. Lexington, Mass., Lexington Books, 1980.

278   Montgomery, R. and Marshall, D. R. (eds.) 'Symposium on housing policy'. *Policy Studies Journal* vol. 8 no. 2 (1979) pp. 203–339.
Special issue of journal on US housing policy.

279   National Association of Housing and Redevelopment Officials. '50 years of housing policy: a NAHRO bibliography'. *Journal of Housing* vol. 41 no. 1 (Jan.–Feb. 1984) pp. 20–2.

280   National Association of Housing Officials. *A housing program for the United States*. Chicago, The Association, 1934.
Pressure group activity ultimately leading to the US Housing Act 1937 and the public housing programme.

281   National Association of Housing Officials. *Housing for the United States after the war*. Chicago, The Association, 1944.

282   National Housing Association. *Housing problems in America*. New York, The Association, 1921?
Proceedings of the Eighth National Conference on Housing, Bridgeport, Dec. 1920.

283   Nenno, M. K. and Brophy, P. C. *Housing and local government*. Washington, DC, International City Management Association, 1982. (Municipal management series).
Housing and community development at local level in US cities.

284   Phares, D. (ed.) *A decent home and environment: housing urban America*. Cambridge, Mass., Ballinger, 1977.

285 Plunz, R. (ed.) *Housing form and public policy in the United States.* New York, Praeger, 1980.
Edited from the proceedings of a seminar held at Columbia University, Graduate School of Architecture and Planning, 1976.

286 Pynoos, J. et al. (eds.) *Housing urban America.* 2nd ed. Chicago, Aldine Publishing Co., 1981.
Readings on US housing policies, including an excellent bibliography.

287 Rasmussen, D. W. and Struyk, R. J. *Housing strategy for the city of Detroit: policy perspectives based on economic analysis.* Washington, DC, Urban Institute, 1981.

288 Rose, A. *Canadian housing policies.* Toronto, Butterworth, 1980.
Discusses the period 1935–80.

289 Roske, M. D. *Housing in transition.* New York, Holt, Rinehart and Winston, 1983.

290 Rouse, J. E. *Urban housing.* Detroit, Gale Research Co., 1978. (Urban studies information guide library).
Guide to sources of information on US housing policy.

291 Sawers, L. and Wachtel, H. M. 'Who benefits from federal housing policies?' In D. Gordon (ed.) *Problems in political economy.* Lexington, Mass., Heath, 1977. pp. 501–7.

292 Schussheim, M. J. (ed.) *Housing — a reader.* Washington, DC, Government Printing Office, 1983.
Broad review of US housing issues prepared by members of the Congressional Research Service. Useful introductory text.

293 Shafor, A. M. and Longfellow, R. E. *Fair share housing: a bibliography.* Chicago, Council of Planning Librarians, 1980. (CPL bibliography no. 38).
Responsibility for sharing of assisted housing units.

294 Smith, L. B. *The anatomy of a crisis: Canadian housing policy in the seventies.* Vancouver, Fraser Institute, 1977.

295   Smith, L. B. 'Canadian housing policy in the seventies'. *Land Economics* vol. 57 no. 3 (Aug. 1981) pp. 338–52.
Increasing state involvement in housing policy and reactions against it.

296   Smith, W. F. (ed.) *Housing America.* Beverly Hills, Sage, 1983. (American Academy of Political and Social Science annals vol. 465).
Essays on US housing issues.

297   Soen, D. (ed.) *New trends in urban planning: studies in housing, urban design and planning.* Oxford, Pergamon, 1979.

298   Solomon, A. P. *Housing the urban poor: a critical analysis of federal housing policy.* Cambridge, MIT Press, 1977.

299   Starr, R. *America's housing challenge: what it is and how to meet it.* Scarborough, Ontario, McGraw-Hill, 1977.
Revised and expanded version of a special issue of the *New Leader.*

300   Sternlieb, G. and Hughes, J. W. *America's housing: prospects and problems.* New Brunswick, Rutgers University, Center for Urban Policy Research, 1980.

301   Strauss, N. *Seven myths of housing.* New York, Knopf, 1944.
Policies for housing in the US after the war.

302   Struyk, R. J. et al. *Federal housing policy at President Reagan's mid-term.* Washington, DC, Urban Institute Press, 1983.

303   Struyk, R. J. and Tuccillo, J. A. 'Defining the federal role in housing: back to basics'. *Journal of Urban Economics* vol. 14 no. 2 (Sept. 1983) pp. 206–23.
The objectives of, and justification for, US federal government intervention in housing, e.g. in low income housing and home ownership policies.

304   United States, Advisory Committee on Intergovernmental Relations. *Housing and community development.* Washington, DC,

The Committee, 1975. (ACIR State Legislative program part 6).

305   United States, Bureau of the Census. *Housing data resources: indicators and sources of data for analyzing housing and neighborhood conditions.* Washington, DC, Government Printing Office, 1980.

306   United States, Department of Housing and Urban Development. *Information sources in housing and community development.* Washington, DC, The Department, 1972.

Directory of organizations, addresses, statistics, periodicals, legislation and bibliographies, rather than a bibliography itself. Useful introduction to the US scene.

307   United States, Department of Housing and Urban Development. *Local housing assistance tools and techniques: a guidebook for local government.* Washington, DC, The Department, 1979.

Prepared jointly by the US conference of mayors, the National Community Development Association and the Urban Land Institute.

308   United States, Department of Housing and Urban Development. *The President's national urban policy report.* Washington, DC, Government Printing Office, 1980.

Report to Congress on urban policy for the 1980s.

309   United States, House, Committee on Banking, Currency and Housing, Subcommittee on Housing and Community Development. *Evolution of the role of the federal government in housing and community development: a chronology of legislative and selected executive actions 1892–1974.* Washington, DC, Government Printing Office, 1975.

310   United States, House, Committee on Banking, Finance and Urban Affairs, Subcommittee on Housing and Community Development. *Future of the housing industry and federal housing policy.* Washington, DC, Government Printing Office, 1982.

311   United States, President's Commission on Housing. *Report of the President's Commission on Housing.* Washington, DC, Government Printing Office, 1982.

312   United States, President's Committee on Urban Housing. *A decent home: the report of the President's Committee on Urban Housing.* Washington, DC, Government Printing Office, 1969.
Chairman: E. F. Kaiser.

313   Vance, M. A. *Housing: a selective bibliography of books published in the United States.* Monticello, Vance Bibliographies, 1981. (Architecture series bibliography A. 579).
Previous edition published 1979.

314   Vernez-Moudon, A. and Sprague, C. 'More than one: a second life for the single-family property'. *Built Environment* vol. 8 no. 1 (1982) pp. 54–9.
Subdivision of housing in the US.

315   Warren, C. R. *The States and urban strategies: a comparative analysis.* Washington, DC, Government Printing Office, 1980.
Prepared for the US Department of Housing and Urban Development, documenting increased state government involvement in urban affairs.

316   Weicher, J. C. *Housing: federal policies and programs.* Washington, DC, American Enterprise Institute for Public Policy Research, 1980.

317   Wheaton, W. L. C. et al. (eds.) *Urban housing.* New York, Free Press, 1966.
Collection of essays on various aspects of housing policy in the US.

318   Wolman, H. *Politics of federal housing.* New York, Dodd, Mead and Co., 1971.

319   Wood, E. E. 'A century of the housing problem'. *Law and Contemporary Problems* Mar. 1934 pp. 127–323.
Social inequality the root of housing problems.

320   Zais, J. P. 'Housing and community development'. In J. L. Palmer and I. V. Sawhill (eds.) *The Reagan experiment.* Washington, DC, Urban Institute, 1982.

1.5 Australasia

321 Australia, Priorities Review Staff. *Report on housing*. Canberra, Australian Government Printer, 1975. (Parliamentary paper no. 261).

322 Australian Institute of Urban Studies. *Bibliography of urban studies in Australia*. Canberra, The Institute, annual since 1969.

323 Australian Institute of Urban Studies. *Housing for Australia: philosophy and policies*. Canberra, The Institute, 1975. (AIUS publication no. 58).
Report of a task force, recommending a programme to alleviate Australia's housing crisis.

324 Australian Institute of Urban Studies. *Housing policy in the Perth region: density and form*. Canberra, The Institute, 1983. (AIUS publication no. 110).

325 Burnley, I. H. (ed.) *Urbanization in Australia: the post war experience*. Cambridge University Press, 1974.
Part II 'The impact and consequences of urbanization: urban residential and social structure'.

326 Carter, R. A. 'Commonwealth housing policies: the effect of commonwealth housing policies on lower income groups'. *Australian Economic Review* Third quarter 1980 pp. 18–23.

327 Carter, R. A. 'Housing policy in the 1970s'. In R. B. Scotton and H. Ferber (eds.) *Public expenditure and social policy in Australia, vol. II, the first Fraser years 1976–78*. Melbourne, Longman Cheshire, 1980.

328 Hope, B. R. '1–100,000: forty-two years of housing by the state'. *New Zealand Architect* no. 5 (Oct. 1978) pp. 24–39.
Work of the government departments responsible for housing since 1936.

329 Jones, M. A. *Housing and poverty in Australia*. Melbourne University Press, 1972.

330 Kemeny, J. *Privatised city: critical studies in Australian housing and urban structure.* University of Birmingham, Centre for Urban and Regional Studies, 1983. (Occasional paper no. 10).

331 Kilmartin, L. and Thorns, D. C. *Cities unlimited: the sociology of urban development in Australia and New Zealand.* Sydney, Allen and Unwin, 1978. (Studies in society 1)
'The urban housing system' (pp. 103–25).

332 Lawrence, R. 'The quest for an ideal: housing policies in Australia'. *Architect Australia* vol. 68 no. 5 (Nov. 1979) pp. 57–60.

333 Lockhart, T. L. 'Housing in Tasmania'. *Voluntary Housing* vol. 11 no. 5 (Sept.–Oct. 1979) pp. 12–13.
Work of the Tasmanian Department of Housing and Construction since 1945.

334 Neutze, M. *Australian urban policy.* Sydney, Allen and Unwin, 1978.
Post war housing policies described (pp. 92–115).

335 Neutze, M. 'Housing'. In P. N. Troy (ed.) *Equity in the city.* Sydney, Allen and Unwin, 1982.
Australian situation.

336 New Zealand, National Housing Commission. *Housing in New Zealand: five yearly report.* Wellington, The Commission, latest ed. 1983.

337 New Zealand, Royal Commission on Housing. *Report.* Wellington, NZ Government Printer, 1971.

338 Pugh, C. *Intergovernmental relations and the development of Australian housing policies.* Canberra, Australian National University, Centre for Research on Federal Financial Relations, 1976. (Monograph no. 15).

339 Rowley, E. M. 'Housing'. In R. Goldstein and R. Alley (eds.) *Labour in power: promise and performance.* Wellington, Price Milburn for New Zealand University Press, 1975. pp. 81–95.

Implementation of housing policy and the influence of the building industry in New Zealand.

340   Stretton, H. 'Housing policy'. In P. Scott (ed.) *Australian cities and public policy.* Melbourne, Georgian House, 1979. pp. 107–22.

341   Williams, P. 'Institutions, agents and structures: the organisation and management of housing provision in Australia'. In C. Adrian (ed.) *Urban service provision in Australia: institutional process and geographic outcome.* London, Croom Helm, 1984.

1.6   Africa, Asia and Latin America

342   Abiodun, J. O. 'Housing problems in Nigerian cities'. *Town Planning Review* vol. 47 (Oct. 1976) pp. 339–47.

343   Abu-Lughod, J. and Hay, R. (eds.) *Third world urbanization.* Chicago, Maaroufa Press, 1977.
Contains section on housing, squatting and the self-help principle with four articles.

344   Adedibu, A. A. 'The impact of government policy on indigenous housing in Ilorin, Nigeria'. *Ekistics* vol. 48 no. 287 (Mar.–Apr. 1981) pp. 133–7.

345   *Aspects of housing in Malaysia.* Kuala Lumpur, International Development Research Centre, 1975. (South East Asian Low Cost Housing Study monograph).

346   Astbury, S. 'Social goal'. *Asian Building and Construction* (Dec. 1982) pp. 19–41.
Provision of shelter for all people in Asia including the poorest. Includes interview with Prime Minister of Sri Lanka on his programme for urban and rural housing.

347   Atkinson, G. A. 'Mass housing in rapidly developing tropical areas'. *Town Planning Review* vol. 31 (1960–1) pp. 86–101.

348   Bacon, E. 'A report on urban housing policies, conditions

in the People's Republic of China'. *Journal of Housing* vol. 34 (Feb. 1977) pp. 77–9.

349   Barbar, A. M. *Housing in the Arab world: a bibliography.* Chicago, Council of Planning Librarians, 1978. (Exchange bibliography no. 1520).

350   Bell, G. (ed.) *Strategies for human settlements: habitat and environment.* Honolulu, University of Hawaii Press, 1976.
Emphasises link between housing and environment, using material assembled for the Habitat Conference, Vancouver, 1976.

351   Bhaskara Rao, B. *Housing and habitat in developing countries.* New Delhi, Newman Group of Publishers for the Indian Institute of Management, 1979.
Concentrates mainly on India.

352   Bhaskara Rao, B. 'Housing 2000 AD: a long range perspective for India'. *Urban and Rural Planning Thought* vol. 18 no. 1 (Jan. 1975).

353   Bhoosan, B. S. *Towards alternative settlement strategies.* New Delhi, Heritage, 1980.
Case studies of small and intermediate centres in Argentina, India, Nigeria and Sudan.

354   Breese, G. (ed.) *The city in newly developed countries: readings on urbanism and urbanization.* Englewood Cliffs, Prentice-Hall, 1972.

355   Breese, G. *Urbanization in newly developing countries.* Englewood Cliffs, Prentice-Hall, 1966. (Modernisation of traditional societies series).

356   Bromley, R. (ed.) *The urban informal sector: critical perspectives on employment and housing.* Oxford, Pergamon, 1979.

357   Butterworth, D. *Latin American urbanization.* Cambridge University Press, 1981.

358   Caufriez, A. L. 'Operacion sitio: a housing solution for progressive growth'. *Latin American Urban Research* vol. 2 (1972) pp. 203–10.

359   Chatterjee, L. *Housing in Indonesia.* Free University Amsterdam, 1979.

360   Chiu, H. L. 'Four decades of housing policy in Thailand'. *Habitat International* vol. 8 no. 2 (1984) pp. 31–42.

361   Daktil, F. H. (ed.) *Housing problems in developing countries: proceedings of the IAHS International Conference 1978.* 2 vols. Chichester, Wiley, 1979.
Conference held in Dhahran, Saudi Arabia and sponsored by the International Association of Housing Science and the University of Petroleum and Minerals, Dhahran.

362   Davis, L. G. *Housing problems in selected African cities: an introductory bibliography.* Monticello, Council of Planning Librarians, 1977. (Exchange bibliography no. 1205).

363   De Souza, A. (ed.) *The Indian city.* Delhi, Manohar, 1978.

364   De Souza, J. B. 'Urban planning and our housing problems'. *Urban and Rural Planning Thought* vol. 18 no. 1 (Jan. 1975).
Housing policies in India.

365   Dewar, D. et al. *Housing: a comparative evaluation of urbanism in Cape Town.* Totowa, Rowman and Littlefield, 1976.

366   Dewar, D. and Ellis, G. *Housing policy in South Africa: with particular reference to the Western Cape.* Cape Town, 1979.

367   Dewar, D. and Ellis, G. *Low income housing policy in South Africa.* Lansdowne, Citadel Press, 1979.

368   Dietz, A. G. H. et al. *Housing in Latin America.* Cambridge, Mass., MIT Press, 1965.

369   Drakakis-Smith, D. *Urbanisation, housing and the development process.* London, Croom Helm, 1981.

370   Drakakis-Smith, D. W. and Fisher, W. B. *Housing in Ankara.*
University of Durham, Department of Geography, 1975. (Occasional publication no. 7).

371   Dwyer, D. J. (ed.) *The city in the Third World: a reader.*
London, Macmillan, 1974.

372   Dwyer, D. J. 'Housing provision in Hong Kong'. In D. J.
Dwyer (ed.) *Asian urbanization: Hong Kong casebook.* Hong Kong
University Press, 1971. pp. 33–47.

373   Dwyer, D. J. *People and housing in Third World cities: perspectives on the problem of spontaneous settlements.* London, Longmans,
1975.
Includes material on Hong Kong, Caracas and Calcutta.

374   Frieden, B. 'The search for a housing policy in Mexico
City'. *Town Planning Review* vol. 36 (1965) pp. 75–90.

375   Friedmann, J. and Wulff, R. *The urban transition.* London,
Edward Arnold, 1976.
Problems of urbanization in Third World cities.

376   Fuller, R. B. 'Accommodating human unsettlement'. *Town
Planning Review* vol. 49 no. 1 (Jan. 1978) pp. 51–60.
Importance of the Habitat Conference, Vancouver, 1976.

377   Gilbert, A. (ed.) *Urbanization in contemporary Latin America.*
Chichester, Wiley, 1982.

378   Gilbert, A. and Gugler, J. *Cities, poverty and development:
urbanization in the third world.* Oxford University Press, 1982.

379   Gilbert, A. G. and Ward, P. M. 'Housing in Latin American
cities'. In D. T. Herbert and R. J. Johnston (eds.) *Geography and the
urban environment: progress in research and applications vol. 1.*
Chichester, Wiley, 1978. pp. 295–318.

380   Gilbert, A. and Ward, P. M. *Housing, the state and the poor:
policy and practice in three Latin American cities.* Cambridge University Press, 1985.

381 Goodrich, J. A. 'Housing policies in Central America: political and economic constraints'. *Habitat International* vol. 6 no. 4 (1982) pp. 461–70.

382 Goodstadt, L. F. 'Urban housing in Hong Kong 1945–63'. In I. C. Jarvie (ed.) *Hong Kong: a society in transition.* London, Routledge and Kegan Paul, 1969. pp. 257–98.

383 Gosschalk, B. 'South America: a glimpse of its urban and housing needs'. *Housing Review* vol. 28 no. 6 (Nov.–Dec. 1979) pp. 164–5.

384 Grigsby, W. G. and Ko, Z. Y. 'Housing policy for Korea: some preliminary observations'. In G. C. Lim (ed.) *Urban planning and spatial strategies in rapidly changing societies.* Princeton University Press, 1983.

385 Grimes, O. F. *Housing for low income urban families: economics and policy in the developing world.* Washington, DC, World Bank, 1976.

386 Groak, S. *Action planning and responsive design: issues of housing, building, planning and development of the Third World.* Oxford, Pergamon, 1983.

387 Gunn, A. M. *Habitat: human settlements in an urban age.* Oxford, Pergamon, 1978.
Problems facing world settlement, using data collected for the Habitat Conference, Vancouver, 1976.

388 Hake, A. *African metropolis: Nairobi's self-help city.* Brighton, Sussex University Press, 1977.

389 Hallaron, S. A. *Urbanization in the developing nations: a bibliography compiled for the 1960s and 1970s.* Monticello, Council of Planning Librarians, 1976. (Exchange bibliography no. 1181).

390 Haramoto, E. 'Chilean housing experience'. *Planning Outlook* vol. 21 no. 1 (Spring 1978) pp. 16–27.

391 Hardoy, J. E. and Misra, R. P. *Shelter provision in developing countries.* Chichester, Wiley, 1978.

392　Hardoy, J. E. and Satterthwaite, D. *Shelter: need and response: housing land and settlement policies in seventeen Third World nations.* Chichester, Wiley, 1981.

393　Harris, J. R. 'A housing policy for Nairobi'. In J. Hutton (ed.) *Urban challenge in East Africa.* Nairobi, East African Publishing House, 1972.

394　'Housing in Africa: problems and prospects'. *Planning and Administration* vol. 4 no. 1 (Spring 1977) pp. 100–19.
Two papers prepared for the African Regional Conference on Human Settlements, Cairo, 1975.

395　'Housing in Cuba'. *Community Action* no. 55 (Sept.–Oct. 1981) pp. 24–6.

396　'Housing in the Philippines'. *NEDA Journal of Development* vols. 1–2, nos. 2–4 (1974–5).
Special issue on various aspects of housing policy, published by the National Economic and Development Authority, Manila, and containing a large bibliography.

397　'Housing in the Suez Canal towns'. *Third World Planning Review* vol. 3 no. 2 (May 1981) pp. 141–200.
Three articles on Port Said, Ismailia and Suez.

398　Hutton, J. (ed.) *Urban challenge in East Africa.* Nairobi, East African Publishing House, 1972.
Contains several articles on housing policy, finance and market in Kenya, Tanzania and Uganda.

399　Jaycox, E. V. K. 'Housing the poor: the task ahead in developing countries'. *Urban Ecology* vol. 2 no. 4 (Nov. 1977) pp. 305–25.

400　Johnstone, M. 'Housing policies in Third World cities: a review'. *Australian Geographical Studies* vol. 14 (1976) pp. 153–66.

401　Johnstone, M. 'Housing policy and the urban poor in peninsular Malaysia'. *Third World Planning Review* vol. 5 no. 3 (Aug. 1983) pp. 249–71.

402 Johnstone, M. 'Urban housing and housing policy in peninsular Malaysia'. *International Journal of Urban and Regional Research* vol. 8 no. 4 (Dec. 1984) pp. 497–529.

403 Jorgenson, N. O. *Housing policy guidelines for African countries.* 2nd ed. University of Nairobi, Housing Research and Development Unit, 1978.

404 Keare, D. H. and Jiminez, E. *Progressive development and affordability in the design of urban shelter projects.* Washington, DC, World Bank, 1983.

405 Keare, D. H. and Parris, S. *Evaluation of Shelter programs for the urban poor: principal findings.* Washington, DC, 1982. (World Bank staff working paper 547).

406 Klaassen, L. H. and Burns, L. S. 'The position of housing in national economic and social policy'. In *Capital formation for housing in Latin America.* Washington, DC, Pan American Union, 1963. pp. 108–19.

407 Knapp, E. et al. *Housing problems in the Third World: theoretical terms of reference, methodology and four case studies in Bogotá, Jakarta, Nairobi and Kasama.* University of Stuttgart, Institute of Town Planning, 1984. (Working report 39).
   Bilingual (English and German) study of self-help settlements for low income communities in three continents.

408 Koenigsberger, O. 'Housing in the national development plan: an example from Nigeria'. *Ekistics* vol. 30 (1970) pp. 393–7.

409 Kulaba, S. M. *Housing, socialism and national development in Tanzania: a policy framework.* Rotterdam, Bouwcentrum International Education, 1981.
   Future housing policy in Tanzania should be geared more towards indigenous resources and demands.

410 Kusnetzoff, F. 'Housing policies or housing politics? An evaluation of the Chilean experience.' *Journal of Interamerican Studies and World Affairs* vol. 17 (1975) pp. 281–310.

411   Laquian, A. A. *Basic housing: policies for urban sites, services and shelter in developing countries.* Ottawa, International Development Research Centre, 1983.
Evaluates projects supported by the World Bank in El Salvador, Philippines, Senegal and Zambia.

412   Lea, J. P. 'Comparative policies towards housing in Sub-Saharan Africa'. *South African Journal of African Affairs* vol. 6 nos. 1–2 (1976) pp. 44–52.

413   Leung, C. K. et al (eds.) *Hong Kong: dilemmas of growth.* Hong Kong University, Centre of Asian Studies, 1980.
Contains several useful articles, notably on new town policy in Hong Kong.

414   Linn, J. *Cities in the developing world: policies for their equitable and efficient growth.* New York, Oxford University Press for the World Bank, 1983.
Especially pp. 120–90 on urban housing: land, services and shelter.

415   Lowder, S. *Inside Third World cities.* London, Croom Helm, 1984.
Ch. 6 'Housing the urban population'.

416   Maasdorp, G. and Humphreys, A. S. B. *From shantytown to township: an economic study of African poverty and rehousing in a South African city.* Cape Town, Juta, 1975.
Study of Durban metropolitan area.

417   McConnell, S. 'Chinese urbanisation'. *Town and Country Planning* vol. 50 no. 3 (Mar. 1981) pp. 84–7.
Settlement policy and housing around Shanghai.

418   McGee, T. G. *The urbanisation process in the Third World.* London, Bell, 1972.

419   Mackenzie, D. R. and Kerst, E. W. *A bibliographic overview of housing in developing countries.* Monticello, Council of Planning Librarians, 1977. (Exchange bibliographies 1225, 1226 and 1227).

420 Manalad-Santiago, A. 'Reorganising for housing and urban development'. *Philippine Journal of Public Administration* vol. 13 (1969) pp. 214–32.

421 Marcussen, L. *Settlement in Turkey: a report on the politics of housing and urbanization.* Copenhagen, Royal Danish Academy of Art, School of Architecture, 1982.
Part II examines different Turkish housing systems and policies.

422 Marga Institute. *Housing in Sri Lanka.* Colombo, Marga Publications, 1976.

423 'Meeting world housing needs'. *Ekistics* vol. 41 no. 242 (Jan. 1976) pp. 1–63.
Special issue, containing several articles.

424 Misra, R. P. (ed.) *Habitat Asia: issues and responses. Vol. 1, India* by B. S. Bhoosan and R. P. Misra; *Vol. 2, Indonesia and the Philippines* by D. Suri et al.; *Vol. 3, Japan and Singapore* by R. Varma and N. N. Sastry. New Delhi, Concept Publishing, 1979.

425 Misra, R. P. and Bhoosan, B. S. *Human settlements in Asia: public policies and programmes.* New Delhi, Heritage, 1980.

426 Mitchell, R. E. *Housing, urban growth and economic development.* Pasadena, Oriental Book Store, 1972. (Asian folklore and social life monograph no.31).
Concentrates largely on housing in China.

427 Moochtar, R. 'Urban housing in Indonesia'. *Habitat International* vol. 4 no. 3 (1979).

428 Morrison, M. K. and Gutkind, P. C. *Housing the urban poor in Africa.* New York, Syracuse University, 1982. (Foreign and comparative studies program African series no. 37).

429 Mumtaz, B. 'Problems in programme implementation'. *Habitat International* vol. 6 no. 4 (1982) pp. 527–32.
Housing policies in developing countries.

430   Murison, H. and Lea, J. P. (eds.) *Housing in Third World countries: perspectives on policy and practice.* London, Macmillan, 1979. (Macmillan international college editions).
Papers from the International Workshop on Housing in Third World Countries, Australia, 1978.

431   Nathalang, W. *Housing in Thailand.* Bangkok, Applied Science Research Corporation of Thailand, 1973? (South East Asian Low Cost Housing Study).

432   Nerfin, M. 'Towards a housing policy'. *Journal of Modern African Studies* vol. 3 (1965) pp. 543–65.

433   Ocampo, R. B. 'Development of Philippine housing policy and administration'. *Philippine Journal of Public Administration* vol. 22 (Jan. 1978) pp. 1–18.
Covers the period 1945–59.

434   O'Connor, A. *The African city.* London, Hutchinson, 1983.

435   Payne, G. K. *Urban housing in the Third World.* London, Leonard Hill, 1977.

436   Peattie, L. R. 'Housing policy in developing countries: two puzzles'. *World Development* vol. 7 (1979) pp. 1017–22.

437   'Perspectives on Habitat: the United Nations Conference on Human Settlements'. *Ekistics* vol. 42 no. 252 (Nov. 1976) pp. 251–311.
Several papers on various aspects of housing in developing countries.

438   Pryor, E. G. 'Environmental quality and housing policy in Hong Kong'. *Pacific Viewpoint* vol. 16 no. 2 (1975) pp. 195–207.

439   Pryor, E. G. *Housing in Hong Kong.* 2nd rev. ed. Oxford University Press, 1983.

440   Qadeer, M. A. 'Successful housing planning for Third World countries must be indigenous'. *Journal of Housing* vol. 37 no. 3 (Mar. 1980) pp. 142–6.

441   Rakodi, C. *Housing and the urban poor in Lusaka.* Cardiff, University of Wales Institute of Science and Technology, 1980. (Papers in planning research 121).

442   Rimmer, P. J. et al (eds.) *Studies of food, shelter and transport in the Third World: challenging the unconventional wisdom.* Canberra, Australian National University, Department of Human Geography, 1978. (Monograph no. 12).

443   Roberts, B. *Cities of peasants.* London, Edward Arnold, 1978.

444   Rogers, A. and Williamson, J. G. 'Migration, urbanization and Third World development: an overview'. *Economic Development and Cultural Change* vol. 30 no. 3 (Apr. 1982) pp. 463–82.
Introductory article to special issue of journal on Third World migration and urbanization.

445   Rondinelli, D. A. and Ruddle, E. *Urbanization and rural development.* New York, Praeger, 1978.

446   Rosser, C. 'Housing and urban change in Calcutta'. In D. J. Dwyer (ed.) *The city as a centre of change in Asia.* Hong Kong University Press, 1972. pp. 179–90.

447   Rothenburg, I. F. 'Administrative decentralization and the implementation of housing policy in Colombia'. In M. S. Grindle (ed.) *Politics and policy implementation in the Third World.* Princeton University Press, 1980. pp. 145–69.

448   Rothenburg, I. F. '"Symbolic schemes" and housing policy for the poor: lessons from Colombia, Mexico, Chile and Hong Kong'. *Comparative Urban Research* vol. 8 no. 2 (1981) pp. 48–75.

449   Salua, A. T. 'Nigeria's housing policies and programmes: a preliminary assessment'. *Planning and Administration* vol. 7 no. 1 (Spring 1980) pp. 49–56.
Housing problems, government policies and housing investment in Nigeria.

450   Schmertz, M. F. 'Housing in Islam'. *Architectural Record* no. 8 (Aug. 1979) pp. 87–92.

Report of the Jakarta Conference on the housing of poor Muslims.

451 Schwerdtfeger, F. W. *Traditional housing in African cities: a comparative study of housing in Zaria, Ibadan and Marrakech.* Chichester, Wiley, 1982.
Looks at the relationship between cultural factors, land tenure, family systems and economics and their effect on development of traditional housing in urban Africa.

452 Shankland Cox Partnership. *Third World urban housing: aspirations, resources, programmes, projects.* Watford, Building Research Establishment, 1977.

453 Sharp, D. 'The housing problems of Lesotho'. *Voluntary Housing* vol. 11 no. 2 (Mar.–Apr. 1979) pp. 11–12.

454 Simon, J. C. *Housing in Ghana.* Monticello, Vance Bibliographies, 1979. (Public administration series no. P-221).

455 Singh, P. K. B. 'A study of housing and urban planning in Delhi'. *Journal of Administration Overseas* vol. 17 (Oct. 1978) pp. 256–69.

456 Slater, G. 'Chinese approach to housing development reveals planning-modernization alternatives'. *Journal of Housing* vol. 38 no. 5 (May 1981) pp. 256–61.
Housing policy and practice in China.

457 Solow, A. A. 'Housing in Latin America'. *Town Planning Review* vol. 38 (1967–8) pp. 83–102.

458 South Africa, Commission of Enquiry into Housing Matters. *Report.* Pretoria, Government Printer, 1977.
The Fouché Commission.

459 Stephens-Rioja, K. 'Land and shelter: important issues for a growing metropolis'. *Built Environment* vol. 8 no. 2 (1982) pp. 108–16.
Study of Mexico City.

460   Strachan, A. J. 'Housing patterns and values in a medium sized Third World city: Georgetown, Guyana'. *Tijdschrift voor Economische en Sociale Geografie* vol. 72 no. 1 (1981) pp. 40–6.

461   Stren, R. *Housing the urban poor in Africa: policy, politics and bureaucracy in Mombasa.* Berkeley, University of California, Institute of International Studies, 1978.

462   Stren, R. E. *Urban inequality and housing policy in Tanzania: the problem of squatting.* Berkeley, University of California Press, 1975. (Research series no. 24).

463   Stretton, H. *Urban housing policy in Papua New Guinea.* Boroko, Institute of Applied Social and Economic Research, 1979. (Monograph 8).

464   Swan, P. J. (ed.) *Seven Asian experiences in housing the poor.* Bangkok, Asian Institute of Technology, 1980.

465   Syagga, P. M. 'The implementation of housing policy in Kenya'. *Housing* vol. 14 no. 12 (Dec. 1978) pp. 12–13.
       Housing policies before independence, the role of the National Housing Corporation and housing development.

466   Tan, S. H. and Sendut, H. (eds.) *Public and private housing in Malaysia.* Kuala Lumpur, Heinemann, 1979.
       Collection of articles on various aspects of Malaysian housing policy.

467   Thurston, L. *Urban housing analysis and housing policy in developing countries: selected references.* Chicago, Council of Planning Librarians, 1983. (Bibliography no. 120).

468   Turin, D. A. 'Housing in Africa: some problems and major policy issues'. In A. A. Nevitt (ed.) *The economic problems of housing.* London, Macmillan, 1967. pp. 200–14.

469   Turner, A. (ed.) *The cities of the poor: settlement planning in developing countries.* London, Croom Helm, 1980.

470   Turner, J. F. C. 'Housing in three dimensions: terms of reference for the housing question redefined'. *World Development*

vol. 6 nos. 9–10 (1978) pp. 1135–45. Reprinted in Bromley, R. (ed.) *The urban informal sector: critical perspectives on employment and housing policies.* Oxford, Pergamon, 1979.
Discusses whether governments in developing countries should supply or support housing.

471   Turner, J. F. C. 'Housing priorities, settlement patterns and urban development in modernising countries'. *Journal of the American Institute of Planners* vol. 34 (1968) pp. 354–63.

472   Turner, J. F. C. 'Who should do what about housing?' In A. Gilbert (ed.) *Urbanization in contemporary Latin America.* Chichester, Wiley, 1982. pp. 191–204.

473   United Nations. *Housing in Africa.* New York, United Nations, 1965.
Includes sections on construction, finance and policy.

474   United Nations. *Report of Habitat: United Nations Conference on Human Settlements, Vancouver, 31 May–11 June 1976.* New York, United Nations, 1976.

475   United Nations, Centre for Human Settlements. *Residential circumstances of the urban poor in developing countries.* New York, Praeger, 1981.

476   United Nations, Department of Economic and Social Affairs. *Housing policy guidelines for developing countries.* New York, United Nations, 1976.

477   United Nations, Department of Economic and Social Affairs. *Integration of housing into national development plans: systems approach.* New York, United Nations, 1974.

478   United Nations, Department of Economic and Social Affairs. *Pilot housing project in Central America.* New York, United Nations, 1974.

479   United Nations, Economic Commission for Africa. *Human settlements in Africa: the role of housing and building.* Addis Ababa, United Nations, 1976.

480   United States, Agency for International Development. *5th conference on housing in Africa, Monrovia, Liberia, May 1978.* Washington, DC, The Agency, 1978.

481   United States, Agency for International Development. *8th conference on housing in Africa.* Washington, DC, The Agency, 1982.
Held at the University of Botswana, Gaborone with a theme 'towards self-reliance in housing'.

482   United States, Agency for International Development. *Preparing a national housing policy.* Washington, DC, The Agency, 1974.

483   United States, Agency for International Development. *Sub-regional conference on housing in Africa.* Washington, DC, The Agency, 1980.
Held in Abidjan, Ivory Coast with a special theme of project implementation.

484   United States, General Accounting Office. *The challenge of meeting shelter needs in less developed countries.* Washington, DC, The Office, 1977.
Report to Congress by the Comptroller General.

485   Walsh, A. C. 'The search for an appropriate housing policy in Fiji'. *Third World Planning Review* vol. 6 no. 2 (May 1984) pp. 185–200.

486   Ward, P. 'Housing and population growth in Latin American cities'. In W. T. S. Gould and R. Lawton (eds.) *Planning for population change.* London, Croom Helm, 1984.

487   Ward, P. M. 'Informal housing: conventional wisdoms reappraised'. *Built Environment* vol. 8 no. 2 (1982) pp. 85–94.
Third World housing.

488   Werlin, H. H. 'Nairobi's politics of housing'. *African Review* vol. 3 no. 4 (1973) pp. 611–29.

489   Wilsher, P. and Righter, R. *The exploding cities.* London, Deutsch, 1975.

Problems of urbanization in developing countries.

490 Wong, L. S. (ed.) *Housing in Hong Kong: a multi-disciplinary study*. London, Heinemann Educational, 1978.

491 World Bank. *Housing*. Washington, DC, The Bank, 1975. (Sector policy paper).
Housing policies for developing countries.

492 World Bank. *Shelter*. Washington, DC, The Bank, 1980. (Poverty and basic needs series).

493 Yeh, S. H. K. and Laquian, A. A. (eds.) *Housing Asia's millions*. Ottawa, International Development Research Centre, 1979.

2
Housing market

This section is concerned with the theoretical studies of housing and the social, political and economic forces which govern its provision. It therefore includes works on demographic patterns, social theory, urban sociology, housing demand and preference, residential mobility, house prices and housing economics, all of which make up what has been termed the 'housing market'. Reference should also be made to sections 3 'Construction and energy conservation', 4 'Housing finance' and 12 'Social aspects'.

2.1 International and comparative

494 Ball, M. 'Housing provision and the economic crisis'. *Capital and Class* vol. 17 (1982) pp. 66–77.

495 Botman, J. J. *Dynamics of housing and planning: a regional simulation model.* The Hague, Nijhoff, 1981.

496 Bourne, L. 'Housing supply and housing market behaviour in residential development'. In D. Herbert and R. Johnston (eds.) *Social areas in cities, vol. 1, spatial processes and form.* Chichester, Wiley, 1976.

497 Bourne, L. S. and Biernacki, C. M. *Urban housing markets, housing supply and the spatial structure of residential change: a working bibliography.* University of Toronto, Centre for Urban and Community Studies, 1978. (Bibliographic series report no. 6).
 Over 600 entries, unannotated but with useful cross-references.

498   Bourne, L. and Hitchcock, J. *Urban housing markets: recent directions in research and policy.* University of Toronto Press, 1978.

499   Cardoso, A. and Short, J. R. 'Forms of housing production: initial formulations'. *Environment and Planning A* vol. 15 no. 7 (July 1983) pp. 917–28.

500   Castells, M. *The urban question.* London, Edward Arnold, 1977.
Seminal work for the French school of urban sociology; pp. 145–69 cover housing policy.

501   Clark, W. A. V. (ed.) *Modelling housing market research.* London, Croom Helm, 1982.
Papers originally prepared for a seminar at the University of California, Los Angeles.

502   Clarke, S. and Ginsburg, N. 'The political economy of housing'. *Kapitalistate* nos. 4–5 (Summer 1976) pp. 66–99.

503   Dicken, P. and Lloyd, P. E. *Modern western society: a geographical perspective on work, home and well-being.* London, Harper and Row, 1981.
Ch. 4 'Finding a home: geographical perspectives on the housing market' (pp. 213–80).

504   Duncan, S. S. 'Housing policy, the methodology of levels, and urban research: the case of Castells'. *International Journal of Urban and Regional Research* vol. 5 no. 2 (1981) pp. 231–54.

505   Fletcher, C. 'The relevance of domestic property to sociological understanding'. *Sociology* vol. 10 (1976) pp. 451–68.

506   Goldfield, D. R. 'Suburban development in Stockholm and the United States: a comparison of form and function'. In *Growth and transformation of the modern city.* Stockholm, Swedish Council for Building Research, 1979. pp. 139–56.

507   Grieson, R. E. (ed.) *The urban economy and housing.* Aldershot, Gower, 1983.

508   Harloe, M. and Lebas, E. (eds.) *City, class and capital: new developments in the political economy of cities and regions.* London, Edward Arnold, 1981.

509   Harvey, D. 'Labor, capital and class struggle around the built environment in advanced capitalist societies'. In K. Cox (ed.) *Urbanization and conflict in market societies.* Chicago, Maaroufa Press, 1978. pp. 9–37.

510   Harvey, D. *Social justice and the city.* London, Edward Arnold, 1975.

511   Lakshmanan, T. R. et al. 'Housing consumption and level of development: a cross-national comparison'. *Economic Geography* vol. 54 (July 1978) pp. 222–33.

512   Lebas, E. et al. 'Urban and regional sociology in advanced industrial societies: a decade of Marxist and critical perspectives'. *Current Sociology* vol. 30 no. 1 (Spring 1982) pp. 1–271.
Special issue containing review articles of urban studies and a bibliography from several countries. Includes housing.

513   Leonard, S. 'Urban managerialism: a period of transition?' *Progress in Human Geography* vol. 6 (1982) pp. 190–215.
Review of the literature and assessment of current theory.

514   Marcuse, P. 'Building house theory: notes on some recent work'. *International Journal of Urban and Regional Research* vol. 6 no. 1 (1982) pp. 115–20.

515   Mitchell, R. E. 'Sociological research on the economic myths of housing'. *Social Problems* vol. 22 (Dec. 1974) pp. 259–79.
Examines popular assumptions on the socio-economic aspects of the housing market.

516   Nesslein, T. S. 'Alternative decision-making models for housing: the question of efficiency'. *Kyklos* vol. 36 no. 4 (1983) pp. 604–33.
Housing resource allocation under the market model, the central planning model and the welfare state model.

517   Pickvance, C. G. 'Life-cycle, housing tenure and intra-urban residential mobility: a causal model'. *Sociological Review* vol. 21 no. 2 (1973) pp. 279–97.

518   Popenoe, D. *The suburban environment: Sweden and the United States*. University of Chicago Press, 1977.

519   Racki, J. et al. 'Housing systems analysis: an aid to policy development'. *Ekistics* vol. 24 no. 227 (1974) pp. 281–6.

520   Short, J. 'Residential mobility'. *Progress in Human Geography* vol. 2 (1978) pp. 419–47.

521   Stevens, B. J. 'Employment, permanent income and the demand for housing'. *Journal of Urban Economics* vol. 6 no. 4 (Oct. 1979) pp. 480–500.
Housing market behaviour and demand patterns in the US and West Germany.

2.2   Europe

522   Byrne, D. 'Dublin — a case study of housing and the residual working class'. *International Journal of Urban and Regional Research* vol. 8 no. 3 (Sept. 1984) pp. 402–20.

523   Clark, W. A. V. et al. 'Housing consumption and residential mobility'. *Annals of Association of American Geographers* vol. 7 no. 1 (Mar. 1984) pp. 29–43.
Relationship between households and the housing stock in Tilburg, Netherlands.

524   Duncan, S. S. *Housing provision in advanced capitalism: Sweden in the 1970s*. Brighton, University of Sussex, 1978. (Urban and regional studies working paper no. 10).

525   Duncan, S. S. *Housing reform, the capitalist state and social democracy*. Brighton, University of Sussex, 1978. (Urban and regional studies working paper no. 9).
A general overview of housing in the capitalist state is followed by an examination of the Swedish case.

526   Folin, M. 'Housing development processes in Europe: some hypotheses from a comparative analysis'. In M. Ball et al. (eds.) *Land rent, housing and urban planning: a European perspective.* London, Croom Helm, 1985. pp. 46–70.

527   Hegedus, J. and Tosics, I. 'Housing classes and housing policy: some changes in the Budapest housing market'. *International Journal of Urban and Regional Research* vol. 7 no. 4 (Dec. 1983) pp. 467–94.

528   Jennings, R. *Some aspects of new house prices in Ireland.* Dublin, National Institute for Physical Planning and Construction Research, 1983.

529   Kreibich, V. and Petri, A. 'Locational behaviour of households in a constrained housing market'. *Environment and Planning A* vol. 14 no. 9 (Sept. 1982) pp. 1195–210.
Locational behaviour in the Stuttgart conurbation in West Germany.

530   Loikkanen, H. A. *Housing demand and intra-urban mobility decisions: a search approach.* Helsinki, Societas Scientarum Fennica, 1982. (Commentationes scientarum socialum 17).
Presents a model of the demand for rental housing and applies it to the introduction of a rent allowance scheme in Finland.

531   Nesslein, T. S. 'The Swedish housing model: an assessment'. *Urban Studies* vol. 19 (1982) pp. 235–46.

532   Rietveld, P. 'Vacancies and mobility in the housing market: an exploratory analysis'. *Environment and Planning A* vol. 16 no. 5 (May 1984) pp. 673–87.
Vacancies in the Netherlands housing market in the period 1966–81.

533   Topalov, C. 'Prices, profits and rents in residential development: France 1960–1980'. In M. Ball et al. (eds.) *Land rent, housing and urban planning: a European perspective.* London, Croom Helm, 1985. pp. 25–45.

534   Wermuth, M. J. 'Hierarchical effects of personal household and residential location characteristics on individual activity demand'. *Environment and Planning A* vol. 14 no. 9 (Sept. 1982) pp. 1252–64.
New research on residential location in West Germany.

2.3   United Kingdom

535   Ball, M. 'The development of capitalism in housing provision'. *International Journal of Urban and Regional Research* vol. 5 no. 2 (1981) pp. 145–77.
Development of the main features of capitalist housing provision in 19th century Britain.

536   Ball, M. 'Forms of housing production — the birth of a new concept or the creation of a cul de sac?' *Environment and Planning A* vol. 16 no. 2 (Feb. 1984) pp. 261–8.

537   Ball, M. J and Kirwan, R. M. 'Accessibility and supply constraints in the urban housing market'. *Urban Studies* vol. 14 no. 1 (Feb. 1977) pp. 11–32.
Survey of the owner occupied housing market in Bristol.

538   Ball, M. J. and Kirwan, R. M. *The economics of an urban housing market.* London, Centre for Environmental Studies, 1975.
Case study of Bristol.

539   Bassett, K. and Short, J. *Housing and residential structure: alternative approaches.* London, Routledge and Kegan Paul, 1980.
Ecological, neo-classical, institutional and Marxist approaches to the study of housing policy.

540   Berry, M. *Marxist approaches to the housing question.* University of Birmingham, Centre for Urban and Regional Studies, 1979. (Research memorandum 69).

541   Bird, H. 'Residential mobility and preference patterns in the public sector of the housing market'. *Transactions of the Institute of British Geographers* new series vol. 1 (1976) pp. 20–33.

542   Blakemore, K. *An econometric model of the UK housing market 1970–82*. London, Henley Centre for Forecasting, 1985.
Sensitivity of market to interest rates and causes of home price increases.

543   Boddy, M. and Gray, F. 'Filtering theory, housing policy and the legitimation of inequality'. *Policy and Politics* vol. 7 no. 1 (Jan. 1979) pp. 39–54.
Criticism of filtering theory.

544   Booth, P. 'Housing as a product: design guidance and residential satisfaction in the private sector'. *Built Environment* vol. 8 no. 1 (1982) pp. 20–4.

545   Buckley, R. M. 'A simple theory of the UK housing sector'. *Urban Studies* vol. 19 no. 3 (Aug. 1982) pp. 303–11.
An econometric model of the UK housing market.

546   Building Societies Association. *The determination and control of house prices*. London, The Association, 1981.
Papers and proceedings of a seminar held in London, Jan. 1981.

547   Building Societies Association. *The housing market in the 1980s*. London, The Association, 1980.

548   Butler, S. *More effective than bombing: government intervention in the housing market*. Kirkcaldy, Adam Smith Institute, 1979.

549   Cadman, D. and Austin-Crowe, L. *Property development*. 2nd ed. London, Spon, 1983.

550   Charles, S. *Housing economics*. London, Macmillan, 1977.
Concise, simple introduction for non-economists.

551   Cockburn, C. *The local state: management of cities and people*. London, Pluto Press, 1977.
Local government and politics in a British city.

552   Conference of Socialist Economists. *Housing, construction and the state*. London, The Conference, 1980.

Collected papers from the Political Economy of Housing Workshop.

553 Conference of Socialist Economists. *Political economy and the housing question.* London, The Conference, 1975.
Collected papers from the Political Economy of Housing Workshop.

554 Conference of Socialist Economists. *Housing and class in Britain.* London, The Conference, 1976.
Collected papers from the Political Economy of Housing Workshop.

555 Cornford, A. J. *The market for owned houses in England and Wales since 1945: prices, building and finance.* Farnborough, Saxon House, 1979.
Time series analysis of trends in the private market.

556 Coupe, R. T. and Morgan, B. S. 'Towards a fuller understanding of residential mobility: a case study in Northampton, England'. *Environment and Planning A* vol. 13 no. 2 (Feb. 1981) pp. 201–15.

557 Couper, M. and Brindley, T. 'Housing classes and housing values'. *Sociological Review* vol. 23 (Aug. 1975) pp. 563–76.
Describes a multiple value system with reference to housing preferences in Bath.

558 Cowley, J. *Housing for people or for profit?* London, Stage 1, 1979.
Radical attack on capitalist housing policies.

559 Damer, S. *Property and class relations in Victorian Glasgow.* Glasgow University, Department of Social and Economic Research, 1976. (Discussion paper no. 15).

560 Dickens, P. 'Social change, housing and the state: some aspects of class fragmentation and incorporation 1915–1946'. In M. Harloe (ed.) *Urban change and conflict.* London, Centre for Environmental Studies, 1977. (Conference paper series no. 19).

Examines some of the difficulties associated with radical studies of housing and the vagaries of the economy and capital.

561 Donnison, D. and Murie, A. 'Housing and class in Britain: the debate continues'. *Social Policy and Administration* vol. 18 no. 2 (Summer 1984) pp. 168–71.

562 Duncan, S. S. *The housing crisis and the structure of the housing market.* Brighton, University of Sussex, 1976. (Urban and regional studies working paper 2).

563 Duncan, S. S. 'The housing question and the structure of the housing market'. *Journal of Social Policy* vol. 6 no. 4 (Oct. 1977) pp. 385–412.
Attempts to link the nature of the housing crisis to the structure of the housing market.

564 Dunleavy, P. *Urban political analysis.* London, Macmillan, 1980.
Review of sociological theories of urban politics.

565 Ermisch, J. 'Demographic changes and housing infrastructure investment'. In D. Eversley and W. Kollmann (eds.) *Population change and social planning.* London, Edward Arnold, 1981.

566 Ermisch, J. 'An economic theory of household formulation: theory and evidence from the General Household Survey'. *Scottish Journal of Political Economy* vol. 28 (Feb. 1981) pp. 1–19.

567 Evans, A. W. *The economics of residential location.* London, Macmillan, 1973.

568 Eversley, D. 'Demographic change and the demand for housing'. In M. Buxton and E. Craven (eds.) *The uncertain future: demographic change and social policy.* London, Centre for Studies in Social Policy, 1976.

569 Farmer, M. K. and Barrell, R. 'Entrepreneurship and government policy: the case of the housing market'. *Journal of Public Policy* vol. 1 no. 3 (Aug. 1981) pp. 307–32.

Continued subsidies in the UK housing market reduce potential business investment.

570   Fleming, M. C. and Nellis, J. G. *House price statistics for the United Kingdom: a survey and critical review of recent developments.* Loughborough University, Department of Economics, 1984.

571   Fleming, M. and Nellis, J. 'House prices in the United Kingdom: the problems of measurement'. *National Westminster Bank Quarterly Review* (Nov. 1984) pp. 43–52.

572   Fleming, M. C. and Nellis, J. G. 'The inflation of house prices in Northern Ireland in the 1970s'. *Economic and Social Review* (Dublin) vol. 13 (Oct. 1981) pp. 1–19.

573   Fleming, M. C. and Nellis, J. G. 'The interpretation of house price statistics for the United Kingdom'. *Environment and Planning A* vol. 13 no. 9 (Sept. 1981) pp. 1109–24.

574   Forrest, R. and Kemeny, J. 'Middle class housing careers: the relationship between furnished renting and home ownership'. *Sociological Review* vol. 30 no. 2 (May 1982) pp. 208–22.

575   Forrest, R. and Williams, P. 'Commodification and housing: emerging issues and contradictions'. *Environment and Planning A* vol. 16 no. 9 (Sept. 1984) pp. 1163–80.

576   Ginsburg, N. *Class, capital and social policy.* London, Macmillan, 1979.
Chapters on private housing, the state and the working class.

577   Hadjimatheou, G. *Housing and mortgage markets: the UK experience.* Farnborough, Saxon House, 1976.
Econometric study of the housing market.

578   Hamnett, C. 'The new geography of housing'. *New Society* vol. 66 no. 1099 (8 Dec. 1983) pp. 396–8.
Changing spatial trends in UK housing.

579   Hamnett, C. 'Regional variations in house prices and house price inflation 1969–81'. *Area* vol. 15 no. 2 (1983) pp. 97–109.

580 Harloe, M. 'The recommodification of housing'. In M. Harloe and E. Lebas (eds.) *City, class and capital: new developments in the political economy of cities and regions.* London, Edward Arnold, 1981. pp. 17–50.

Describes long term withdrawal from state regulation of housing provision towards the private sector.

581 Harloe, M. and Paris, C. 'The decollectivization of consumption: housing and local government finance in England and Wales 1979–1981'. In I. Szelenyi (ed.) *Cities in recession: critical responses to the urban policies of the new right.* London, Sage, 1984. (Sage studies in international sociology vol. 30). pp. 70–98.

582 Harvey, J. *The economics of real property.* London, Macmillan, 1981.

Ch. 12 (pp. 194–227) in particular refers to housing policy.

583 Hawkins, C. *Britain's economic future: an immediate programme for revival.* Brighton, Wheatsheaf, 1983.

Contains chapters entitled 'Housing in chaos', 'Mortgage reforms' and the 'Case for reforming housing'.

584 Hole, W. V. and Poutney, M. T. *Trends in population, housing and occupancy rates 1861–1961.* London, HMSO, 1971.

Household formation and headship rates.

585 Holmans, A. E. 'A forecast of effective demand for housing in Great Britain'. *Social Trends* no. 1 (1970) pp. 33–42.

586 Holmans, A. 'Housing careers of recently married couples'. *Population Trends* no. 24 (Summer 1981) pp. 10–14.

587 Hyman, C. and Markowski, S. 'Speculation and inflation in the market for house-building land in England and Wales'. *Environment and Planning A* vol. 12 no. 10 (Oct. 1980) pp. 1119–30.

Discusses the property boom of 1971–3 and its subsequent collapse.

588 Ineichen, B. 'The housing decisions of young people'. *British Journal of Sociology* vol. 31 no. 2 (June 1981) pp. 252–8.

589 Jenkins, S. P. and Maynard, A. K. 'Intergenerational conti-
nuities in housing'. *Urban Studies* vol. 20 no. 4 (Nov. 1983) pp.
431–8.
Data from the Rowntree Follow-up Study to provide evidence
on the housing status of parents and children.

590 Johnson, J. H. et al. *Housing and the migration of labour.*
Farnborough, Saxon House, 1974.

591 King, D. *Forecasting local housing requirements: a renewal of
interest in the demographic approach.* Chelmsford, Chelmer Institute
of Higher Education, 1984. (Chelmer working papers in environmental planning no. 6).

592 Kirby, A. *Education, health and housing: an empirical investigation of resource accessibility.* Farnborough, Saxon House, 1979.
Develops a model of residential location which emphasizes the
realities of social and market forces.

593 Kirby, A. *The inner city: causes and effects.* London, Retail
Planning Associates, 1978.

594 Kirby, A. M. 'Housing market studies: a critical review'.
Institute of British Geographers Transactions vol. 1 (1976) pp 2–7.

595 Leaper, R. A. B. (ed.) *Health, wealth and housing: some recent
developments.* Oxford, Blackwell, 1980.

596 Lomax, D. F. 'The banks and the housing market'. *National
Westminster Bank Quarterly Review* Feb. 1982 pp. 2–12.

597 McAvinchey, I. D. and Maclennan, D. 'A regional comparison of house price inflation rates in Britain 1967–76'. *Urban
Studies* vol. 19 no. 1 (Feb. 1982) pp. 43–57.

598 Maclennan, D. *Housing economics: an applied approach.*
Harlow, Longman, 1982.
Highly quantitative economic text.

599 Maclennan, D. 'Information, space and the measurement
of housing preferences and demand'. *Scottish Journal of Political
Economy* vol. 24 no. 2 (June 1977) pp. 97–115.

600 Maclennan, D. 'Some thoughts on the nature and purpose of urban house price studies'. *Urban Studies* vol. 14 no. 1 (Feb. 1977) pp. 59–72.
Examines implicit assumptions in hedonic studies of urban house prices. Review of literature.

601 Maclennan, D. and Clapham, D. 'The social market'. *Roof* vol. 7 no. 6 (Nov.–Dec. 1982) pp. 14–15
Discusses the social market approach to housing provision.

602 Madge, J. and Brown, C. *First homes: a survey of the housing circumstances of young married couples.* London, Policy Studies Institute, 1981.

603 Mayes, D. G. *The property boom: the effects of building society behaviour on house prices.* Oxford, Martin Robertson, 1979.
Examines the particular circumstances surrounding the boom in house prices in the early 1970s.

604 Mellor, J. R. *Urban sociology in an urbanized society.* London, Routledge and Kegan Paul, 1977. (International library of sociology).
Includes discussion of housing question in Britain.

605 Moorhouse, H. F. and Chamberlain, C. W. 'Lower class attitudes to property: aspects of the counter ideology'. *Sociology* vol. 8 no. 3 (1974) pp. 387–405.

606 Morcombe, K. N. *The residential development process: housing policy and theory.* Aldershot, Gower, 1984. (Studies in urban and regional policy no. 1).

607 Moreton, C. G. N. and Tate, J. C. 'The vacancy reserve'. *Town Planning Review* vol. 46 no. 1 (Jan. 1975) pp. 5–30.
Subtracting vacant properties from dwelling stock ignores value of economic surplus. Total approach advocated: data from Birmingham.

608 Murie, A. and Forrest, R. *Housing market processes and the inner city.* London, Social Science Research Council, 1980. (Inner city in context series no. 10).

609   Murie, A. and Forrest, R. 'Wealth, inheritance and housing policy'. *Policy and Politics* vol. 8 no. 1 (Jan. 1980) pp. 1–19.
Accumulation of wealth through housing.

610   Nellis, J. G. and Longbottom, J. A. *The determination of house prices in the UK*. Loughborough University, Department of Economics, 1980. (Occasional research paper no. 38).

611   Nellis, J. G. and Longbottom, J. A. 'An empirical analysis of the determination of house prices in the United Kingdom'. *Urban Studies* vol. 18 no. 1 (Feb. 1981) pp. 9–21.

612   'A new index of average house prices'. *Economic Trends* no. 348 (Oct. 1981) pp. 134–8.
How DOE's house price index differs in operation from those of building societies.

613   Nicholson, R. V. and Topham, N. 'The determinants of investment in housing by local authorities: an econometric approach'. *Journal of Royal Statistical Society Series A* vol. 134 (1971) pp. 273–320.

614   Norman, P. 'Managerialism: a review of recent work'. In M. Harloe (ed.) *Proceedings of the conference on urban change and conflict*. London, Centre for Environmental Studies, 1975. (Conference paper 14).

615   Pahl, R. *Whose city?* London, Penguin, 1975.
Contains misgivings about his original urban managerialism ideas.

616   Pahl, R. E. et al. 'The housing market'. In R. E. Pahl et al. *Structures and processes of urban life*. 2nd ed. Harlow, Longman, 1983. pp. 62–80.

617   Palmer, D. and Gleave, D. 'Employment, housing and mobility in London'. *London Journal* vol. 7 no. 2 (Winter 1981) pp. 177–93.

618   Palmer, D. and Gleave, D. 'Housing and labour mobility: the British experience'. In L. J. Walden (ed.). *Housing policy: the*

just price and the role of the public housing sector: papers and discussions from two British–Scandinavian seminars. Gavle, National Swedish Institute for Building Research, 1981. (Bulletin M81:24). pp. 135–60.

619   Payne, J. and Payne, G. 'Housing pathways and stratification: a study of life chances in the housing market'. *Journal of Social Policy* vol. 6 part 2 (1977) pp. 129–56.

620   Pickvance, C. G. (ed.) *Urban sociology: critical essays.* London, Tavistock, 1976.
Good introduction to the French school of urban sociology, containing many new translations.

621   Pratt, G. 'Class analysis and urban domestic property: a critical re-examination'. *International Journal of Urban and Regional Research* vol. 6 no. 4 (1982) pp. 481–501.
Returns to the theory of housing classes to examine differences between those who own property and those who do not.

622   Pritchard, R. M. *Housing and the spatial structure of the city: residential mobility and the housing market in an English city since the industrial revolution.* Cambridge University Press, 1976.
Case study of Leicester.

623   Reade, E. J. 'Residential decay, household movement and class structure'. *Policy and Politics* vol. 10 no. 1 (1982) pp. 27–45.

624   Richardson, H. W. et al. *Housing and urban spatial structure: a case study.* Farnborough, Saxon House, 1975.
Studies house prices and the urban spatial structure in Edinburgh.

625   Ricketts, M. 'Housing policy: towards a public choice perspective'. *Journal of Public Policy* vol. 1 no. 4 (Oct. 1981) pp. 501–22.

626   Ricketts, M. 'Local authority housing investment and finance: a test of the theory of regulation'. *Manchester School of Economic and Social Studies* vol. 51 no. 1 (Mar. 1983) pp. 45–62.

627   Robinson, R. *Housing economics and public policy.* London, Macmillan, 1979.

Application of economic theory to housing provision.

628 Robson, B. T. 'Housing, empiricism and the state'. In D. T. Herbert and D. M. Smith (eds.) *Social problems and the city: geographical perspectives.* Oxford University Press, 1979. pp. 66–83.

629 Rodger, R. G. 'The invisible hand: market forces, housing, and the urban form in Victorian cities'. In D. Fraser and A. Sutcliffe (eds.) *The pursuit of urban history.* London, Edward Arnold, 1983. pp. 190–211.
   Origins and history of Scottish tenements.

630 Rose, D. et al. 'Ideologies of property: a case study'. *Sociological Review* vol. 24 (1976) pp. 699–730.

631 Saunders, P. 'Beyond housing classes: the sociological significance of private property rights and means of consumption'. *International Journal of Urban and Regional Research* vol. 8 no. 2 (1984) pp. 202–27.

632 Saunders, P. 'Domestic property and social class'. *International Journal of Urban and Regional Research* vol. 2 no. 2 (June 1978) pp. 233–51.

633 Saunders, P. *Social theory and the urban question.* London, Hutchinson, 1981.

634 Saunders, P. *Urban politics: a sociological interpretation.* London, Hutchinson, 1979. Reprinted London, Penguin, 1980.

635 Shelter. *And I'll blow your house down. Housing need in Britain: present and future.* London, Shelter, 1980.

636 Short, J. R. 'Residential mobility in the private housing market of Bristol'. *Institute of British Geographers Transactions* vol. 3 no. 4 (1978) pp 533–47.

637 Stafford, D. *The economics of housing policy.* Rev. ed. London, Croom Helm, 1980.

Proposes a housing market based on consumer preferences, angled towards owner occupation.

638   Stone, P. A. *Urban development in Britain: standards, costs and resources 1964–2004, vol. 1, population trends and housing.* Cambridge University Press, 1970.

639   Taylor, P. J. and Hadfield, H. 'Housing and the state: a case study and structuralist interpretation'. In K. R. Cox and R. J. Johnston (eds.) *Conflict, politics and the urban scene.* Harlow, Longman, 1982. pp. 241–63.

640   Thomas, M. 'Construction of an index of housing need based on data from the National Dwelling and Housing Survey'. *Environment and Planning A* vol. 15 no. 6 (June 1983) pp. 769–79.
Describes the construction of an index to measure levels of housing need in the London Borough of Tower Hamlets.

641   Thorns, D. C. 'The implications of differential rates of capital gain from owner-occupation for the formation and development of housing classes'. *International Journal of Urban and Regional Research* vol. 5 no. 2 (1981) pp. 205–17.

642   Thorns, D. C. 'Industrial restructuring and change in the labour and property markets in Britain'. *Environment and Planning A* vol. 14 no. 6 (June 1982) pp. 745–63.

643   True, C. 'The economic rationale for government intervention in housing'. *Social Policy and Administration* vol. 13 no. 2 (Summer 1979) pp. 124–37.

644   United Kingdom, Department of Employment. *Family expenditure survey.* London, HMSO, annual.
Consumer expenditure on a number of housing variables.

645   United Kingdom, Department of the Environment, Housing Services Advisory Group. *Assessment of housing requirements.* London, The Department, 1977.
Guidance to local housing authorities on assessing housing needs.

646 United Kingdom, Department of the Environment, Housing Services Advisory Group. *The assessment of housing requirements: case studies.* London, The Department, 1979.

647 United Kingdom, National Economic Development Office. *BMRB housing consumer survey: a survey of attitudes towards current and alternative housing policies 1976.* London, HMSO, 1977.

648 United Kingdom, Office of Population Censuses and Surveys. *General household survey.* London, HMSO, annual.
Annual analysis of social characteristics of households, including occasional surveys on, e.g., housing satisfaction and tenure preferences.

649 United Kingdom, Scottish Development Department. *Assessing housing need: a manual of guidance.* London, HMSO, 1977.

650 United Kingdom, Scottish Development Department. *Local housing needs and strategies: a case study of the Dundee Sub-Region.* Edinburgh, HMSO, 1976.

651 University of Birmingham, Centre for Urban and Regional Studies, Housing Monitoring Team. *Housing price analysis: monitoring the private housing market.* Birmingham, The Centre, 1980. (Research memorandum 83).

652 Watson, C. J. et al. *Estimating local housing needs: a case study and discussion of methods.* University of Birmingham, Centre for Urban and Regional Studies, 1973. (Occasional paper 24).

653 Webster, D. 'A "social market" answer on housing'. *New Society* 12 Nov. 1981 pp. 269–72.

654 Weinstein, E. T. A. 'The movement of owner-occupied households between regions'. *Regional Studies* vol. 9 no. 2 (1975) pp. 137–57.

655 Whitbread, M. and Bird, H. 'Rent surplus and the evaluation of residential environments'. *Regional Studies* vol. 7 (1973) pp. 193–223.

656   Whitehead, C. M. E. 'Privatisation and housing'. In J. Le Grand and R. Robinson (eds.) *Privatisation and the welfare state.* London, Allen and Unwin, 1984. pp. 116–32.
Privatization of public housing in UK as economic policy or political ideology.

657   Whitehead, C. *The UK housing market: an econometric model.* Farnborough, Saxon House/Lexington Books, 1974.
In this overview of the workings of the UK housing market, some attention is given to factors that determine the construction of residential property.

658   Williams, P. 'Restructuring urban managerialism: towards a political economy of resource allocation'. *Environment and Planning A* vol. 14 (1982) pp. 95–105.

659   Williams, P. 'The role of institutions in the inner London housing market: the case of Islington'. *Transactions of the Institute of British Geographers* new series vol. 1 (1976) pp. 72–82.

2.4   North America

660   Alberts, W. W. and Kerr, H. S. 'The rate of return from investing in single family housing'. *Land Economics* vol. 57 no. 2 (May 1981) pp. 230–42.
Rates of return on owner occupied housing versus renting in US sample.

661   Barton, S. E. 'The urban housing problem: Marxist theory and community organizing'. *Review of Radical Political Economy* vol. 9 (Winter 1977) pp. 16–30.

662   Beaton, W. P. and Sossamon, L. B. 'Housing integration and rent supplements to existing housing'. *Professional Geographer* vol. 34 no. 2 (May 1982) pp. 147–55.

663   Buckley, R. M. (ed.) *Capital markets and the housing sector: perspectives on financial reform.* Cambridge, Mass., Ballinger, 1977.
Econometric analysis of financial institutions in the US housing market. Papers prepared for a study conducted by the US Department of Housing and Urban Development.

664   Carman, E. C. and Smith, D. A. 'Housing demand in the eighties: reports of its demise are exaggerated'. *Urban Law and Policy* vol. 6 no. 2 (Dec. 1983) pp. 107–31.
Demographic and financial factors affecting US housing demand during the 1980s.

665   Carvalho, M. 'On the determinants of residential property values'. *Plan Canada* vol. 16 nos. 3–4 (Sept.–Dec. 1976) pp. 190–7.
Factors influencing the local housing market in Winnipeg.

666   Clark, W. (ed.) *Modelling housing market research.* London, Croom Helm, 1982.

667   Clark, W. A. V. and Moore, E. G. (eds.) *Residential mobility and public policy.* Beverly Hills, Sage, 1980. (Urban affairs annual reviews vol. 19).
Based on a conference held at the University of California, Los Angeles, Nov. 1979.

668   Clark, W. A. V. and Onaka, J. L. 'Life cycle and housing adjustment as explanations of residential mobility'. *Urban Studies* vol. 20 part 1 (Feb. 1983) pp. 47–57.

669   Coleman, R. P. 'Patterns in housing market goals by socio-economic class and life stages'. In R. A. Dentler (ed.) *Urban problems: perspectives and solutions.* Chicago, Rand McNally, 1977. pp. 256–69.

670   De Jong, G. F. 'Residential preferences and migration'. *Demography* vol. 14 (1977) pp. 169–78.

671   De Leeuw, F. and Struyk, R. J. *The web of urban housing: analysing policy with a market simulation model.* Washington, DC, Urban Institute, 1975.
Policy simulations for metropolitan areas in the US.

672   Deutschmann, H. D. 'The residential location decision: study of residential mobility'. *Socio-economic Planning Sciences* vol. 6 (1972) pp. 349–64.

673   Dougherty, A. and Van Order, R. 'Inflation, housing costs

and the consumer price index'. *American Economic Review* vol. 72 no. 1 (Mar. 1982) pp. 154–64.
Cost of US housing measured against the US Consumer Price Index.

674 Fisch, O. 'Dynamics of the housing market'. *Journal of Urban Economics* vol. 4 no. 4 (Oct. 1977) pp. 428–47.
Derivation of rent values of the stock of the housing market.

675 Fisher, E. M. *Housing markets and congressional goals.* New York, Praeger, 1975. (Praeger special studies).
Criticism of assumptions made by US federal government in the Housing Act 1968.

676 Follian, J. R. 'Does inflation affect real behavior? The case of housing'. *Southern Economic Journal* vol. 48 no. 3 (1982) pp. 570–82.

677 Foote, N. N. *Housing choices and housing constraints.* New York, McGraw-Hill, 1960.

678 Frieden, B. *The environmental protection hustle.* Cambridge, Mass., MIT Press, 1979.
Effects of environmental issues on housing developments and the housing market in California.

679 Friedman, J. 'Housing consumption under a constrained income transfer'. *Journal of Urban Economics* vol. 11 no. 3 (May 1982) pp. 253–71.
Evidence from the Housing Allowance Demand Experiment, a US housing assistance programme.

680 Gold, D. E. *Housing market discrimination: causes and effects of slum formation.* New York, Praeger, 1980. (Praeger special studies).
Study of New York.

681 Goldberg, M. A. 'Housing and land prices in Canada and the US'. In L. B. Smith and M. Walker (eds.) *Public property: the Habitat debate continued.* Vancouver, Fraser Institute, 1977. pp. 207–54.

682   Goldberg, M. A. *The housing problem: a real crisis? A primer on housing markets, policies and problems.* Vancouver, University of British Columbia Press, 1983.

683   Goldberg, M. A. and Gau, G. W. (eds.) *North American housing markets into the twenty-first century.* Cambridge, Mass., Ballinger, 1983.
Issues of housing demand, supply and finance in US and Canadian contexts, from papers originally presented at a symposium at the University of British Columbia, Vancouver, 1981.

684   Goodman, J. L. 'Housing consumption disequilibrium and local residential mobility'. *Environment and Planning A* vol. 8 no. 8 (Dec. 1976) pp. 855–74.
Economic theory of local residential mobility developed from US data.

685   Goodman, J. L. *Urban residential mobility: places, people and policy.* Washington, DC, Urban Institute, 1978.

686   Grebler, L. *Large scale housing and real estate firms: analysis of a new business enterprise.* London, Pall Mall, 1974.

687   Grebler, L. and Mittelbach, F. G. *The inflation of house prices: its extent, causes and consequences.* Lexington, Mass., Lexington Books, 1979. (Lexington books special series in real estate and urban land economics).

688   Greendale, A. and Knock, S. F. (eds.) *Housing costs and housing needs.* New York, Praeger, 1976. (Praeger special studies in US economic, social and political issues).
Papers presented at a conference entitled 'Decent housing: a promise to keep' and sponsored by the Inter-religious Coalition for Housing, Washington, DC, Apr. 1975.

689   Grier, G. 'Population dynamics, housing economics and the future of the American habitat'. *Habitat* vol. 2, nos. 1–2 (1977) pp. 143–55.

690   Grigsby, W. G. *Housing markets and public policy.* Philadelphia, University of Pennsylvania Press, 1963.

691   Hendershott, P. H. 'Real user costs and the demand for single family housing'. *Brookings Papers on Economic Activity* no. 2 (1980) pp. 401–52.
Evidence from the US in 1979–80.

692   Hensher, D. A. *Housing demand and tenure choice: data emphasis and an annotated bibliography.* Monticello, Vance Bibliographies, 1980. (Public administration series bibliography no. 395).

693   Houstoun, L. O. 'Market trends reveal housing choices for the 1980s'. *Journal of Housing* vol. 38 (Feb. 1981) pp. 73–9.

694   Ingram, G. K. (ed.) *Residential location and urban housing markets.* Cambridge, Mass., Ballinger, 1977.

695   King, M. 'An econometric model of tenure choice and demand for housing as a joint decision'. *Journal of Public Economics* vol. 14 (1980) pp. 137–59.

696   Kristoff, F. S. et al. 'Federal housing policies: subsidized production, filtration and objectives'. *Land Economics* vol. 48 no. 4 (1972) pp. 309–20.
Key text on filtration theory.

697   Leigh, W. A. 'Economic depreciation of the residential housing stock of the United States 1950–1970'. *Review of Economics and Statistics* vol. 62 no. 2 (May 1980) pp. 200–6.

698   Lewis, E. L. (ed.) *Housing decisions.* Rev. ed. South Holland, Ill., Goodheart, 1984.

699   McCarthy, K. F. 'The household life cycle and housing choices'. *Papers of the Regional Science Association* vol. 37 (1976) pp. 55–80.

700   McDonald, J. F. *Economic analysis of an urban housing market.* New York, Academic Press, 1979. (Studies in urban economics).
Wide review of urban housing market models followed by a concentrated focus on the Chicago housing market.

701   Mayo, S. K. 'Theory and estimation in the economy of housing demand'. *Journal of Urban Economics* vol. 10 no. 1 (July 1981) pp. 95–116.

702   Michelson, W. *Environmental choice, human behavior and residential satisfaction.* New York, Oxford University Press, 1977.
Reasons for choice and location of housing and behavioural aspects. Study in Toronto.

703   Miron, J. R. *Housing affordability and willingness to pay.* University of Toronto Press, 1984. (Research paper no. 154).

704   Muth, R. F. *Cities and housing.* University of Chicago Press, 1969.
Theory of residential location by income.

705   Myers, D. 'Housing allowances, submarket relationships and the filtering process'. *Urban Affairs Quarterly* vol. 11 (Dec. 1975) pp. 215–40.

706   Myers, D. 'Turnover and filtering of postwar single-family houses'. *Journal of the American Planning Association* vol. 50 no. 3 (Summer 1984) pp. 352–8.

707   Newman, S. J. and Duncan, G. J. 'Residential problems, dissatisfaction and mobility'. *Journal of the American Planning Association* vol. 45 no. 2 (Apr. 1979) pp. 154–66.
Perceived satisfaction with housing and the neighbourhood and residential mobility in US cities.

708   Orr, L. L. *Income, employment and urban residential location.* New York, Academic Press, 1975.

709   Ozanne, L. and Struyk, R. *Housing from the existing stock: comparative economic analysis of owner-occupants and landlords.* Washington, DC, Urban Institute, 1976.

710   Palm, R. 'Financial and real estate institutions in the housing market: a study of recent house price changes in the San Francisco Bay Area'. In D. T. Herbert and R. J. Johnston (eds.)

Geography and the urban environment vol. 2. Chichester, Wiley, 1979. pp. 83–124.

711   Palm, R. I. 'Homeownership cost trends'. *Environment and Planning A* vol. 9 no. 7 (July 1977) pp. 795–804.
Influences on house prices in San Francisco.

712   Pollakowski, H. O. *Urban housing markets and residential location.* Lexington, Mass., Lexington Books, 1982.
Examines the effect on housing prices and choices of public service provision and amenities.

713   Quigley, J. M. and Weinberg, D. H. 'Intra-urban residential mobility: a review and synthesis'. *International Regional Science Review* vol. 2 (1977) pp. 41–66.

714   Reid, M. *Housing and income.* University of Chicago Press, 1962.

715   Ricks, B. *National housing models.* Lexington, Mass., Heath, 1974.

716   Rosen, K. T. *California housing markets in the 1980s: demand, affordability and policies.* Cambridge, Mass., Oelgeschlager, Gunn and Hain, 1984.
Housing problems in California.

717   Rosen, K. T. *Seasonal cycles in the housing market: patterns, costs and policies.* Cambridge, Mass., MIT Press, 1979.

718   Rossi, P. H. *Why families move.* 2nd ed. Beverly Hills, Sage, 1980.
Seminal work on residential mobility.

719   Salins, P. D. *The ecology of housing destruction: economic effects of public intervention in the housing market.* New York University Press for the International Center for Economic Policy Studies, 1980.
Study of New York.

720   Sands, G. *Land-office business: land and housing prices in*

rapidly growing metropolitan areas. Lexington, Mass., Lexington Books, 1982.

721 Sands, G. and Bower, L. L. *Housing turnover and housing policy: case studies of vacancy chains in New York State.* New York, Praeger, 1976.
Housing opportunities created by new housing in New York, Buffalo and Rochester.

722 Schafer, R. *The suburbanization of multifamily housing.* Lexington, Mass., Lexington Books, 1975.
Forces influencing role and location of multifamily construction in the US since 1900.

723 Schnidman, F. and Silverman, A. (eds.) *Housing supply and affordability.* Washington, DC, Urban Land Institute, 1983.

724 Schwartz, S. I. et al. 'Suburban growth controls and the price of new housing'. *Journal of Environmental Economics and Management* vol. 8 no. 4 (Dec. 1981) pp. 303–20.
Effect of growth controls on the price of new houses in California.

725 Smith, L. B. 'A model of the Canadian housing and mortgage markets'. *Journal of Political Economy* vol. 77 (1969) pp. 795–816.

726 Smith, L. B. *The postwar Canadian housing and residential mortgage markets and the role of government.* University of Toronto Press, 1974.

727 Smith, T. R. and Clark, W. A. V. 'Housing market search behavior and expected utility theory: 1: measuring preferences for housing'. *Environment and Planning A* vol. 14 no. 5 (May 1982) pp. 681–98.
Housing market search in Los Angeles.

728 Sogaard, G. A. and Tremblay, K. R. *Empirical research on housing satisfactions: an annotated bibliography.* Monticello, Vance Bibliographies, 1980. (Public administration series bibliography no. P-590).

US material.

729   Speare, A. et al. *Residential mobility, migration and metropolitan change.* Cambridge, Mass., Ballinger, 1975.

730   Steele, M. *The demand for housing in Canada.* Ottawa, Statistics Canada, 1979. (Census analytical study).

731   Stegman, M. A. (ed.) *Housing and economics: the American dilemma.* Cambridge, Mass., MIT Press, 1970.

732   Stegman, M. A. *Housing investment in the inner city: the dynamics of decline.* Cambridge, Mass., MIT Press, 1972.

733   Stokes, C. J. and Fisher, E. M. *Housing market performance in the United States.* New York, Praeger, 1976.

734   Stone, M. E. 'Housing and the American economy: a Marxist analysis'. In P. Claval (ed.) *Urban and regional planning in an age of austerity.* New York, Pergamon, 1980. pp. 81–108.

735   Straszheim, M. R. *An econometric analysis of the urban housing market.* New York, National Bureau of Economic Research, 1975.

736   Timms, D. *The urban mosaic: toward a theory of residential differentiation.* Cambridge University Press, 1971.

737   Tuccillo, J. *Housing and investment in an inflationary world: theory and evidence.* Washington, DC, Urban Institute, 1980.

738   Tuccillo, J. A. and Villani, K. E. (eds.) *House prices and inflation.* Washington, DC, Urban Institute Press, 1981.

739   United States, Department of Housing and Urban Development. *Families and housing markets: obstacles to locating suitable housing.* Washington, DC, Government Printing Office, 1980.
    Special problems of families with children.

740   United States, Department of Housing and Urban Development. *Projections of housing consumption in the US 1980–2000, by*

a cohort method. Washington, DC, Government Printing Office, 1980. (Annual housing survey studies no. 9).
Feasibility of making housing projections based on current data.

741   Urban Land Institute. *The affordable community: adapting today's communities to tomorrow's needs: the report on development choices for the 1980s.* Washington, DC, The Institute, 1982.

742   Varady, D. P. 'Determinants of residential mobility decisions'. *Journal of the American Planning Association* vol. 49 no. 2 (Spring 1983) pp. 184–99.

743   Varady, D. P. 'Residential mobility in the urban homesteading demonstration neighborhoods'. *Journal of the American Planning Association* vol. 50 no. 3 (Summer 1984) pp. 346–51.

744   Wandersman, A. and Moos, R. H. 'Assessing and evaluating residential environments: a sheltered living environments example'. *Environment and Behavior* vol. 13 no. 4 (July 1981) pp. 481–508.

745   Weicher, J. C. 'Urban housing policy'. In P. Mieskowski and M. Straszheim (eds.) *Current issues in urban economics.* Baltimore, Johns Hopkins University Press, 1979.

746   Weicher, J. C. et al. *Metropolitan housing needs for the 1980s.* Washington, DC, Urban Institute Press, 1982.
Housing demand in the US.

747   Weisbrod, G. and Vidal, A. 'Housing search barriers for low-income renters'. *Urban Affairs Quarterly* vol. 16 no. 4 (June 1981) pp. 465–82.
Obstructions to residential mobility in two US cities.

748   Williams, J. A. 'The multifamily housing solution and housing type preferences'. *Social Science Quarterly* vol. 52 no. 3 (1971) pp. 543–59.

749   Zikmund, J. and Dennis, D. E. *Suburbia: a guide to information sources.* Detroit, Gale, 1979.

2.5 Australasia

750   Abelson, P. W. 'Property prices and the value of amenities'. *Journal of Environmental Economics and Management* vol. 6 no. 1 (Mar. 1979) pp. 11–28.
Effects of variables on house prices in Sydney.

751   Bell, C. 'On housing classes'. *Australian and New Zealand Journal of Sociology* vol. 13 (1977) pp. 36–40.

752   Bell, C. 'Towards a political economy of housing'. In E. L. Wheelwright and K. Buckley (eds.) *Essays in the political economy of Australian capitalism vol. 2*. Sydney, Australian and New Zealand Book Co., 1978.

753   Berry, M. 'Posing the housing question in Australia: elements of a theoretical framework for a Marxist analysis of housing'. *Antipode* vol. 13 no. 1 (1981) pp. 3–14.

754   Burke, T. and Hancock, L. *Housing and the family.* Melbourne, Institute of Family Studies, 1983.
Changing trends in family structure in Australia and effects on housing market.

755   Dao, D. T. and McMurray, J. A. *Housing preferences in New Zealand: an overview.* Wellington, New Zealand National Housing Commission, 1977. (Research paper 77/3).

756   Gibbings, M. J. *Housing preferences in the Brisbane area.* Canberra, Australian Institute of Urban Studies, 1973.

757   Johnston, J. A. *Demographic change and housing need.* Wellington, New Zealand National Housing Commission, 1978.

758   Johnston, J. A. *Housing needs assessment — a regional emphasis.* Wellington, New Zealand National Housing Commission, 1980. (Research paper 80/1).

759   Kendig, H. *Buying and renting: household moves in Adelaide.* Canberra, Australian Institute of Urban Studies, 1981. (AIUS publication no. 91).

760   Kendig, H. L. 'Housing careers, life cycle and residential mobility: implications for the housing market'. *Urban Studies* vol. 21 no. 3 (Aug. 1984) pp. 271–83.
Movement of households through the housing market in Adelaide: concept of a housing career.

761   King, R. *The dimensions of housing need in Australia.* University of Sydney, Ian Fell Bequest, 1973. (Occasional paper no. 3).

762   New Zealand, National Housing Commission. *New Zealand's housing requirements 1976–86.* Wellington, The Commission, 1976. (Commission paper 1/76).

763   Smith, B. N. P. and Thorns, D. C. *Constraints, choices and housing environments.* Wellington, New Zealand National Housing Commission, 1979. (Research paper 79/1).
Housing need, demand and residential mobility in New Zealand.

2.6   Africa, Asia and Latin America

764   Angel, S. et al. *Land for housing the poor.* Singapore, Select Books, 1983.

765   Araud, C. et al. *Studies on employment in the Mexican housing industry.* Paris, Organisation for Economic Co-operation and Development, 1973.

766   Asiama, S. O. 'The land factor in housing for low income urban settlers: the example of Madina, Ghana'. *Third World Planning Review* vol. 6 no. 2 (May 1984) pp. 171–84.

767   Baross, P. 'Analysis of housing production systems — Bandung, Indonesia'. *Openhouse* vol. 4 no. 4 (1979) pp. 44–61.

768   Batley, R. *Power through democracy: urban political analysis in Brazil.* Aldershot, Gower, 1983.

769   Borukhov, E. et al. 'Housing prices and housing preferences in Israel'. *Urban Studies* vol. 15 (1978) pp.187–200.

770   Edwards, M. 'Residential mobility in a changing housing market: the case of Bucaramanga, Colombia'. *Urban Studies* vol. 20 no. 2 (May 1982) pp. 131–45.

771   Eng, T. S. 'Residential choice in public and private housing in Singapore'. *Ekistics* vol. 45 no. 270 (June 1978) pp. 246–9.

772   Gabriel, S. A. 'A note on housing market segmentation in an Israeli development town'. *Urban Studies* vol. 21 (May 1984) pp. 189–94.

773   Gauhan, T. O. *Some economic and political characteristics of the low income housing market in Bogotá, Colombia and their implications for public policy alternatives.* Houston, Rice University, Program of Development Studies, 1975.

774   Ha, S.-K. and Merrett, S. 'Assessing housing consumption requirements: the case of Seoul'. *Third World Planning Review* vol. 6 no. 4 (Nov. 1984) pp. 331–7.

775   Jaramillo, S. and Schteingart, M. 'Capital accumulation and housing production in Latin America 1960–80'. In J. Walton (ed.) *Capital and labour in the urbanized world.* London, Sage, 1985. pp. 176–94.

776   Johnstone, M. 'Conventional housing provision in peninsular Malaysia: spatial distortions in a developing economy'. *Habitat International* vol. 5 (1981) pp. 337–59.

777   Lakshmanan, T. R. et al. 'Housing requirements and national resources: implications of the UN World Model'. *Habitat* vol. 2 nos. 3–4 (1977) pp. 277–90.

778   Lea, J. P. 'Underlying determinants of housing location: a case study from Swaziland'. *Journal of Modern African Studies* vol. 11 (1973) pp. 211–25.

779   Merrett, S. 'The assessment of housing consumption requirements in developing countries'. *Third World Planning Review* vol. 6 no. 4 (Nov. 1984) pp. 319–29.

780   Payne, G. K. 'Housing agents in the towns of Papua New Guinea'. *Built Environment* vol. 8 no. 2 (1982) pp. 125–37.

781   Rodwin, L. 'Measuring housing needs in developing countries'. In H. W. Eldredge (ed.) *Taming megalopolis vol. 2*. New York, Praeger, 1967. pp. 1011–17.

782   Tipple, A. G. 'Housing need and implementation strategy for Kumasi: lessons from Zambia'. *Planning Outlook* vol. 23 no. 2 (1981) pp. 67–77.
Housing need in Kumasi, Ghana and lessons from similar policies in Zambia.

783   World Bank. *The Bertaud model: a model for the analysis of alternatives for low income shelter in the developing world.* Washington, DC, The Bank, 1981. (Urban Development Department technical paper no. 2).

784   Yeh, S. H. K. 'Housing conditions and housing needs in Singapore'. *Malaysian Economic Review* vol. 14 no. 2 (1974) pp. 47–71.

3

Construction and energy conservation

Sources of information on construction and energy conservation are limited to those which have a direct association with the determination or expression of housing policy. Included, therefore, are works on the organization of the housebuilding industry, political influences on housebuilding, the effects of political decisions on the shape and size of housing design, housebuilding land availability, housing maintenance, and changes in housing policy induced by the need for energy conservation measures. Reference should also be made to sections 2 'Housing market', 4 'Housing finance' and 14 'Special needs'.

3.1 International and comparative

785   Armitage, J. S. *Guide to international organisations of interest to the construction industry.* London, Construction Industry Research and Information Association, 1982.

786   Burns, L. S. and Grebler, L. 'Resource allocation to housing investment: a comparative international study'. *Economic Development and Cultural Change* vol. 25 no. 1 (Oct. 1976) pp. 95–121.
   Share of residential construction in the total output of countries at various stages of development.

787   Farmer, P. *Energy conservation in building 1973–1983: a bibliography of European and American literature on government,*

*commercial and domestic buildings.*Bedford, Technical Communications, 1983.

788   Josey, J. L. 'Increased mobility and energy conservation through concurrent housing and transportation planning'. *International Journal for Housing Science and its Applications* vol. 4 no. 4 (1980) pp. 297–301.
    Efficient housing developments are energy saving.

789   King, A. D. *The bungalow: the production of a global culture.* London, Routledge and Kegan Paul, 1984.

790   Klingberg, T. and Wickman, K. *Energy trends and policy impacts in seven countries.* Gavle, National Swedish Institute for Building Research, 1984. (Bulletin M84:12).

791   Leach, G. and Pellew, S. *Energy conservation in housing.* London, International Institute for Environment and Development, 1982.

792   O'Sullivan, P. et al. 'Low energy houses: some issues in matching design, construction and use'. *International Journal for Housing Science and its Applications* vol. 6 no. 4 (1982) pp. 361–75.
    Changes in housing design criteria in response to the energy crisis.

793   Scott, D. and Sridurangkatum, S. 'A comparative study of housing construction methods'. *Building and Environment* vol. 15 no. 1 (1980) pp. 27–31.

794   Snell, J. E. et al. 'Energy conservation in new housing design'. *Habitat* vol. 2 nos. 1–2 (1977) pp. 59–72.

795   Turner, G. 'Energy conservation: horizons and determiners'. *International Journal for Housing Science and its Applications* vol. 5 no. 2 (1981) pp. 159–68.

796   United Kingdom, Department of the Environment, Building Research Establishment. *Energy conservation in the built environment: symposium.* London, Construction Press, 1976.

Proceedings of the symposium of the International Council for Building Research Studies and Documentation.

797   United Nations, Department of Economic and Social Affairs, Centre for Housing, Building and Planning. *Design of low-cost housing and community facilities, vol. 2, basic housing case studies.* New York, United Nations, 1975.

798   United States, Department of Housing and Urban Development. *Housing and urban development energy research abroad: a bibliography.* Washington, DC, The Department, 1980.

799   Ural, O. (ed.) *Construction of lower-cost housing.* New York, Wiley, 1980.

800   Ural, O. (ed.) *Energy resources and conservation related to built environment.* 2 vols. New York, Pergamon, 1980.
Proceedings of the International Conference on Energy Resources and Conservation related to the Built Environment, Miami Beach, Florida, Dec. 1980.

3.2   Europe

801   Anthony, K. H. 'Public and private space in Soviet cities'. *Landscape* vol. 23 no. 2 (1979) pp. 20–5.
Priority given to design and maintenance of housing in the USSR compares badly with public space.

802   Clark, E. 'Housing policies and new construction: a study of chains of moves in Southwest Skane'. *Scandinavian Housing and Planning Research* vol. 1 no. 1 (Feb. 1984) pp. 3–14.
Construction policies most suited to Sweden's housing policy goals.

803   Datel, R. E. *A selected annotated bibliography of works on Western European building conservation, housing and inner cities.* Monticello, Vance Bibliographies, 1980. (Architecture series bibliography no. A-396).

804   Ginatempo, N. 'The structural contradictions of the building industry in Italy and the significance of the new housing

legislation'. *International Journal of Urban and Regional Research* vol. 3 no. 4 (1979) pp. 465–91.

805   Hekhaus, H. H. et al. *Main characteristics for energy saving in low cost housing. Summary report.* Luxembourg, European Communities Commission, 1983. (Document no. EUR 8370).

806   Jager, F. *Solar energy applications in houses: performance and economics in Europe.* Oxford, Pergamon, 1981.

807   Jantzen, E. B. and Kaaris, H. 'Danish low-rise housing'. *Scandinavian Housing and Planning Research* vol. 1 no. 1 (Feb. 1984) pp. 27–42.
Low density housing research in Denmark has led to development of small, varying, low rise housing units.

808   Klingberg, T. (ed.) *Effects of energy conservation programs.* Gavle, National Swedish Institute for Building Research, 1984. (Bulletin M84:2).

809   Klingberg, T. (ed.) *Energy conservation in rented buildings.* Gavle, National Swedish Institute for Building Research, 1984. (Bulletin M84:11).

810   McCarthy, J. A. *Private housebuilding in Ireland 1976–1981.* Dublin, National Institute for Physical Planning and Construction Research, 1982.

811   Scholten, H. 'Planning for housing construction and population distribution in the Netherlands'. *Town Planning Review* vol. 55 no. 4 (Oct. 1984) pp. 405–19.

812   Sharp, D. 'Public appeal'. *Building* vol. 243 no. 7266 (5 Nov. 1982) pp. 30–3.
Efforts to brighten dull French housing estates.

3.3   United Kingdom

813   Aspinall, P. J. 'The internal structure of the house-building industry in nineteenth century cities'. In J. H. Johnson and C. G.

Pooley (eds.) *The internal structure of the nineteenth century British city*. London, Croom Helm, 1981. pp. 81–114.

814   Association of Metropolitan Authorities. *Defects in housing, part 1, non-traditional dwellings of the 1940s and 1950s*. London, The Association, 1983.

815   Association of Metropolitan Authorities. *Defects in housing, part 2, industrialised and system built dwellings of the 1960s and 1970s*. London, The Association, 1984.

816   Association of Metropolitan Authorities. *Defects in housing, part 3, repair and modernisation of traditional built buildings*. London, The Association, 1985.

817   Ball, M. 'British housing policy and the housebuilding industry'. *Capital and Class* no. 4 (Spring 1978) pp. 78–99.
Using Marxist analytical techniques, argues that Britain's continuing housing crisis can be traced back to the low productivity of the country's housebuilding industry.

818   Beer, A. 'Development control and design quality, part 2, attitudes to design'. *Town Planning Review* vol. 54 no. 4 (Oct. 1983) pp. 383–404.

819   Beer, A. R. 'The external environment of housing areas'. *Built Environment* vol. 8 no. 1 (1982) pp. 25–9.

820   Bowley, M. *The British building industry*. Cambridge University Press, 1966.
Assesses the role of various professionals involved in the construction process, with particular reference to technological change in the industry.

821   Bradfield, V. J. 'Construction industry information sources'. *Architect and Surveyor* vol. 58 no. 5 (Oct.–Nov. 1983) pp. 4–9.

822   Bradfield, V. (ed.) *Information sources in architecture*. London, Butterworth, 1983.
Guide to various sources of information in architecture with substantial attention to housing.

823   Construction Industry Research and Information Association. *CIRIA guide to sources of construction information.* 4th ed. London, The Association, 1984.

824   Diacon, D. *Residential housing and nuclear attack: the ineffectiveness of current civil defence measures.* London, Croom Helm, 1984.
Assesses the effectiveness of UK housing against possible nuclear attack.

825   Edwards, A. M. *The design of suburbia.* London, Penbridge Press, 1981.

826   Esher, L. *A broken wave: the rebuilding of England 1940–1980.* London, Allen Lane, 1981.
Architectural history of England since the war.

827   Fleming, M. C. *Construction and the related professions.* Oxford, Pergamon, 1980. (Reviews of UK statistical sources vol. 12).
Detailed analysis of statistical sources for the construction industry.

828   Fraser, R. and Evans, R. W. 'A study of Scottish housebuilding performance'. *Construction Papers* vol. 1 no. 2 (1981) pp. 17–27.

829   Gaskell, S. M. *Building control: national legislation and the introduction of local bye-laws in Victorian England.* London, Bedford Square Press, 1984.

830   *House's guide to the construction industry.* London, House Information Services, irregular.
Reference book for the construction industry in Britain. Latest edition (8th) 1981–2.

831   *Kemp's property industry yearbook.* Birmingham, Kemp's, annual.
Up to date information on estate agents, property developers and professional bodies in Britain.

832   Leach, G. *Energy-related statistics for UK dwellings.* London,

International Institute for Environment and Development, 1981. Report to the Joint Research Centre for the European Community.

833 Leach, G. *A low energy strategy for the United Kingdom.* London, International Institute for Environment and Development, 1979. See 'Domestic sector' (pp. 82–122).

834 Lewis, J. P. *Building cycles and Britain's growth.* London, Macmillan, 1965.
Traces the impact of investment in building production on Britain's economic performance from the Middle Ages. The final chapter speculates on the prospects of the industry and of the economy as a whole until the year 2000.

835 National House Building Council. *Private house building statistics.* Amersham, The Council, quarterly.
Includes data on the prices of new dwellings, and building starts by region.

836 Nicholls, D. C. et al. *Private housing development process: a case study.* London, Department of the Environment, 1981. (Inner cities research programme 4).

837 Nicholls, D. C. et al. 'The risk business: developers' perceptions and prospects for housebuilding in the inner city'. *Urban Studies* vol. 19 no. 4 (Nov. 1982) pp. 331–41.
Discusses principal results from a study of residential developers and role in housing development process in Nottingham.

838 Pezzey, J. *An economic assessment of some energy conservation measures in housing and other buildings.* Watford, Building Research Establishment, 1985.
Cost effectiveness of various energy saving measures in housing.

839 Planning Exchange. *Modernisation of non-traditional housing*

of the 1944–55 period. Glasgow, The Exchange, 1983. (Forum report 33).
Papers presented at a Planning Exchange seminar, Dec. 1982.

840   Powell, C. G. *An economic history of the British building industry 1815–1979.* London, Methuen, 1982.

841   Property Services Agency, Library. *Engergy conservation in building design: an annotated bibliography.* 2nd ed. London, 1980.

842   Richardson, H. W. and Aldcroft, D. H. *Building in the British economy between the two wars.* London, Allen and Unwin, 1968.

843   Romig, F. and Leach, G. *Energy conservation in UK dwellings: domestic sector survey and insulation.* London, International Institute for Environment and Development, 1977.

844   Rydin, Y. *Residential development and the planning system: a study of the housing land system at the local level.* Oxford, Pergamon, 1985. (Progress in planning vol. 24 part 1).

845   Saul, S. B. 'Housebuilding in England 1890–1914'. *Economic History Review* vol. 15 (1962) pp. 119–37.

846   Scoffham, E. R. *The shape of British housing.* London, George Godwin, 1984.
Historical study of the architecture of housing especially in post-war Britain.

847   Sherratt, A. F. C. (ed.) *Experience of energy conservation in buildings.* London, Construction Press, 1981.

848   Smyth, H. *Land banking, land availability and planning for private housebuilding.* University of Bristol, School for Advanced Urban Studies, 1982. (Working paper 23).

849   Smyth, H. *Land supply, housebuilders and government policies.* University of Bristol, School for Advanced Urban Studies, 1984. (Working paper 43).

850   United Kingdom, Department of the Environment. *The future of building control in England and Wales.* London, HMSO, 1981. (Cmnd. 8179).

851 United Kingdom, Department of the Environment. *Study of the availability of private housebuilding land in Greater Manchester 1978–1981.* London, HMSO, 1979.

The most recent of several official investigations of land availability for private housebuilding.

852 United Kingdom, Department of the Environment, Building Research Establishment. *Energy conservation: a study of energy consumption in buildings and possible means of saving energy in housing.* Watford, The Establishment, 1975. (Current paper 56/75).

853 United Kingdom, Department of the Environment, Building Research Establishment. *Quality in traditional housing.* 3 vols. London, The Department, 1982.

Analyses faults in housing construction.

854 United Kingdom, Department of the Environment, Building Research Establishment. *Timber framed housing — a technical appraisal.* Watford, The Establishment, 1983.

Provides reassurance on some contemporary criticisms of timber framed housing.

855 United Kingdom, Department of the Environment, Housing Development Directorate. *The quality of local authority housing schemes.* London, HMSO, 1974. (HDD occasional paper 1/74).

Report of a pilot survey to assess the quality of public sector housing built in the first four years of the operation of the housing cost yardstick (1967–71).

856 United Kingdom, Department of the Environment, Housing Development Directorate. *Value for money in local authority housebuilding programmes.* London, HMSO, 1978.

In the Simon, Banwell and Wood traditions, proposes reforms in the management of local authority contracts which would make for more efficient and effective building programmes.

857 United Kingdom, Department of the Environment, Housing Services Advisory Group. *The client role in public sector housebuilding.* London, The Department, 1978.

858 United Kingdom, House of Commons, Environment Committee. *Green belt and land for housing.* London, HMSO, 1984. (First report, HC 275, Session 1983–84).
Discusses possible use of green belt land for new housebuilding.

859 United Kingdom, Local Government Board. *Report of the committee to consider questions of building construction in connection with the provision of dwellings for the working classes.* London, HMSO, 1918. (Cd. 9191).
The Tudor Walters report, which recommended densities of housing construction for rural and urban areas.

860 United Kingdom, Ministry of Health, Central Housing Advisory Committee. *Design of dwellings. Report of the design of dwellings sub committee.* London, Ministry of Health, 1944.
The Dudley report, which recommended improved housing standards from inter-war dwellings.

861 United Kingdom, Ministry of Works. *House construction. Report by an interdepartmental committee.* London, HMSO, 1943. (Post-war building studies no. 1).
The first Burt report.

862 United Kingdom, Ministry of Works. *House construction. Second report by an interdepartmental committee.* London, HMSO, 1945. (Post-war building studies no. 23).
The second Burt report.

863 United Kingdom, Ministry of Works. *House construction. Third report by an interdepartmental committee.* London, HMSO, 1947. (Post-war building studies no. 25).
The third Burt report.

864 United Kingdom, National Economic Development Office. *Construction to 1990.* London, The Office, 1985.
Latest in a series of forecasts for the construction industry in the UK.

865 United Kingdom, National Economic Development

Office. *The public client and the construction industries.* London, HMSO, 1975.

The Wood report. Examines purchasing policies and practices in the public sector as they affect the construction industry.

866   United Kingdom, National Economic Development Office. *The public sector infrastructure: the making of spending decisions.* London, The Office, 1985.

Highlights the need for public investment in the infrastructure, including housing.

867   United Kingdom, Scottish Local Authorities Special Housing Group. *Housing maintenance manual, vol. 1, parts 1–5, structure and finishes.* Edinburgh, The Group, 1980.

868   University College London, Bartlett School of Architecture and Planning. *The production of the built environment.* London, The School, 1979.

Proceedings of the first Bartlett summer school.

869   University of Birmingham, Centre for Urban and Regional Studies, Housing Monitoring Team. *The housebuilding industry and changes in the market for housebuilding work: a review of the British experience in the 1970s.* Birmingham, The Centre, 1981. (Research memorandum 87).

870   University of Birmingham, Centre for Urban and Regional Studies, Housing Monitoring Team. *New housebuilding and housing strategies: a report of the public/private sector housing forum.* Birmingham, The Centre, 1980. (Research memorandum 82).

871   University of Birmingham, Centre for Urban and Regional Studies, Housing Monitoring Team. *The role of the local authority in land programming and the process of private residential development.* Birmingham, The Centre, 1980. (Research memorandum 80).

872   Wilkinson, R. K. and Archer, C. 'Uncertainty, prices and the supply of housing'. *Policy and Politics* vol. 5 no. 1 (Sept. 1976) pp. 63–74.

Factors influencing the private house building industry.

3.4 North America

873 Brown, D. M. *Building codes and residential construction: an annotated bibliography.* Monticello, Vance Bibliographies, 1980. (Architecture series bibliography A-334).

874 Canada Mortgage and Housing Corporation. *Energy conservation in new small residential buildings.* Ottawa, The Corporation, 1981.

875 Catania, P. J. 'The impact of solar energy on Canada's housing market'. *International Journal for Housing Science and its Applications* vol. 5 no. 3 (1981) pp. 217–23.

876 Connolly, E. 'Single-family housing conversions: a strategy for increasing the housing supply'. *Journal of Housing* vol. 39 no. 2 (Mar.–Apr. 1982) pp. 40–2.
   Ideas to increase the supply of homes in the US by legalizing the conversion of single family units into more units.

877 Crosbie, M. J. *Industrialized building for housing in the United States.* Monticello, Vance Bibliographies, 1980. (Architecture series bibliography A-449).

878 Downs, A. *Energy costs, urban development and housing.* Washington, DC, Brookings Institution, 1984.

879 Eichler, N. 'House building in the 1980s.' *Annals of the American Academy of Political and Social Science* vol. 465 (1983) pp. 35–44.

880 Horowitz, C. F. *The new garden apartment: current market realities of an American housing form.* New Brunswick, Rutgers University, Center for Urban Policy Research, 1983.

881 Pommer, R. 'The architecture of urban housing in the United States during the early 1930s'. *Society of Architectural Historians Journal* vol. 37 no. 4 (1978) pp. 235–64.

882 United States, Congressional Office of Technical Assessment. *Residential energy conservation.* Washington, DC, Government Printing Office, 1979.

883 United States, Department of Commerce, Bureau of the Census. *Housing construction statistics 1889 to 1964.* 1966. Reprinted Philadelphia, Ayer, 1976. (America in two centuries series).

884 United States, Department of Housing and Urban Development. *Energy management for housing managers: vol. 1, participant's workbook; vol. 2, instructor's guide.* Washington, DC, The Department, 1980.

885 United States, General Accounting Office. *National standards needed for residential energy conservation. Department of Housing and Urban Development: report to the Congress by the Comptroller General of the United States.* Washington, DC, The Office, 1975.

886 Untermann, R. and Small, R. *Site planning for cluster housing.* New York, Van Nostrand Reinhold, 1977.
Low rise, medium density, cluster environments in North America.

887 Urban Land Institute. *Residential development handbook.* Washington, The Institute, 1978. (Community builders handbook series).

3.5 Africa, Asia and Latin America

888 Agrawal, P. K. 'Low-cost timber cluster-housing'. *International Journal for Housing Science and its Applications* vol. 3 no. 2 (1979) pp. 85–95.
Low cost housing, using local resources, in Malaysia.

889 Al-Alak, B. and Ford, J. D. *The housebuilding market in the Middle East.* London, Graham and Trotman, 1979.

890 Bakr, T. A. 'The Saudi Egyptian Construction Company: an example of Pan-Arab co-operation to solve housing problems'. *International Journal for Housing Science and its Applications* vol. 3 no. 2 (1979) pp. 129–35.
Concentrates on middle and upper income housing.

891   Bindal, M. 'Privacy requirement and its effect on housing design'. *International Journal for Housing Science and its Applications* vol. 6 no. 4 (1982) pp. 301–12.
Assesses privacy requirements in dwellings with special reference to Turkey.

892   Caminos, H. and Goethart, R. *Urbanization primer: project assessment, site analysis, design criteria for site and services or similar dwelling environments in developing areas with documentary collection of photographs on urbanization.* Cambridge, Mass., MIT Press, 1978.

893   Childers, V. E. 'Transferring housing technology'. *International Journal for Housing Science and its Applications* vol. 3 no. 2 (1979) pp. 111–18.
Transfer of knowledge and technology from US firms to housing needs in developing countries.

894   'Energy conservation in human settlements'. *Ekistics* vol. 45, no. 269 (May 1978) pp. 163–211.
Special issue containing several articles.

895   Ferchiou, R. 'The indirect effects of new housing construction in developing countries'. *Urban Studies* vol. 19 no. 2 (May 1982) pp. 167–76.
Effects of new construction on old housing stock. Evidence from Mexico and Tunisia.

896   Ganesan, S. *Growth of housing and construction sectors: key to employment creation.* Oxford, Pergamon, 1979. (Progress in planning vol. 12 part 1).
Development of the housing and construction sectors of developing countries, especially for employment creation. Case study of Sri Lanka.

897   Gokhale, R. G. 'Appropriate technology for urban housing in India'. *International Journal for Housing Science and its Applications* vol. 3 no. 2 (1979) pp. 137–42.
Substandard housing in India and how appropriate technology and modern techniques can help.

898   Hendry, J. and McKie, R. 'The maintenance of low cost

housing'. *International Journal for Housing Science and its Applications* vol. 4 no. 6 (1980) pp. 525–36.

899   Hoek-Smit, M. C. 'Institutional constraints in the development of informal housing areas'. *Build Kenya* vol. 2 no. 16 (July 1977) pp. 18–29.

900   Knauer, B. 'Industrialised building in developing countries'. *Building Research and Practice* vol. 10 no. 5 (Sept.–Oct. 1982) pp. 276–85.

901   Kreimer, A. 'Emergency, temporary and permanent housing after disasters in developing countries'. *Ekistics* vol. 46 no. 279 (Nov.–Dec. 1979) pp. 361–5.

902   Madhava Rao, A. G. (ed.) *Modern trends in housing in developing countries*. London, Spon, 1984.
Papers presented at the advanced course on modern trends in housing, Structural Engineering Research Centre, Madras.

903   Martin, R. 'Poverty and professionals'. *RIBA Journal* vol. 91 no. 7 (July 1984) pp. 31–42.
Low income housing in developing countries with case studies from Egypt, Lesotho and Nigeria.

904   Moriarty, P. 'The case for traditional housing in tropical Africa'. *Habitat International* vol. 4 no. 3 (1979) pp. 285–90.

905   Moustapha, A. F. and Costa, F. J. 'Al Jarudiyah: a model for low rise/high density development in Saudi Arabia'. *Ekistics* vol. 48 no. 287 (Mar.–Apr. 1981) pp. 100–8.

906   Pama, R. P. et al (eds.) *Low income housing: technology and policy*. Bangkok, Asian Institute of Technology, 1977.

907   Ramaswamy, G. S. 'A critical assessment of current industrialized building systems for mass housing in Trinidad and Tobago'. *International Journal for Housing Science and its Applications* vol. 4 no. 3 (1980) pp. 233–52.

908   Rao, G. L. 'Appropriate housing'. *Mazingira* no. 12 (1979) pp. 4–38.

Co-operation between developing countries needed to find appropriate technology for housing construction.

909   Sinha, I. B. 'Emergency for the saviour building technology in Africa'. *International Journal for Housing Science and its Applications* vol. 3 no. 2 (1979) pp. 97–102.
Need for prefabricated systems of housing to provide faster construction for low income housing in Africa.

910   Sinha, I. B. 'A solution to the problem of low-income group housing in developing countries by use of prefabricated system'. *International Journal for Housing Science and its Applications* vol. 3 no. 6 (1979) pp. 445–60.
Recommends industrialized housing techniques as low cost housing for developing countries.

911   Strassmann, W. P. *Housing and building technology in developing countries.* East Lansing, Michigan State University, Graduate School of Business Administration, 1978.

912   Sulzer, H. D. 'Cluster-shell design for lowest cost housing'. *International Journal for Housing Science and its Applications* vol. 6 no. 4 (1982) pp. 313–27.
Alternatives to self help housing schemes.

913   United Kingdom, Department of the Environment, Building Research Establishment. *Building in hot climates: a selection of overseas building notes.* London, HMSO, 1980.

914   Yahya, D. *House registration handbook: a manual for registered houses and pests in unplanned settlements.* Washington, DC, World Bank, 1982. (Urban Development Department technical paper no. 4).

915   Zaw, W. 'System approach for mass housing production for low income people in Burma'. *Openhouse* vol. 3 no. 1 (Mar. 1978) pp. 40–53.

4

Housing finance

Included in this section are general works on housing finance and the role of governments in resource allocation for housing development. References to finance for particular housing tenures are listed elsewhere in, for instance, sections 6 'Home purchase finance', 9 'Public housing' and 11 'Alternative tenures', while rebates and allowances are discussed in the following section.

4.1 International and comparative

916 Boleat, M. *Housing finance: an international study.* London, Building Societies Association, 1982.

917 Boleat, M. *National housing finance systems — a comparative study.* London, International Union of Building Societies and Savings Associations and Croom Helm, 1984.

918 Falk, K. L. *Housing problems and tax policies: an international comparison.* Washington, DC, National Association of Housing and Redevelopment Officials, 1969.

919 Howenstine, E. J. *Attacking housing costs: foreign policies and strategies.* New Brunswick, Rutgers University, Centre for Urban Policy Research, 1983.
Compares housing costs in industrialized countries and describes policies to make housing more affordable to all.

920 Howenstine, E. J. *Housing costs in the United States and other*

industrialized countries 1970–77. Washington, DC, Department of Housing and Urban Development, 1979.

921   Mandelker, D. R. *Housing subsidies in the United States and England.* New York, Bobbs-Merrill, 1973.
Particularly useful for the US situation.

922   Organisation for Economic Co-operation and Development. *Flexibility in housing finance.* Paris, The Organisation, 1975.

923   Organisation for Economic Co-operation and Development. *Housing finance: present problems: three reports.* Paris, The Organisation, 1974.
Reports by the working party on housing finance.

924   Organisation for Economic Co-operation and Development. *Taxes on immovable property.* Paris, The Organisation, 1983.
Report by the Committee on Fiscal Affairs and the Ad Hoc Group on Urban Problems. Reviews property taxes and policies in 15 OECD countries.

925   Priemus, H. (ed.) *Who will pay the housing bill in the eighties?* Delft University Press, 1983.
Papers of the IFHP World Congress Workshop, Oslo, 1982.

926   Pugh, C. 'Co-operation, co-ownership, voluntary social housing finance polices and widening possibilities'. *Annals of Public and Co-operative Economy* vol. 48 (July–Sept. 1977) pp. 343–70.
Housing finance in Norway, Sweden, Britain and Australia.

927   Stokes, B. *Global housing prospects: the resource constraints.* Washington, DC, Worldwatch Institute, 1981. (Worldwatch paper 46).

928   Sweet, M. L. and Walters, S. G. *Mandatory housing finance programs: a comparative international analysis.* New York, Praeger, 1976. (Praeger special studies in US economic, social and political issues).

929   United Nations, Department of International Economic

and Social Affairs. *Non-conventional financing of housing for low-income households*. New York, United Nations, 1978.

930   United States, Department of Housing and Urban Development. *Housing finance institutions abroad: a directory*. Washington, DC, The Department, 1979.

931   Whitbread, M. *Housing finance policies: an international review*. London, Centre for Environmental Studies, 1975.

4.2   Europe

932   Cardis, G. P. and Robinson, H. *Monetary corrections, thrift institutions and housing finance*. Chicago, International Union of Building Societies and Savings Associations, 1983.
Housing finance in West Germany.

933   Englund, P. and Persson, M. 'Housing prices and tenure choice with asymmetric taxes and progressivity'. *Journal of Public Economics* vol. 19 no. 3 (Dec. 1982) pp. 271–90.
Changes in relative costs of owner occupation and rented housing in Sweden.

934   Ghorra-Gobin, C. 'The subsidized housing system in France'. *Planning and Administration* vol. 10 no. 1 (Spring 1983) pp. 47–56.
Development of housing policy in France, especially the reforms of 1977 and 1982.

935   Howenstine, E. J. 'The changing roles of housing production subsidies in European national housing policy'. *Land Economics* vol. 51 no. 1 (Feb. 1975) pp. 86–94.

936   Jennings, R. 'Irish housing subsidies'. *Administration* vol. 28 no. 4 (1980) pp. 409–22.

937   Johnson, L. J. *The reorganisation of central–local relations in housing: an examination of English experiences with HIP system and their relevance for the Netherlands*. Oxford Polytechnic, Department of Town Planning, 1982. (Working paper no. 62).

938   McKeon, J. and Jennings, R. *Public subventions to housing in Ireland.* Dublin, National Institute for Physical Planning and Construction Research, 1978.

939   Ratzda, A. D. 'Land banking in Stockholm: an evaluation of municipal residential leasehold as a public finance and housing subsidy instrument'. *American Planning Association Journal* vol. 47 no. 3 (1981) pp. 279–88.

940   'Reform of housing finance in France: the Barre report'. *Local Finance* vol. 6 no. 1 (Feb. 1977). English summary pp. 17–23.
Major recommendations of committee to investigate financing of housing construction in France .

941   Renaud, B. *Housing finance: the French contractual savings scheme.* Washington, DC, World Bank, 1982. (Internal paper).

942   Simonis, U.E. 'Public financing of housing and urban development in West Germany'. In F. Kunst (ed.) *Housing and labour immigrants: problems and policies in West German metropolitan areas.* Berlin Technical University, 1982. (Working paper 21). pp. 25–32.

943   Smigel, S. E. 'Trends and problems in European housing finance'. *HUD International* 1974. (Information series 26).

944   Welfeld, H. H. *European housing subsidy systems.* Washington, DC, Department of Housing and Urban Development, 1972.

4.3   United Kingdom

945   Aughton, H. *Housing finance: a basic guide.* London, Shelter, 1981.
Concise and clear guide.

946   Bramley, G. et al. *Developments in housing finance.* University of Bristol, School for Advanced Urban Studies, 1981. (Working paper 24).

Brief review of the Housing Act 1980 subsidy system, block grant, HIPs and housing benefit.

947   Bramley, G. et al. *Housing strategies and investment programmes.* University of Bristol, School for Advanced Urban Studies, 1980. (Working paper no. 7).

948   Bucknall, B. *Housing finance.* London, Chartered Institute of Public Finance and Accountancy, 1985.
Comprehensive review of the public and private sectors in the UK.

949   Building Societies Association. *Housing finance into the 1990s.* London, The Association, 1985.
Working party report on future prospects for owner occupation, tenure preferences and the role of building societies.

950   Community Development Project. *Profits against houses: an alternative guide to housing finance.* London, CDP Information and Intelligence Unit, 1976.

951   Crine, A. and Wintour, J. 'HIPs: the vital statistics'. *Roof* vol. 5 no. 2 (Mar.–Apr. 1980) pp. 52–4.
Housing investment programmes probably represent the richest source of housing information in Britain. This first ever published analysis reveals many startling facts.

952   Doling, J. 'Housing finance and the British city'. *Area* vol. 14 no. 1 (1982) pp. 33–8.

953   Ermisch, J. 'Housing finance: principles and facts'. *Policy Studies* vol. 5 part 2 (Oct. 1984) pp. 1–23.

954   Gibson, J. G. 'Block grant and subsidies'. *Roof* vol. 6 no. 4 (July–Aug. 1981) pp. 19–20.
Explains the new block grant system as it affects housing.

955   Gibson, J. G. *The new housing subsidy system and its interaction with the block grant.* University of Birmingham, Institute of Local Government Studies, 1981.

956   Goss, S. and Lansley, S. *What price housing? A review of housing subsidies and proposals for reform.* London, SHAC, 1981. (Research report 4).

957   Grey, A. et al. *Housing rents, costs and subsidies.* 2nd rev. ed. London, Chartered Institute of Public Finance and Accountancy, 1981.
Inequalities and anomalies in housing subsidies and proposals for reform.

958   Hepworth, N. C. *The finance of local government.* 7th ed. London, Allen and Unwin, 1984.
Standard text.

959   Holmes, C. 'Housing expenditure: how it breaks down'. *Roof* May 1976 pp. 73–6.
Although slightly dated, provides a valuable review of the annual public expenditure white paper.

960   Hughes, G. A. 'The distributional effects of housing taxation and subsidies in Britain'. In L. J. Walden (ed.) *Housing policy: the just price and the role of the public housing sector: papers and discussions from two British–Scandinavian seminars.* Galve, National Swedish Institute for Building Research, 1981. (Bulletin M81:24). pp. 79–110.

961   Hughes, G. A. 'Housing and the tax system'. In G. A. Hughes and G. M. Heal (eds.) *Public policy and the tax system.* London, Allen and Unwin, 1980. pp. 67–105.

962   Hughes, G. A. 'Housing income and subsidies'. *Fiscal Studies* vol. 1 no. 1 (Nov. 1979) pp. 20–38.

963   Institute for Fiscal Studies. *Housing finance.* London, The Institute, 1975.

964   Kilroy, B. *Housing finance: organic reform.* London, Labour Economic Finance and Taxation Association, 1978.

965   Kilroy, B. 'Housing finance: why so privileged?' *Lloyds Bank Review* no. 133 (July 1979) pp. 37–52.

966   Kilroy, B. 'Public expenditure on housing'. In A. Walker (ed.) *Public expenditure and social policy: an examination of social spending and social priorities.* London, Heinemann, 1982. pp. 113–36.

967   Leather, P. 'Housing (dis?) investment programmes'. *Policy and Politics* vol. 11 no. 2 (1983) pp. 215–29.

968   Needleman, L. *The economics of housing.* London, Staples Press, 1965.
Remains an important work for students of housing finance and subsidies.

969   Nevitt, A. A. *Housing, taxation and subsidies: a study of housing in the United Kingdom.* London, Nelson, 1966.
Still provides a useful framework for the study of housing finance in Britain.

970   O'Sullivan, A. J. 'Misconceptions in the current housing subsidy debate'. *Policy and Politics* vol. 12 no. 2 (Apr. 1984) pp. 119–44.

971   Prentice, R. 'The governance of British public housing investment in the late 1970s: central encouragement of comparative local diversity'. *Environment and Planning C* (Aug. 1984) pp. 325–41.

972   Robinson, R. *Housing tax expenditures, subsidies and the distribution of income.* Brighton, University of Sussex, 1980. (Urban and Regional Studies working paper 19).

973   Rosenthal, L. 'The regional and income distribution of the council house subsidy in the United Kingdom'. *Manchester School of Economic and Social Studies* no. 2 (June 1977) pp. 127–40.

974   Royal Town Planning Institute. *Housing investment programmes.* London, The Institute, 1980.

975   Shelter. *Housing and the economy: a priority for reform.* London, Shelter, 1982.

976   Shelter. *Public expenditure on housing: who benefits?* London, Shelter, 1977.

977   Shelter (Scotland). *Dead end street.* Edinburgh, Shelter (Scotland), 1981.
Reviews the effects of public expenditure cuts on Scottish housing.

978   Shelter (Scotland). *Housing finance in Scotland.* Edinburgh, Shelter (Scotland), 1981.

979   United Kingdom, Committee to Review the Functioning of the Financial Institutions. *Report.* London, HMSO, 1980. (Cmnd. 7937).
The Wilson report, published with several appendices. Contains sections on building society activity.

980   United Kingdom, Department of the Environment. *The Government's reply to the third report from the Environment Committee, Session 1980–81, HC 383.* London, HMSO, 1981. (Cmnd. 8435).
Reply to report on DOE housing policies.

981   United Kingdom, Department of the Environment. *Housing strategies and investment programmes: arrangements for 1978/79.* London, HMSO, 1977. (Circular 63/77).
Introduced the HIP system and described its objectives.

982   United Kingdom, Department of the Environment. *Housing strategies and investment programmes: arrangements for 1979/80.* London, HMSO, 1978. (Circular 38/78).
Further guidance on HIP submissions, assessment of housing need and preparation of local housing strategy statement.

983   United Kingdom, Department of the Environment. *Housing subsidies and accounting manual 1981.* Rev. ed. London, HMSO, 1982.

984   United Kingdom, House of Commons, Environment Committee. *DOE's housing policies: enquiry into Government's expenditure plans 1981–82 to 1983–84 and the updating of the committee's*

first report for the session 1979/80. London, HMSO, 1981. (Third report, HC 383, Session 1980–81).

985 United Kingdom, House of Commons, Environment Committee. *Enquiry into implications of Government's expenditure plans 1980–81 to 1983–84 for the housing policies of the Department of the Environment: together with the proceedings of the committee, minutes of evidence and appendices.* London, HMSO, 1980. (First report, HC 714, Session 1979–80).

986 United Kingdom, Ministry of Housing and Local Government. *Housing revenue accounts: report of the working party on the housing revenue account.* London, HMSO, 1969.
    Delafons report on local authority housing revenue accounts.

987 United Kingdom, Scottish Office. *The reform of housing finance in Scotland.* Edinburgh, HMSO, 1971. (Cmnd. 4727).

988 Warburton, M. *Housing finance: the case for reform.* London, Catholic Housing Aid Society, 1983. (Occasional paper no. 8).

989 Watson, C. et al. 'Housing investment programmes and the private sector'. *Local Government Studies* vol. 5 no. 6 (Nov.–Dec. 1979) pp. 41–52.

990 Webster, D. 'New council and private housing: can the subsidy cost argument be settled?' *CES Review* no. 3 (May 1978) pp. 38–44.
    Relative costs of public and private sector building programmes: analysis of DOE evidence.

991 Wilding, P. 'Housing subsidies 1906–1914'. *Social and Economic Administration* vol. 6 no 1 (1972) pp. 3–17.

4.4 North America

992 Aaron, H. J. *Shelter and subsidies: who benefits from federal housing policies?* Washington, DC, Brookings Institution, 1972. (Studies in social economics).

993   Betnun, N.S. *Housing finance agencies: a comparison between states and HUD.* New York, Praeger, 1977.

994   Boleat, M. *The Canadian housing finance system.* 2nd ed. London, Building Societies Association, 1980.

995   Brooks, M. E. *Housing equity and environmental protection: the needless conflict.* Washington, DC, American Institute of Planners, 1976.

996   Bunce, H. L. et al. *Effects of the 1980 census on community development funding.* Washington, DC, Department of Housing and Urban Development, 1983.

997   Colton, K. W. 'The future of the nation's housing finance system: reform or paralysis'. *American Institute of Planners Journal* vol. 44, no. 3 (July 1978) pp. 306–16.
Housing finance system in the US and proposals for reform.

998   Colton, K. W. 'Housing finance in the 1980s: economic factors indicate future directions'. *Journal of Housing* vol. 38 no. 1 (Jan. 1981) pp. 15–20.
A review of US housing finance in the 1980s.

999   De Leeuw, F. and Ozanne, L. 'The impact of the federal income tax on investment in housing'. *Survey of Current Business* vol. 59 (Dec. 1979) pp. 50–61.
Effects of taxation on owner occupied and rental housing in the US.

1000   Downs, A. *Federal housing subsidies: how are they working?* Lexington, Mass., Heath, 1973.
Study by the Real Estate Research Corporation.

1001   Feins, J. D. and Lane, T. S. *How much for housing? New perspectives on affordability and risk.* Cambridge, Mass., Abt Books, 1981.
Housing costs in the US.

1002   Fernsler, J. P. 'Tax-exempt financing for housing: HUD and local governments in joint venture with public and private owners and lenders'. *Urban Lawyer* vol. 11 no. 3 (Summer 1979) pp. 429–34.

1003 Gainer, W. 'Subsidised housing production: profiting from past errors'. *Journal of Housing* vol. 40 no. 3 (May–June 1983) pp. 77–9.
Shortcomings of housing subsidy programmes in the US.

1004 Harris, W. T. 'Property tax circuit breakers: good causes but bad economics'. *American Journal of Economics and Sociology* vol. 42 no. 2 (Apr. 1983) pp. 209–16.
Reduction of rates of property tax for low income households and the elderly in a number of US states.

1005 Hendershott, P. H. and Villani, K. E. *Housing finance in the United States in the year 2001*. Cambridge, Mass., National Bureau of Economic Research, 1981. (NBER working paper no. 739).

1006 Hoben, J. E. 'Affordable housing: what states can do'. *Urban Land* vol. 42 no. 4 (Apr. 1983) pp. 20–3.
Actions which may be taken by US state governments to reduce housing costs, including private sector involvement.

1007 Howell, J. T. 'Project syndication: how it works'. *Journal of Housing* vol. 41 (July–Aug. 1984) pp. 107–11.
Advantages and disadvantages of syndication (the process of selling limited partnership interests in income producing properties) as solution to US housing problem.

1008 Mahrer, L. L. 'Financing housing: innovative systems'. *International Journal for Housing Science and its Applications* vol. 8 no. 2 (1984) pp. 113–23.
Alternative methods of private sector housing finance in the US.

1009 Rabinowitz, A. *Urban real estate finance*. Chicago, Council of Planning Librarians, 1979. (Bibliography no. 26).

1010 Sears, C. E. 'Problems and prospects for housing finance'. *Urban Land* vol. 41 no. 9 (Sept. 1982) pp. 11–17.

Housing finance in the US.

1011 Seiders, D. F. 'Changing patterns of housing finance'. *Federal Reserve Bulletin* vol. 67 (June 1981) pp. 461–72.

1012 Smith, L. B. 'Housing assistance: a re-evaluation'. *Canadian Public Policy* vol. 7 (Summer 1981) pp. 454–63.

1013 Stegman, M. A. 'Housing finance agencies: are they crucial instruments of state government?' *American Institute of Planners Journal* vol. 40 (Sept. 1974) pp. 307–20.

1014 Sternlieb, G. et al. *Tax subsidies and housing investment: a fiscal cost-benefit analysis.* New Brunswick, Rutgers University, Center for Urban Policy Research, 1976 .
Three housing programmes in New York.

1015 Struyk, R. J. and Khadduri, J. 'Saving the housing assistance plan: improving incentives to local governments'. *Journal of the American Planning Association* vol. 46 no. 4 (Oct. 1980) pp. 387–97.
Describes the HAP process prepared by each community in its application for block grant.

1016 Tuccillo, J. A. and Goodman, J. L. *Housing finance — a changing system in the Reagan era.* Washington, DC, Urban Institute, 1983.

1017 United States, Congressional Budget Office. *Housing finance: federal programs and issues: staff working paper.* Washington, DC, Government Printing Office, 1976.
Contemporary problems of mortgage credit and housing investment finance and federal housing finance programmes.

1018 United States, Department of Housing and Urban Development. *Budgeting procedures for housing managers: vol. 1, participant's workbook; vol. 2, instructor's guide.* Washington, DC, The Department, 1980.

1019 United States, Department of Housing and Urban Development. *Final report of the Task Force on Housing Costs.* Washington, DC, The Department, 1978.

Chairman: W. J. White. Programme of action to reduce or stabilize housing costs to the consumer in rented and owner occupied housing in the US.

1020   United States, Senate, Committee on Banking, Housing and Urban Affairs, Subcommittee on Housing and Urban Affairs. *Federal role in conventional home financing.* Washington, DC, Government Printing Office, 1981.
Current status in home finance and role of the secondary mortgage market.

1021   Urban Land Institute. *Reducing the development costs of housing: actions for state and local governments: proceedings of the HUD national conference on housing costs.* Washington, DC, Department of Housing and Urban Development, 1979.

1022   Vance, M. A. *Property tax: a bibliography.* Monticello, Vance Bibliographies, 1981. (Public administration bibliography P. 795).

1023   Weicher, J. C. 'Housing block grants for the United States'. *Urban Law and Policy* vol. 4 no. 3 (Sept. 1981) pp. 269–83.
Housing finance from federal government to state and local governments.

1024   White, W. J. 'What price shelter?' *Urban Land* vol. 37 no. 7 (July–Aug. 1978) pp. 9–13.
Rising housing costs in the US led to the creation of the Task Force on Housing Costs by the Department of Housing and Urban Development. Outline of its role.

1025   Windsor, D. *Fiscal zoning in suburban communities.* Lexington, Mass., Lexington Books, 1979.
Fiscal implications of suburban exclusionary practices in New Jersey.

1026   Worsham, J. R. *Government and state housing finance agencies: a selected bibliography.* Monticello, Vance Bibliographies, 1979. (Public administration series bibliography no. P–349).

1027   Zech, C. E. 'Fiscal effects of urban zoning'. *Urban Affairs Quarterly* vol. 16 (Sept. 1980) pp. 49–58.

How urban fiscal zoning may affect low income housing in the US.

4.5 Australasia

1028   Australia, Committee of Inquiry into the Australian Finance System. *Final report.* Canberra, Australian Government Publishing Service, 1981.
The Campbell report.

1029   Australia, Committee of Inquiry into Housing Costs. *The cost of housing: report: vol. 1, report; vol. 2, proceedings of the key issue seminars; vol. 3, report of commissioned studies.* Canberra, Australian Government Publishing Service, 1978. (Parliamentary papers 270–2, 1978).
The Eyers report.

1030   Australia, Department of Environment, Housing and Community Development. *Finance for new houses.* Canberra, Australian Government Publishing Service, 1976.

1031   Australian Bureau of Statistics. *Survey of housing occupancy and costs.* Canberra, The Bureau, 1981.

1032   Building Societies Association. 'Housing finance and the final report of the committee of inquiry into the Australian financial system'. In *Studies in building society activity 1980–81.* London, The Association, 1982. pp. 160–2.

1033   Butler, G. J. et al. 'Determinants of housing expenditure in Australia'. *Environment and Planning A* vol. 16 no. 8 (Aug. 1984) pp. 1099–113.

1034   Hill, M. *Housing finance in Australia.* Melbourne University Press, 1959.

1035   Hill, M. R. 'Housing finance institutions'. In R. R. Hirst and R. H. Wallace (eds.) *The Australian capital market.* Melbourne, Cheshire, 1974. pp. 332–65.

1036   Housing Corporation of New Zealand. *Home finance.* Wellington, The Corporation, 1983.

1037   Sharpe, I. G. 'Housing finance costs in Australia'. *Australian Quarterly* vol. 45 no. 2 (1975) pp. 71–83.

1038   'Sources of housing finance in New Zealand'. *Reserve Bank of New Zealand Bulletin* vol. 41 (Apr. 1978) pp. 117–24.

4.6   Africa, Asia and Latin America

1039   Awotona, A. A. 'Financing appropriate housing in Nigeria'. *Ekistics* vol. 44 (Aug. 1977) pp. 100–5.

1040   Bahl, R.W. (ed.) *The taxation of urban property in less developed countries.* Madison, University of Wisconsin Press, 1979.
   Public finance text.

1041   Batley, R. *The Brazilian national housing bank: establishment and adaptation.* University of Birmingham, Institute of Local Government Studies, Development Administration Group, 1979. (Occasional paper 6).

1042   Bienefeld, M. and Binhammer, H. 'Tanzanian housing finance and housing policy'. In J. Hutton (ed.) *Urban challenge in East Africa.* Nairobi, East African Publishing House, 1972.

1043   Boleat, M. 'Housing finance in developing countries'. In M. Boleat *National housing finance systems.* London, Croom Helm, 1985. pp. 18–39.

1044   Christian, J. W. *Housing finance for developing countries.* Chicago, International Union of Building Societies and Savings Associations, 1980.

1045   Devas, N. 'Financing urban land development for low income housing: an analysis with particular reference to Jakarta, Indonesia'. *Third World Planning Review* vol. 5 no. 3 (Aug. 1983) pp. 209–25.

1046   Elliott, S. M. *Financing Latin American housing*. New York, Praeger, 1968.

1047   Gilbert, R. T. 'An evaluation of British housing aid provided by the Ministry of Overseas Development'. *Journal of Administration Overseas* vol. 19 no. 2 (Apr. 1980) pp. 73–87.

1048   Grebler, L. 'Possibilities of international financing of housing in underdeveloped areas'. In B. Kelly (ed.) *Housing and economic development*. Cambridge, Mass., MIT Press, 1955.

1049   Ichimura, S. 'Economic growth, savings and housing finance in Japan'. *Journal of Economic Studies* vol. 8 no. 3 (1981) pp. 41–64.

1050   Jagatheesan, N. 'Housing finance in Malaysia'. In S. H. Tan and H. Sendut (eds.) *Public and private housing in Malaysia*. Kuala Lumpur, Heinemann, 1979.

1051   Jorgenson, N. O. *Housing finance for low income groups: with special reference to developing countries*. Rotterdam, Bouwcentrum, 1977.

1052   Knocke, J. *Financing housing for urban low income households in Africa — a matter of technical building codes?* Gavle, National Swedish Institute for Building Research, 1982. (Bulletin M82:1).

1053   Korell, M. L. 'Housing finance in Asia and the Pacific nations: poverty, inflation among hurdles to better living'. *Federal Home Loan Bank Board Journal* vol. 12 (June 1979) pp. 18–23.

1054   Onibokun, G. A. 'Housing finance in Nigeria: a critical survey of private and public sources'. *Town Planning Review* vol. 42 (1971) pp. 277–92.

1055   Osterbrauck, W.-D. 'The provision of house-building finance in developing countries, part 1'. *Chartered Building Societies Institute Journal* vol. 35 no. 143 (Feb. 1981) pp. 19–20, 43.
    Problems of financing house building in developing countries.

1056   Osterbrauck, W.-D. 'The provision of house-building

finance in developing countries, part 2'. *Chartered Building Societies Institute Journal* vol. 35 no. 144 (Apr. 1981) pp. 86–8.
West Germany's role in providing finance for housing.

1057   Prakash, V. and Sah, J. P. 'Financing housing and urban development'. In L. Jakobson and V. Prakash (eds.) *Metropolitan growth: public policy for South and Southeast Asia.* New York, Wiley, 1974. (Southeast Asia urban studies series).

1058   Ramachandran, A. 'Human settlement finance and management'. *Habitat* vol. 6 no. 3 (1982) pp. 267–300.

1059   Renaud, B. *Housing and financial institutions in developing countries: an overview.* Washington, DC, World Bank, 1984. (Staff working paper 642).

1060   Reynolds, C. W. and Carpenter, R. T. 'Housing finance in Brazil: towards a new distribution of wealth'. In A. Cornelius and F. M. Trueblood (eds.) *Urbanisation and inequality: the political economy of urban and rural development in Latin America.* Beverly Hills, Sage, 1975. (Latin American urban research vol. 5). pp. 147–76.

1061   Sandilands, R. J. *Monetary correction and housing finance in Colombia, Brazil and Chile.* Farnborough, Gower, 1980.

1062   Solaun, M. 'On the effects of subsidized house and apartment living in Colombia'. *American Institute of Planners Journal* vol. 42 no. 4 (Oct. 1976) pp. 427–37.
Reactions to a housing project.

1063   United States, Agency for International Development. *Sixth conference on housing in Africa.* Washington, DC, The Agency, 1979.
Held in Rabat, Morocco, with a theme of housing finance.

1064   Wegener, R. H. 'Low income housing finance: an integrated approach'. *Habitat International* vol. 6 no. 4 (1982) pp. 425–39.

5

Rebates and allowances

Works on government measures to alleviate financial disadvantage and hardship in housing policy are covered in this section. The widespread existence of attempts to achieve more equitable distribution of resources in housing policy to more disadvantaged groups in industrialized countries is sufficient to justify the inclusion of this section, although in general housing policies in developing countries have not yet reached the level of sophistication to introduce such policies. Reference should also be made to sections 4 'Housing finance' and 9 'Public housing'.

5.1 International and comparative

1065 Hetzel, O. et al. 'Making allowances for housing costs: a comparison of British and US experiences'. *Urban Law and Policy* vol. 1 no. 3 (July 1978) pp. 229–73.
Comparison of British rent allowances with the US Experimental Housing Allowance Program.

1066 Trutko, J. *A comparison of the Experimental Housing Allowance Program and Great Britain's rent allowance program.* Washington, DC, Urban Institute, 1978.

5.2 Europe

1067 Lawson, R. and Stevens, C. 'Housing allowances in West Germany and France'. *Journal of Social Policy* vol. 3 no. 3 (July 1974) pp. 213–34.

5.3   United Kingdom

1068   Clark, B. et al. *Nobody's benefit — a survey of the housing benefit scheme.* London, Child Poverty Action Group, 1984.

1069   Hemming, R. and Hills, J. 'The reform of housing benefits'. *Fiscal Studies* vol. 4 no. 1 (Mar. 1983) pp. 48–65.

1070   Hill, M. 'The implementation of housing benefit'. *Journal of Social Policy* vol. 13 no. 3 (July 1984) pp. 297–320.

1071   Jones, H. et al. *Glasgow tenants' grant scheme: an assessment.* Edinburgh, Scottish Office, Central Research Unit, 1983.

1072   Kemp, P. *The cost of chaos: a survey of the housing benefit scheme.* London, SHAC, 1984.

1073   Kemp, P. *Housing benefit: the way forward.* London, SHAC, 1984.

1074   Kemp, P. and Raynsford, N. (eds.) *Housing benefit: the evidence.* London, Housing Centre Trust, 1984.
Publication of 16 submissions to the Government's housing benefit review.

1075   Legg, C. and Brion, M. *The administration of the rent rebate and rent allowance scheme.* London, Department of the Environment, 1976.
Outline of the system which existed before the introduction of housing benefit.

1076   Local Government Training Board. *Guide to housing benefits.* Luton, The Board, 1983.

1077   Local Government Training Board. *Housing benefit: a training package.* Luton, The Board, 1982.

1078   McGurk, P. and Raynsford, N. *A guide to housing benefits.* Rev. ed. London, Institute of Housing/SHAC, 1983.
Comprehensive guide to the new housing benefit for administrators and housing aid agencies.

1079   Means, R. and Hill, M. 'The administration of rent rebates'. *Journal of Social Welfare Law* July 1982 pp. 193–208.

1080   Oxford Centre for Local Government Studies. *Understanding housing benefit*. Rev. ed. Abingdon, The Centre, 1984.
Layman's guide.

1081   Ritchie, J. and Matthews, A. *Take up of rent allowances: an in-
depth study*. London, Social and Community Planning Research,
1982.
Results of a DOE commissioned study into the operation of
the rent allowance scheme.

1082   SHAC. *Home owners: your guide to housing benefits*. London,
1983.
Practical guide for low income owner occupiers.

1083   United Kingdom, Department of the Environment. *Advisory Committee on Rent Rebates and Rent Allowances. Report no. 1*.
London, HMSO, 1974.

1084   United Kingdom, Department of the Environment. *Advisory Committee on Rent Rebates and Allowances. Report no. 2*. London,
HMSO, 1977.

1085   United Kingdom, Department of the Environment. *Advisory Committee on Rent Rebates and Rent Allowances. Report no. 3
(Final report)*. London, HMSO, 1983.

1086   United Kingdom, Department of Health and Social
Security. *The housing benefit scheme: implementation*. London,
HMSO, 1982.
Official guide to the scheme introduced in the Social Security
and Housing Benefits Act 1982.

1087   United Kingdom, House of Commons, Committee of
Public Accounts. *Housing benefits scheme*. London, HMSO, 1985.
(Sixth report, Session 1984–85, HC 78).

1088   United Kingdom, National Audit Office. *Report by the
Comptroller and Auditor General. Department of Health and Social*

Security: housing benefits scheme. London, HMSO, 1984. (Session 1983–84, HC 638).

1089   Walker, R. L. 'Temporal aspects of claiming behaviour: renewal of rent allowances'. *Journal of Social Policy* vol. 9 no. 2 (Apr. 1980) pp. 207–22.

5.4   North America

1090   Barnett, C. L. and Lowry, I. S. *How housing allowances affect housing prices: housing assistance supply experiment.* New York, Rand Corporation, 1979.
Report of an experiment in Wisconsin and Indiana 1970–4.

1091   Bendick, M. 'Voucher versus income versus services: an American experiment in housing policy'. *Journal of Social Policy* vol. 11 no. 3 (July 1982) pp. 365–78.
Evaluates lessons of Experimental Housing Allowance Program and contrasts three major housing policy alternatives.

1092   Bradbury, K. L. and Downs, A. (eds.) *Do housing allowances work?* Washington, DC, Brookings Institution, 1981. (Brookings studies in social experimentation).

1093   Carlson, D. and Heinberg, J. *How housing allowances work.* Washington, DC, Urban Institute, 1978.

1094   Falk, K. 'Housing allowances in theory and practice: implications for a Canadian plan'. *Habitat* vol. 25 no. 4 (1982) pp.10–15.
Issues in designing and implementing a national housing allowance programme for Canada.

1095   Frieden, B. J. 'Housing allowances: an experiment that worked'. *Public Interest* no. 59 (Spring 1980) pp. 15–35.
Housing allowances to the poor rather than building subsidized housing have proved successful.

1096   Friedman, J. and Weinberg, D. H. *The economics of housing vouchers.* New York, Academic Press, 1982.

Report on the US Experimental Housing Allowance Program to determine the effectiveness of housing vouchers for low income private sector tenants.

1097   Friedman, J. and Weinberg, D. H. (eds.) *The great housing experiment.* Beverly Hills, Sage, 1983. (Urban affairs annual reviews vol. 24).
Report on the US Experimental Housing Allowance Program.

1098   Hamilton, W. L. *A social experiment in program administration: the Housing Allowance Administrative Agency Experiment.* Cambridge, Mass., Abt Associates, 1979.

1099   Kennedy, S. D. *Final report of the Housing Allowance Demand Experiment.* Cambridge, Mass., Abt Associates, 1980.

1100   Khadduri, J. et al. 'Welfare reform and housing assistance: a national policy debate'. *Journal of the American Institute of Planners* vol. 44 no. 1 (Jan. 1978) pp. 2–12.
Cash transfer to the poor to provide decent housing under the Carter administration criticized.

1101   Lowry, I. S. (ed.) *Experimenting with housing allowances: findings of a ten-year study of housing assistance for low-income families, with implications for national housing policy.* Cambridge, Mass., Oelgeschlager, Gunn and Hain, 1983.
Final report of the US Housing Assistance Supply Experiment.

1102   Murray, M. P. 'A potential hazard of housing allowances for public housing'. *Journal of Urban Economics* vol. 4 no. 2 (Apr. 1977) pp. 119–34.
Possible effects of the introduction of a national housing allowance for public housing tenants in the US.

1103   Nolon, J. R. 'Re-examining federal housing programs in a time of fiscal austerity: the trend toward block grants and housing allowances'. *Urban Lawyer* vol. 14 no. 2 (Spring 1982) pp. 249–82.
Review of 1981 change in US federal housing policy from construction of new housing to subsidies for existing houses

and rent allowances for the poor, and likely effects on low income households.

1104   Olsen, E. O. and Reeder, W. J. 'Does HUD pay too much for Section 8 existing housing?' *Land Economics* vol. 57 no. 2 (May 1981) pp. 243–51.
Possible results of lowering government subsidy and raising rents to low income families in privately owned rental housing.

1105   Rosen, H. S. *Housing behavior and the Experimental Housing Allowance Program: what have we learned?* Boston, National Bureau of Economic Research, 1981. (Working paper no. 657).

1106   Stein, J. M. 'Determining utility allowances for US public housing tenants'. *Habitat International* vol. 6 no. 4 (1982) pp. 487–93.
Inadequate help with energy costs.

1107   Struyk, R. J. and Bendick, M. (eds.) *Housing vouchers for the poor: lessons from a national experiment.* Washington, DC, Urban Institute, 1981.
History of the US Experimental Housing Allowance Program.

1108   Trend, M.G. *Housing allowances for the poor: a social experiment.* Boulder, Westview, 1978.
Experiment conducted in North Dakota in which monthly housing allowances were paid to low income families to buy houses.

1109   United States, Department of Housing and Urban Development. *Experimental Housing Allowance Program: conclusion: the 1980 report.* Washington, DC, Government Printing Office, 1980.

1110   United States, Department of Housing and Urban Development. *Housing for low income families: HUD's new section 8 Housing Assistance Payments Program.* Washington, DC, The Department, 1976.

1111   United States, Department of Housing and Urban Development. *A summary report of current findings from the Experimental Housing Allowance Program.* Washington, DC, The Department, 1978.

Response of low income households to state assistance with housing allowances.

1112 Urban Systems Research and Engineering. *The costs of HUD multifamily housing programs: a comparison of the development, financing and life cycle costs of section 8, public housing and other major* . *HUD programs.* 2 vols. Washington, DC, Department of Housing and Urban Development, 1982.

1113 Weaver, R. C. 'Housing allowances'. *Land Economics* vol. 51 (Aug. 1975) pp. 247–57.

1114 Worsham, J. P. *An overview of the experimental housing allowance and assistance supply programs in bibliographical form.* Monticello, Vance Bibliographies, 1980. (Public administration series bibliography no. P-415).

1115 Zais, J. P. et al. *Modifying section 8: implications from experiments with housing allowances.* Washington, DC, Urban Institute, 1979.
Likely effects of three changes to the lower income housing assistance programme in the US.

5.5 Australasia

1116 Albon, R. 'The defunct housing allowance experiment: some assumptions and oversights'. *Australian Journal of Management* vol. 4 (Apr. 1979) pp. 1–11.

1117 Albon, R. 'To have and to hold: experimentation in Australia with a housing allowance scheme'. *Australian Journal of Management* vol. 2 (Oct. 1977) pp. 95–104.
Comparison of the Australian housing allowance voucher experiment with traditional voucher schemes.

1118 Katz, A. J. and Jackson, W. B. 'The Australian housing allowance voucher experiment: a venture in social policy development'. *Social and Economic Administration* vol. 12 (Winter 1978) pp. 197–208.

6

Home purchase finance

Increasing trends towards owner occupation, as documented in the following section on home ownership (to which reference should also be made), have intensified debate over the subsidies given by governments to encourage people to buy their own homes. The means by which homes are purchased, usually but not exclusively in the form of mortgages, is the subject of this section which reviews publications on building societies, mortgages, the role of other financial institutions in the home finance market, and government policies towards mortgage finance.

6.1   International and comparative

1119   Melton, C. R. *Housing finance and home ownership: public policy initiatives in selected countries.* Chicago, International Union of Building Societies and Savings Associations, 1978.

1120   Melton, C. R. *Savings and lending for home ownership.* Chicago, International Union for Building Societies and Savings Associations, 1980.

1121   Phillips, B. H. *Building society finance.* Wokingham, Berks., Van Nostrand Reinhold in association with the Chartered Building Societies Institute, 1983.

6.2 Europe

1122 Burda, W. A. 'The contract system in Germany'. *Chartered Building Societies Institute Journal* vol. 35 no. 148 (Dec. 1981) pp. 251–3.
Practice in mortgages and home loans in West Germany.

1123 Ireland, National Price Commission. *Building societies in Ireland.* Dublin, The Commission, 1972.
The Cleary report.

1124 Kirkham, D. H. 'Housing finance and the financial system in France'. *Chartered Building Societies Institute Journal* vol. 35 no. 146 (Aug. 1981) pp. 157–9.
Various methods of financing owner occupation in France.

1125 Kraus, F. 'UK building societies: the EEC legal scheme'. *Chartered Building Societies Institute Journal* vol. 35 no. 148 (Dec. 1981) pp. 246–9.
Implications for housing credit of moves towards European financial harmonization.

1126 Lehmann, W. *Short history of the German thrift and home ownership movement.* Chicago, International Union of Building Societies and Savings Associations, 1982.

1127 O'Rourke, C. et al. *Problems of delays and expenses associated with private house purchase transactions, report no. 1, building societies and legal requirements.* Dublin, National Institute for Physical Planning and Construction Research, 1982.

1128 Revell, J. 'Housing finance in Europe'. *Three Banks Review* no. 114 (June 1977) pp. 61–77.
Finance for owner occupation in Europe.

6.3 United Kingdom

1129 Ashworth, H. *The building society story.* London, Franey, 1980.

The history of building societies since 1775 by the then chairman of the Nationwide Building Society.

1130   Barnes, P. *Building societies: the myth of mutuality*. London, Pluto Press, 1984.

1131   Barnes, P. and Dodds, C. 'The structure and performance of the UK building society industry'. *Journal of Business Finance and Accounting* vol. 10 no. 1 (Spring 1983) pp. 37–56.

1132   Bassett, K. A. and Short, J. R. 'Patterns of building society and local authority mortgage lending in the 1970s'. *Environment and Planning A* vol. 12 no. 3 (Mar. 1980) pp. 279–300.

1133   Boddy, M. *The building societies*. London, Macmillan, 1980. Very thorough study which puts building societies firmly in the context of housing policy.

1134   Boddy, M. 'Political economy of housing: mortgage-financed owner-occupation in Britain'. *Antipode* vol. 8 no. 1 (Mar. 1976) pp. 15–24.

1135   Boddy, M. 'The public implementation of private housing policy: relations between government and the building societies in the 1970s'. In S. Barrett and C. Fudge (eds.) *Policy and action: essays on the implementation of public policy*. London, Methuen, 1981. pp. 87–104.

1136   Boddy, M. 'The structure of mortgage finance: building societies and the British social formation'. *Transactions of the Institute of British Geographers* new series vol. 1 (1976) pp. 58–71.

1137   Boleat, M. *The Building Societies Association*. London, Building Societies Association, 1979.

1138   Boleat, M. *The building society industry*. London, Allen and Unwin, 1982.

1139   Boleat, M. *The building society support scheme for local authorities*. London, Building Societies Association, 1978.

1140 Building Societies Association. *Building society factbook.*
London, The Association, annual.
Review of the activities and statistics of building societies.

1141 Building Societies Association. *Compendium of building
society statistics.* 5th ed. London, The Association, 1984.

1142 Building Societies Association. *The future constitution and
powers of building societies.* London, The Association, 1983.
The Spalding report. Anticipates Treasury green paper of
1984.

1143 Building Societies Association. *Mortgage finance in the
1980s: report of a working party.* London, The Association, 1980.
The Stowe report. Present and potential sources of building
society funds.

1144 Building Societies Association. *Mortgage repayment difficulties.* London, The Association, 1985.

1145 Building Societies Association. *New legislation for building
societies.* London, The Association, 1984.
Range of activities of building societies as limited by statute
and proposals for reform; Treasury green paper followed.

1146 Building Societies Association. *Studies in building society
activity 1974–79.* London, The Association, 1980.

1147 Cleary, E. J. *The building society movement.* London, Elek
Books, 1965.
Detailed history of building societies from the eighteenth
century.

1148 Davies, G. *Building societies and their branches: a regional
economic survey.* London, Franey, 1981.

1149 Davis, E.P. and Saville, I. D. 'Mortgage lending and the
housing market'. *Bank of England Quarterly Bulletin* vol. 22 no. 3
(Sept. 1982) pp. 390–8.

1150 Douglas, C. M. and Lee, R. G. *The Estate Agents Act 1979.*
London, Sweet and Maxwell, 1979.

1151 Duncan, S. 'Self-help: the allocation of mortgages and the formation of housing sub-markets'. *Area* vol. 8 no. 4 (1976) pp. 307–16.

1152 Equal Opportunities Commission. *It's not your business, it's how the society works.* Manchester, The Commission, 1978.
Experience of married applicants for joint mortgages.

1153 Evans, A. W. *The five per cent sample survey of building society mortgages.* London, HMSO, 1975. (Studies in official statistics no. 26).

1154 Fairest, P. B. *Mortgages.* London, Sweet and Maxwell, 1975. (Modern legal studies).

1155 Ford, J. 'The role of the building society manager in the urban stratification system: autonomy and constraint'. *Urban Studies* vol. 12 no. 3 (Oct. 1975) pp. 295–302.

1156 Gough, T. J. *The economics of building societies.* London, Macmillan, 1982.

1157 Grime, E. K. and Smith, A. G. 'Mortgage allocation in Salford and Manchester'. *Area* vol. 14 (1982) pp. 305–12.

1158 Harrison, M. L. and Stevens, L . *Down-market lending: mortgages and the support scheme in Leeds.* University of Birmingham, Centre for Urban and Regional Studies, 1983. (Occasional paper 7).
Local account of the Support Lending Scheme under which building societies made funds available to local authorities for allocation to particular groups for house purchase.

1159 'The housing finance market: recent growth in perspective'. *Bank of England Quarterly Bulletin* vol. 25 no. 1 (Mar. 1985) pp. 80–91.
Review of bank and building society mortgage lending since 1980. Updates no. 1149.

1160 Jones, C. 'The future of building societies'. *National Westminster Bank Review* May 1984 pp. 33–45.

1161   Karn, V. A. 'Arrears'. *Roof* vol. 8 no. 1 (Jan.–Feb. 1983) pp. 11–14.
Increasing unemployment is producing an escalation in mortgage default.

1162   Kemeny, J. and Thomas, A. D. 'Capital leakage from owner occupied housing'. *Policy and Politics* vol. 12 no. 1 (1984) pp. 13–30.
The extent to which capital gains on housing sales are not reinvested in housing but diverted to general consumption.

1163   King, M. A. and Atkinson, A. B. 'Housing policy, taxation and reform'. *Midland Bank Review* Spring 1980 pp. 7–15.
Assesses the costs and injustices of mortgage interest tax relief and proposes reform.

1164   Local Authorities Management Services and Computer Committee. *Mortgage arrears.* London, The Committee, 1979.

1165   McLeay, E. M. 'Building societies: a question of accountability?' *Public Administration* vol. 62 no. 2 (Summer 1984) pp. 147–60.

1166   Mills, J. *Wurzburg and Mills building society law.* 14th ed. London, Stevens, 1976.
Standard reference work.

1167   Moreton, P. 'Valuations for mortgage purposes'. *Journal of Valuation* vol. 2 no. 2 (Winter 1983–4) pp. 125–36.

1168   Nellis, J. G. and Thom, R. 'The demand for mortgage finance in the United Kingdom'. *Applied Economics* vol. 15 no. 4 (Aug. 1983) pp. 521–9.
Rationing behaviour of building societies in the UK.

1169   Price, S. J. *Building societies: their origins and history.* London, Franey, 1958.
Dull and dry history by their official publisher.

1170   Rigge, M. and Young, M. *Building societies and the consumer.* London, National Consumer Council, 1981.

Consumers' guide to building societies and suggestions for reform.

1171 SHAC. *Buying a home.* London, SHAC, 1983.

1172 Thom, R. 'Housing starts and mortgage availability: evidence from the UK time series'. *Applied Economics* vol. 16 no. 6 (Dec. 1984) pp. 881–93.
Uses UK data from 1958 to 1981 to analyse the relationship between mortgage availability and housing starts.

1173 Thornton, C. E. I. and McBrien, J. P. *Building society law — cases and material.* 2nd ed. London, Sweet and Maxwell, 1975.

1174 United Kingdom, Chief Registrar of Friendly Societies. *Annual report.* London, HMSO, annual.
Reports on the activities of building societies and friendly societies.

1175 United Kingdom, Conveyancing Committee. *Conveyancing simplifications.* London, HMSO, 1985.
Second report of the committee chaired by Professor J. T. Farrand.

1176 United Kingdom, Conveyancing Committee. *Non-solicitor conveyancers: competence and consumer protection.* London, HMSO, 1984.
First report of the committee chaired by Professor J. T. Farrand.

1177 United Kingdom, Joint Advisory Committee on Building Society Mortgage Finance. *The guideline system.* London, Department of the Environment, 1980.
Report on the working of the owner occupied market and on government regulation of building societies.

1178 United Kingdom, Price Commission. *Charges, costs and margins of estate agents.* London, HMSO, 1979. (Cmnd. 7467).

1179 United Kingdom, Treasury. *Building societies: a new framework.* London, HMSO, 1984. (Cmnd. 9316).

Proposals for diversification of building society activity.

1180 University of Birmingham, Centre for Urban and Regional Studies, Housing Monitoring Team. *Building societies and the local housing market*. Birmingham, The Centre, 1982. (Research memorandum 90).

1181 University of Birmingham, Centre for Urban and Regional Studies, Housing Monitoring Team. *The structure and functioning of building societies: a head office view*. Birmingham, The Centre, 1978. (Research memorandum 64).

1182 Weir, S. 'How Labour failed to reform mortgage relief'. *New Society* vol. 46 no. 835 (5 Oct 1978) pp. 14–16.
How a topical issue was handled by the then Labour government.

1183 Weir, S. 'Red line districts'. *Roof* vol. 1 no. 4 (July 1976) pp. 109–14.
Evidence of building societies' failure to lend in inner city areas.

1184 Welham, P. J. 'The tax treatment of owner-occupied housing in the UK'. *Scottish Journal of Political Economy* vol. 29 no. 2 (June 1982) pp. 139–55.

1185 Wilkinson, M. and Wilkinson, R. K. 'The withdrawal of mortgage tax relief: a survey and evaluation of the debate'. *Policy and Politics* vol. 10 no. 1 (1982) pp. 47–63.

1186 Williams, L. 'Building societies and their role in the national economy'. *Royal Society of Arts Journal* vol. 127 no. 5275 (June 1979) pp. 422–75.

1187 Williams, P. 'Building societies and the inner city'. *Institute of British Geographers Transactions* vol. 3 no. 1 (1978) pp. 23–34.

6.4   North America

1188 Ash, T. and Kornhauser, A. L. 'Reduction of transportation through home mortgage subsidies'. *Journal of Advanced*

Transportation vol. 17 no. 2 (Summer 1983) pp. 119–58.
Mortgage subsidies to encourage people to live closer to work.
Results in shorter trips and reduced energy consumption.

1189   Baptiste, K. E. 'Attacking the urban redlining problem'.
Boston University Law Review vol. 56 (Nov. 1976) pp. 989–1019.

1190   Barth, J. R. 'Redlining in housing markets: mortgages and
minorities in the US'. *Journal of Social and Political Studies* vol. 5
(Winter 1980) pp. 221–42.
Techniques for defining, measuring and dealing with
redlining.

1191   Belec, J. 'Origins of state housing policy in Canada — the
case of the Central Mortgage Bank'. *Canadian Geographer* vol. 28
no. 4 (Winter 1984) pp. 377–82.

1192   Benston, G. J. 'Mortgage redlining research: a review and
critical analysis'. In *The regulation of financial institutions*. Boston,
Federal Reserve Bank of Boston, 1979. pp. 144–95.

1193   Black, H. et al. 'Discrimination in mortgage lending'.
American Economic Review Papers and Proceedings vol. 68 (1978) pp.
186–91.

1194   Bradford, C. 'Financing home ownership: the federal role
in neighborhood decline'. *Urban Affairs Quarterly* vol. 14 no. 3
(Mar. 1979) pp. 313–35.

1195   Gold, S. D. 'Homeowner property taxes, inflation and
property tax relief'. *National Tax Journal* vol. 34 (June 1981) pp.
167–84.

1196   Guy, R. F. et al. 'Discrimination in mortgage lending: the
Home Mortgage Disclosure Act'. *Population Research and Policy
Review* vol. 1 (1982) pp. 283–96.

1197   Hood, E. T. and Weed, C. M. 'Redlining revisited: a
neighborhood development bank as a proposed solution'. *Urban
Lawyer* vol. 11 no. 1 (Winter 1979) pp. 139–71.

Revitalization of urban areas is prevented by lack of mortgage finance. Establishment of neighbourhood development bank mooted.

1198   Ittig, P. T. 'Tax subsidy of home ownership'. *Journal of Public Policy* vol. 4 no. 2 (May 1984) pp. 103–10.
Tax treatment of homes as investments with particular reference to the US.

1199   Jaffee, D. M. and Rosen, K. T. 'Mortgage credit availability and residential construction'. *Brookings Papers on Economic Activity* vol. 2 (1979) pp. 333–76.

1200   Kaster, L. R. *Subsidized housing workouts, income tax aspects and certain investor problems.* Washington, DC, Department of Housing and Urban Development, 1975.
Defaults in mortgage payments.

1201   Low, E. 'The red (and green) lining of America'. *Roof* vol. 2 no. 6 (Nov. 1977) pp. 180–1.
Under the Home Mortgage Disclosure Act, loan associations in the US have to disclose home lending policies.

1202   Schafer, R. and Ladd, H. F. *Mortgage lending decisions: criteria and constraints.* 2 vols. Cambridge, Mass., MIT Press and Harvard University Press, 1978.

1203   Smith, L. B. 'Myths and realities in mortgage finance and the housing crisis'. *Canadian Public Policy* vol. 2 (Spring 1976) pp. 240–8.

1204   Stone, M. 'Housing, mortgage lending and the contradictions of capitalism'. In W. Tabb and L. Sawers (eds.) *Marxism and the metropolis.* New York, Oxford University Press, 1978.

1205   United States, Commission on Civil Rights. *Mortgage money: who gets it? A case study in mortgage lending discrimination in Hartford, Connecticut.* Washington, DC, The Commission, 1974. (Clearinghouse publication 48).

1206   United States, Department of Housing and Urban Development. *A guidebook: Home Mortgage Disclosure Act and reinvestment strategies.* Washington, DC, Government Printing Office, 1979.

1207 United States, Department of Housing and Urban Development. *Redlining and disinvestment as a discriminatory practice in residential mortgage loans.* Washington, DC, The Department, 1977.
Prepared by the Center for Urban Studies, University of Illinois.

1208 Vance, M. A. *Mortgage and construction finance: a bibliography.* Monticello, Vance Bibliographies, 1982. (Architecture series A-778).

1209 Walmsley, J. 'Secondary mortgage markets: the wave of the future'. *Banker* vol. 134 no. 704 (Oct. 1984) pp. 21, 23–4.
Structure and operation of the secondary mortgage market in the US.

1210 White, A. G. *Discrimination in housing loans — redlining: a selected bibliography.* Monticello, Council of Planning Librarians, 1976. (Exchange bibliography no. 977).

1211 White, M. J. and White, L. J. 'The tax subsidy to owner-occupied housing: who benefits?' *Journal of Public Economics* vol. 7 no. 1 (Feb. 1977) pp. 111–26.
Incidence and effects of the US federal income tax subsidy of owner occupied housing.

6.5 Australasia

1212 Australian Association of Permanent Building Societies. *Annual report.* Deakin, ACT, The Association, annual.

1213 Australian Bureau of Statistics. *Housing finance for owner occupation.* Canberra, The Bureau, 1983.

1214 Building Societies Association of New Zealand. *Building societies in New Zealand.* Wellington, The Association, 1982.

1215   Burtt, D. J. *The demand for housing in New Zealand, part l, financial organisations in the mortgage market.* Wellington, New Zealand National Housing Commission, 1978. (Research paper 79/4).

1216   Burtt, D. J. *The provision of housing finance with special reference to permanent building societies.* Wellington, New Zealand Institute of Economic Research for the Building Societies Association of New Zealand, 1979.

7

Housing tenure

Housing tenure, or the legal conditions under which housing is occupied, is widely recognized as an important determinant of variables such as housing satisfaction, housing costs, social status, and housing conditions and standards. This section includes references to material on housing tenure as a general concept, and collected works on various forms of housing tenure. References to particular forms of housing tenure may be found in sections 8 'Home ownership', 9 'Public housing' and 11 'Alternative tenures', while discussion of some of the general principles may be found in section 2 'Housing market'.

7.1 International and comparative

1217 Kemeny, J. 'Forms of tenure and social structure: a comparison of owning and renting in Australia and Sweden'. *British Journal of Sociology* vol. 29 no. 1 (Mar. 1978) pp. 41–56.

1218 McAllister, I. 'Housing tenure and party choice in Australia, Britain and the United States'. *British Journal of Political Science* vol. 14 part 4 (Oct. 1984) pp. 509–22.
Housing tenure as a political issue: comparative approach with useful data.

7.2 Europe

1219 Lundqvist, L. J. 'Housing policy and alternative housing tenures: some Scandinavian examples'. *Policy and Politics* vol. 12 no. 1 (Jan. 1984) pp. 1–12.

Conversion of rented dwellings into co-operatives or condominiums and changes in structure of rental tenure increases
tenant influence and decreases need for state housing policies
in Scandinavia.

1220   Lundqvist, L. J. 'Housing tenure experiments in Sweden:
what should be done with renting'. *Housing Review* vol. 32 no. 4
(July–Aug. 1983) pp. 120–2.
As rental housing becomes increasingly unpopular in Sweden,
so it is being converted to other tenures.

1221   Lundqvist, L. J. *Housing tenures in Sweden.* Gavle, National
Swedish Institute for Building Research, 1983.

7.3   United Kingdom

1222   Bagot, P. *A comparative study of three forms of housing tenure.*
University of Edinburgh, Architecture Research Unit, 1971.

1223   Building Societies Association. *Housing tenure.* London,
The Association, 1983.
Historical review of tenure patterns and results of 1983 BMRB
survey into tenure preferences.

1224   Building Societies Association. *Leaseholds — time for a
change.* London, The Association, 1984.
Advocates the replacement of the current system of long
leaseholds with the Australian strata title system.

1225   Darke, J. and Darke, R. *Who needs housing?* London,
Macmillan, 1979.
Chapters on the three main tenures plus an examination of
the role of the professional in housing policy.

1226   Hamnett, C. 'Housing the two nations: socio-tenurial
polarization in England and Wales 1961–81'. *Urban Studies* vol. 21
no. 4 (Nov. 1984) pp. 389–405.

1227   Harrison, A. and Lomas, G. 'Tenure preference: how to
interpret the survey evidence'. *CES Review* no. 8 (Jan. 1980) pp.
20–3.

Review of tenure preference surveys by BMRB and General Household Survey.

1228   Holmans, A. E. 'Housing tenure in England and Wales: the present situation and recent trends'. *Social Trends* no. 9 (1979) pp. 10–19.

1229   Murphy, M. J. 'The influence of fertility, early housing career, and socioeconomic factors on tenure determination in contemporary Britain'. *Environment and Planning A* vol. 16 no. 10 (Oct. 1984) pp. 1303–18.

1230   Saunders, P. R. *Housing tenure and class interests.* Brighton, University of Sussex, 1977. (Urban and regional studies working paper no. 6)

1231   Sullivan, O. and Murphy, M. J. 'Housing pathways and stratification: some evidence from a British national survey'. *Journal of Social Policy* vol. 13 no. 2 (Apr. 1984) pp. 147–65.
   Uses data from OPCS Family Formation Survey to explore e.g. tenure types and transitions between tenures.

7.4   North America

1232   Chi, P. S. K. *Population redistribution and changes in housing tenure status in the United States.* Washington, DC, Department of Housing and Urban Development, 1980. (American housing survey studies no. 4).

1233   Cox, K. 'Housing tenure and neighborhood activism'. *Urban Affairs Quarterly* vol. 18 (1982) pp. 107–29.

1234   Golant, S. M. 'The housing tenure adjustments of the young and the elderly: policy implications'. *Urban Affairs Quarterly* vol. 13 no. 1 (Sept. 1977) pp. 95–108.
   Household trends related to housing needs in the US.

1235   Harloe, M. *Housing management and new forms of tenure in the USA.* London, Centre for Environmental Studies, 1978.

1236 Kent, R. J. 'Housing tenure choice: evidence from time series'. *Journal of Urban Economics* vol. 15 no. 2 (Mar. 1984) pp. 195–209.
Model of choice between owning and renting in the US.

1237 Macrae, C. D. 'The Federal Housing Administration, tenure choice, and residential land use'. *Journal of Urban Economics* vol. 4 no. 3 (July 1977) pp. 360–78.
Movement of households whose costs are reduced by FHA insurance programmes.

1238 Peiser, R. and Brueggeman, W. B. 'Changing patterns in homeowning and renting: the response to economic incentives'. *Appraisal Journal* vol. 50 no. 3 (July 1982) pp. 410–16.
Relative costs of renting and owning property in the US are compared between 1963 and 1978.

1239 Rudel, T. K. and Neaigus, A 'Inflation, new homeowners and downgrading in the 1970s'. *Urban Studies* vol. 21 no. 2 (May 1984) pp. 129–38.
Consumer responses to house price inflation, and tenure movement in the US.

7.5 Australasia

1240 Australian Bureau of Statistics. *Survey of home rental and home ownership.* Canberra, The Bureau, 1979.

1241 Heady, B. and Smith, A. W. 'Owning versus renting in Australia: public and private choices in housing'. In *Housing economics.* Canberra, Australian Government Publishing Service, 1980. pp. 278–85.

1242 Paterson, J. 'Home-owning, home renting and income redistribution'. *Australian Quarterly* vol. 47 no. 4 (1975) pp. 28–36.

8

Home ownership

The proportion of people owning and living in their own property varies greatly from country to country. The reasons for this variation, together with the political ideologies of increasing owner occupation, the sociological aspects of home ownership and the housing policy measures to promote home ownership, are among the issues covered in this section. For works on the financial aspects of owner occupation the user should turn to section 6 'Home purchase finance' while the following section on public housing provides some interesting comparisons on approaches to housing policy.

8.1 International and comparative

1243 Agnew, J. A. 'Home ownership and the capitalist social order'. In M. Dear and A. J. Scott (eds.) *Urbanization and urban planning in capitalist society*. London, Methuen, 1981. pp. 457–80.

1244 Agnew, J. 'Home ownership and identity in capitalist societies'. In J. S. Duncan (ed.) *Housing and identity*. London, Croom Helm, 1981. pp. 60–97.
Includes extensive bibliography.

1245 Boyle, R. and Rich, D. 'Urban policy and the new privatism in the United States and Britain'. *Public Administration Bulletin* no. 45 (Aug. 1984) pp. 22–36.
Discusses whether privatization is part of a coherent strategy and if it can regenerate depressed cities.

1246 Kemeny, J. 'Home ownership and privatization'. *International Journal of Urban and Regional Research* vol. 4 no. 3 (Sept. 1980) pp. 372–88.

1247 Kemeny, J. *The myth of home ownership: private versus public choices in housing tenure*. London, Routledge and Kegan Paul, 1981.
   Uses cross national data to compare home ownership and advocates non-profit housing organizations to reinvest in new housing construction.

1248 Kendig, H. 'Housing tenure and generational equity'. *Ageing and Society* vol. 4 part 3 (Sept. 1984) pp. 249–72.
   Financial impacts of home ownership on older generations in Australia, Britain and the US.

1249 Thorns, D. C. 'The implications of differential rates of capital gain from owner occupation for the formation and development of housing classes'. *International Journal of Urban and Regional Research* vol. 5 (1981) pp. 205–17.

1250 Thorns, D. C. 'Owner-occupation: its significance for wealth transfer and class formation'. *Sociological Review* vol. 29 no. 4 (Nov. 1981) pp. 705–28.
   Data on the owner occupied housing market in Britain and New Zealand.

8.2 Europe

1251 Ball, M. 'The effect of land rent on the relations of production in owner-occupied housing development'. In M. Ball et al. (eds.) *Land rent, housing and urban planning: a European perspective*. London, Croom Helm, 1985.

1252 Howenstine, E. J. 'Innovations in European home ownership policy'. *Construction Review* Apr. 1975 pp. 4–10.

1253 Kemeny, J. 'Urban home ownership in Sweden'. *Urban Studies* vol. 15 no. 3 (Oct. 1978) pp. 313–20.

1254   Schaefer, P. 'Private property: vehicle of the European housing industry'. *Appraisal Journal* July 1981 pp. 409–12.
Private ownership of housing in Western and Eastern Europe.

1255   Schifferes, S. 'Homes rule in Ireland'. *Roof* vol. 3 no. 6 (Nov. 1978) pp. 179–81.
Encouraging owner occupation in Ireland.

1256   Svensson, W. 'Home ownership in Sweden'. *Annals of the American Academy of Social Sciences* no. 197 (May 1938) pp. 154–9.

8.3   United Kingdom

1257   Allen, P. *Shared ownership: a stepping stone to home ownership.* London, HMSO, 1982.
Department of the Environment report on local authority part mortgage/part rental schemes for home ownership.

1258   Ashmore, G. *The owner-occupied housing market.* University of Birmingham, Centre for Urban and Regional Studies, 1975. (Research memorandum 41).
Effects of market and financial fluctuations on building society policy, lending and borrowing patterns.

1259   Ball, M. *Housing policy and economic power: the political economy of owner-occupation.* London, Methuen, 1983.

1260   Cowling, M. and Smith, S. 'Home ownership, socialism and realistic socialist policy'. *Critical Social Policy* no. 9 (Spring 1984) pp. 64–8.
Discusses how socialism comes to terms with the popular trend towards home ownership.

1261   Edel, M. 'Home ownership and working class unity'. *International Journal of Urban and Regional Research* vol. 6 no. 2 (June 1982) pp. 205–22.

1262   Forrest, R. 'The meaning of homeownership'. *Environment and Planning D* vol. 1 no. 2 (1983) pp. 205–16.

Connections betweeen mass home ownership and the means of production in Britain.

1263 Forrest, R. et al. *A foot on the ladder. An evaluation of low cost home ownership initiatives.* University of Bristol, School for Advanced Urban Studies, 1984.

1264 George, A. F. and George, A. *The sale of flats.* 5th ed. London, Sweet and Maxwell, 1984.

1265 Ginsburg, N. 'Home ownership and socialism in Britain: a bulwark against Bolshevism'. *Critical Social Policy* no. 7 (Summer 1983) pp. 34–53.

1266 Ineichen, B. 'Home ownership and manual workers lifestyles'. *Sociological Review* vol. 20 no. 3 (Aug. 1972) pp. 391–412.

1267 Jackson, A. A. *Semi-detached London: suburban development, life and transport.* London, Allen and Unwin, 1973.
Private housing development around the capital.

1268 Jones, C. 'Household movement, filtering and trading up within the owner-occupied sector'. *Regional Studies* vol. 12 no. 5 (1978) pp. 551–61.

1269 Kirkham, A. *Improvement for sale by local authority involvement in the provision of new housing for owner occupation.* London, HMSO, 1983.

1270 Littlewood, J. and Mason, S. *Taking the initiative: a survey of low cost home owners.* London, HMSO, 1984.

1271 Melville-Ross, T. 'Home ownership in the UK in the 1980s'. *Long Range Planning* vol. 14 no. 4 (Aug. 1981) pp. 43–50.
Speculates on the effect of future economic trends on the demand for home ownership and mortgage finance.

1272 Merrett, S. *Owner-occupation in Britain.* London, Routledge and Kegan Paul, 1982.

1273 Murphy, W. T. and Clark, H. *The family home.* London, Sweet and Maxwell, 1983. (Modern legal studies)

Home ownership disputes settled in law.

1274   Oliver, P. et al. *Dunroamin: the suburban semi and its enemies.* London, Barrie and Jenkins, 1981.
A sympathetic study of 1930s suburban housing.

1275   Pawley, M. *Home ownership.* London, Architectural Press, 1978.
Reviews the history of building societies to show the development of owner occupation.

1276   SHAC. *Home ownership in the 1980s: a one-day conference.* London, SHAC, 1980. (Policy paper no. 3).

1277   Simpson, M. A. and Lloyd, T. H. *Middle class housing in Britain.* Newton Abbot, David and Charles, 1977.
Review of the development of more desirable residential areas from the eighteenth century.

1278   Smith, R. 'Advocating owner occupation in the inner city: some lessons from American experience for UK low cost home ownership programmes'. *Planning Outlook* vol. 26 no. 1 (1983) pp. 40–3.

1279   Thompson, F. M. L. (ed.) *The rise of suburbia.* Leicester University Press, 1982.
Essays in the growth of suburbia in English cities in the nineteenth century.

1280   United Kingdom, Department of the Environment, Housing Development Directorate. *Local authorities and building for sale: a handbook on local authority involvement in the provision of new housing for owner-occupation.* London, The Department, 1977. (HDD occasional paper 1/77).
Assesses several schemes where local authorities and private developers have co-operated on build for sale schemes.

1281   United Kingdom, Department of the Environment, Housing Development Directorate. *Starter homes: a report of a DOE survey of new small houses and flats for sale.* London, Department of the Environment, 1980. (HDD occasional paper 2/80).

Report on new, small, cheap homes as first step on the owner occupier ladder.

1282   United Kingdom, Ministry of Housing and Local Government. *Help towards home ownership*. London, HMSO, 1966. (Cmnd. 3163).

1283   Walker, J. B. 'Access to the owner-occupied and local authority sectors: an exploratory analysis'. *Urban Studies* vol. 13 (1976) pp. 311–18.

1284   Wistow, G. 'Managing housing policy: the implementation of policy in the owner-occupied sector'. *Local Government Studies* vol. 4 no. 4 (Oct. 1978) pp. 53–66.

8.4   North America

1285   Bennett, L. 'Privatism and housing policy in the United States'. *Urban Law and Policy* vol. 6 no. 2 (Dec. 1983) pp. 169–84. Privatism in US housing policy since the 1930s and its effect on federal housing polices.

1286   Bradbury, T. 'Housing policy and home ownership in mining towns: Quebec, Canada'. *International Journal of Urban and Regional Research* vol. 9 no. 1 (Mar. 1985) pp. 1–14.

1287   Carliner, G. 'Determinants of home ownership'. *Land Economics* vol. 50 no. 2 (1974) pp. 109–19.

1288   Christian, J. W. and Parliment, T. J. *Home ownership: the American dream adrift*. Chicago, US League of Savings Associations, 1982.

1289   Coons, A. E. and Glaze, B. T. *Housing market analysis and the growth of home ownership*. Columbus, Ohio State University, 1963.

1290   Cunningham, R. P. 'Requiem for FHA is premature'. *Appraisal Journal* vol. 45 no. 1 (Jan. 1977) pp. 95–102.

Achievements of the US Department of Housing and Urban Development's Federal Housing Administration mortgage insurance programmes which have helped increase home ownership.

1291   Duncan, N. G. 'Home ownership and social theory'. In J. S. Duncan (ed.) *Housing and identity*. London, Croom Helm, 1981. pp. 98–134.

1292   Edel, M. et al. *Shaky palaces: home ownership and social mobility in Boston's suburbanization*. New York, Columbia University Press, 1984. (Columbia history of urban life series).
100 years of suburban growth in Boston.

1293   Fredland, D. R. *Residential mobility and home purchase*. Lexington, Mass., Lexington Books, 1974.

1294   *Home ownership: a bibliography*. Monticello, Vance Bibliographies, 1982. (Architecture series A-829).
Mainly US sources.

1295   Marcuse, P. 'Residential alienation, home ownership, and limits of shelter policy'. *Journal of Sociology and Social Welfare* vol. 3 (1975) pp. 181–203.

1296   Ranney, S. I. 'The future price of houses, mortgage market conditions, and the returns to homeownership'. *American Economic Review* vol. 71 no. 3 (June 1981) pp. 323–33.

1297   Rosen, H. S. and Rosen, K. T. 'Federal taxes and homeownership: evidence from time series'. *Journal of Political Economy* vol. 88 (1980) pp. 59–75.

1298   Rubinowitz, L. S. and Trosman, E. 'Affirmative action and the American dream: implementing fair housing policies in federal homeownership programs'. *Northwestern University Law Review* vol. 74 (Nov. 1979) pp. 491–616.

1299   Sternlieb, G. 'The evolution of housing and its social compact'. *Urban Land* vol. 41 no. 12 (Dec. 1982) pp. 17–20.

Growth of home ownership in the US.

1300 Stewart, J. K. 'Subsidy housing: the ownership alternative'. *Journal of Property Management* vol. 48 no. 3 (May–June 1983) pp. 48–51.
New schemes of tenant purchase in the US aim to avoid problems of earlier subsidized home ownership programmes.

1301 Struyk, R. *Urban home ownership: the economic determinants.* Lexington, Mass., Heath, 1976.

1302 Tuccillo, J. et al. 'Home ownership policies and mortgage markets 1960 to 1980'. *Housing Finance Review* vol. 1 (Jan. 1982) pp. 1–21.

1303 United States, Congressional Budget Office. *Home ownership: the changing relationship of costs and incomes, and possible federal roles.* Washington, DC, The Office, 1977.

1304 Walsh, J. A. 'An analysis of intraurban residential ownership patterns'. *Environment and Planning A* vol. 10 no. 1 (Jan. 1978) pp. 17–28.
Models of housing ownership patterns in Canadian cities between 1951 and 1971.

8.5 Australasia

1305 Keifer, D. M. 'The equity of alternative polices for the Australian home owner'. *Economic Record* vol. 54 (1978) pp. 127–39.

1306 Kemeny, J. 'Federal policy favours owners, compounds inequity'. *Royal Australian Planning Institute Journal* vol. 17 no. 4 (Nov. 1979) pp. 223–6.

1307 Kemeny, J. *The great Australian nightmare: a critique of the home ownership ideology.* Melbourne, Georgian House, 1983.

1308 Kemeny, J. 'A political sociology of home ownership in Australia'. *Australian and New Zealand Journal of Sociology* vol. 13 no. 1 (Feb. 1977) pp. 47–52.

1309   Reece, B. F. 'The income tax incentive to owner-occupied housing in Australia'. *Economic Record* vol. 51 (June 1975) pp. 218–31.

1310   Sandercock, L. 'A socialist city in a capitalist society? Property ownership and urban reform in Australia'. *Journal of Australian Political Economy* no. 3 (Sept. 1978) pp. 66–79.

1311   Tucker, S. N. 'An analysis of housing subsidy schemes in Australia'. *Urban Studies* vol. 20 no. 4 (Nov. 1983) pp. 439–53. Measuring the cost of schemes for subsidizing home ownership in Australia.

1312   Williams, P. 'The politics of home ownership'. In J. Halligan and C. Paris (eds.) *Australian urban politics: critical essays.* Melbourne, Longman, 1984.

1313   Yates, D. J. 'The demand for owner occupied housing'. *Australian Economic Papers* vol. 20 (Dec. 1981) pp. 309–24.

8.6   Africa, Asia and Latin America

1314   Awotona, A. A. 'Land ownership and tenure in Nigeria, a major factor in the housing equation'. *Planning Outlook* vol. 21 no. 1 (Spring 1978) pp. 11–15.

1315   Odongo, J. and Lea, J. P. 'Home ownership and rural-urban links in Uganda'. *Journal of Modern African Studies* vol. 15 (1977) pp. 59–73.

1316   Perdomo, R. P. and Nikken, P. 'The law and home ownership in the barrios of Caracas'. In A. Gilbert (ed.) *Urbanization in contemporary Latin America.* Chichester, Wiley, 1982. pp. 205–30.

9
Public housing

Increasing awareness by governments of the need to assume responsibility for the housing of their expanding populations, promoted the development of direct state involvement in housing, and although the form in which such involvement occurs varies widely from country to country, public housing is now an essential ingredient of housing policy all over the world. This section considers works on general public housing policy, housing management issues such as allocation, rents and problem estates, sales of public housing to the private sector, and statistics. Other sections such as 1 'Housing policy: general works', 2 'Housing market', 5 'Rebates and allowances', 7 'Housing tenure' and 12 'Social aspects' contain references on related housing issues.

9.1 International and comparative

1317 Ascher, C. S. *The administration of publicly aided housing.* The Hague, Nijhoff, 1971.
International Institute of Administrative Sciences study.

1318 Brown, J. S. et al. *Public housing and welfare services: a comparative review of developments in Canada, United States and Britain 1947–1963.* Vancouver, University of British Columbia, 1964.

1319 Fuerst, J. S. (ed.) *Public housing in Europe and America.* London, Croom Helm, 1974.

151

Collection of essays by experts from the countries concerned.

1320 Lewis, C. W. and Sternheimer, S. *Soviet urban management: with comparisons to the United States.* New York, Praeger, 1979.

1321 Rose, A. 'The impact of recent trends in social housing policies'. In L.S. Bourne and J. Hitchcock (eds.) *Urban housing markets.* University of Toronto Press, 1978. pp. 261–78.

1322 Turner, J. F. C. 'Approaches to government-sponsored housing'. *Ekistics* vol. 41 no. 242 (Jan. 1976) pp. 4–7.

1323 United Nations, Department of Economic and Social Affairs. *Basics of housing management.* New York, United Nations, 1969.

1324 United Nations, Department of Economic and Social Affairs. *Management of government housing projects.* New York, United Nations, 1976.
Report of the ad hoc group of experts on the financial management of government housing projects, New York, 3–10 Dec. 1974.

9.2 Europe

1325 Dybbroe, O. 'Why "property owning democracy"? Some notes on the defeat of social housing and on the role of the architect planner in capitalist society'. *Habitat International* vol. 4 no. 3 (1979).

1326 Eisenger, P. K. 'French urban housing and the mixed economy: the privatization of the public sector'. *Annals of the American Academy of Political and Social Science* vol. 459 (Jan. 1982) pp. 134–47.

1327 Jacobs, E. M. 'Rent and the charge for public services in Soviet urban public housing'. *Canadian Slavonic Papers* vol. 19 (Mar. 1977) pp. 76–86.

1328 Johansson, A. 'Social housing policy in Sweden'. *Annals of American Academy of Social Sciences* no. 197 (May 1938) pp. 160–70.

1329   Lundqvist, L. J. 'Strategies for the Swedish public housing sector'. *Urban Law and Policy* vol. 6 no. 3 (June 1984) pp. 215–51.
Describes the organization of municipal housing corporations which control Swedish public rental housing.

1330   Pena, D. and Ruiz-Castillo, J. 'Distributional aspects of public rental housing and rent control policies in Spain'. *Journal of Urban Economics* vol. 15 no. 3 (May 1984) pp. 350–70.
Rent control and public housing in Spain.

1331   Priemus, H. 'Rent and subsidy policy in the Netherlands during the seventies'. *Urban Law and Policy* vol. 4 no. 4 (Dec. 1981) pp. 299–355.
Government policy for public housing in the Netherlands.

1332   Sbragia, A. 'Not all roads lead to Rome: local housing policy in the unitary Italian state'. *British Journal of Political Science* vol. 9 no. 3 (July 1979) pp. 315–39.
Public housing in Milan and relations with the central government.

1333   Wackerbarth, D. 'Public housing in the USSR: some comparisons with the work of housing associations in the UK'. *Voluntary Housing* vol. 11 no. 6 (Nov.–Dec. 1979) pp. 14–15, 18–19.
Rehabilitation, alternative forms of tenure and housing for special needs.

1334   Walden, L.-J. (ed.) *Housing policy: the just price and the role of the public housing sector: papers and discussions from the British–Scandinavian seminar at the London School of Economics and CURS, University of Birmingham, January 1981.* Gavle, National Swedish Institute for Building Research, 1981.

1335   Watson, C. J. *Social housing policy in Belgium.* University of Birmingham, Centre for Urban and Regional Studies, 1971. (Occasional paper 19).

1336   Wynn, M. 'San Cosme, Spain: planning and renewal of a state housing area'. *Journal of the American Planning Association* vol. 46 no. 1 (Jan. 1980) pp. 76–87.

Rebuilding of state housing estate in Barcelona and associated problems.

9.3   United Kingdom

1337   Adam Smith Institute. *The Omega file: local government, planning and housing.* London, The Institute, 1983.
Reviews public sector housing and advocates increased private sector involvement.

1338   Alpren, L. *The causes of serious rent arrears.* London, Housing Centre Trust, 1977.
Rent arrears, tenants' problems and local authority responses in a London borough.

1339   Arden, A. *The public tenant's handbook.* London, Allison and Busby, 1985.

1340   Ascher, K. 'The politics of administrative opposition — council house sales and the right to buy'. *Local Government Studies* vol. 9 no. 2 (Mar.–Apr. 1983) pp. 12–20.

1341   Attenburrow, J. J. et al. *The problem of some large local authority estates.* Watford, Building Research Establishment, 1978.
Reviews the literature and uses census indicators in Merseyside to provide objective analysis of housing problems on public sector estates.

1342   Baldwin, J. 'Problem housing estates'. *Social and Economic Administration* vol. 8 no. 2 (1974) pp. 116–35.
Study of two estates in Sheffield, comparison of maintenance of buildings and attitudes of both residents and officials.

1343   Barr, A. W. *Public authority housing.* London, Batsford, 1958.
Reviews the development of British public authority housing during the immediate post-war period.

1344   Bassett, K. et al. 'Council house sales'. *Policy and Politics* vol. 8 no. 3 (1980).

Special issue devoted to council house sales with valuable case studies of practices in individual local authorities.

1345 *Best practice in housing: a guidebook by experts on all that is best in housing policy and management through the United Kingdom.* London, BKT Publications, 1981.
Disappointing, overpriced collection of short papers by experts on housing management issues.

1346 Blaber, A. et al. *Improving delivery of housing and welfare services: a digest of experiences.* London, National Council for Voluntary Organisations, 1982.

1347 Boyne, G. 'The privatisation of public housing'. *Political Quarterly* vol. 55 no. 2 (Apr.–June 1984) pp. 180–7.

1348 Charles, S. T. 'Council house sales'. *Social Policy and Administration* vol. 16 no. 2 (Summer 1982) pp. 104–14.

1349 Chartered Institute of Public Finance and Accountancy. *Capital expenditure and debt financing statistics.* London, The Institute, annual.
Statistics on the housing debt of local authorities, previously known as *Return of outstanding debt.*

1350 Chartered Institute of Public Finance and Accountancy. *Housing management and maintenance statistics.* London, The Institute, annual.
Data for each local authority in England and Wales on number of dwellings and expenditure per dwelling on various categories of management and maintenance.

1351 Chartered Institute of Public Finance and Accountancy. *Housing rent statistics.* London, The Institute, annual.
Data for each local authority on housing stocks and average rents, rebates and allowances.

1352 Chartered Institute of Public Finance and Accountancy. *Housing revenue account statistics.* London, The Institute, annual.
Statistics of local authority housing accounts.

1353 Chartered Institute of Public Finance and Accountancy. *Local government comparative statistics*. London, The Institute, annual.
Comparative statistics on a wide range of issues for each local authority in England and Wales.

1354 Chartered Institute of Public Finance and Accountancy. *Review of the right to buy provisions of the Housing Act 1980 and subsequent developments*. London, The Institute, 1984.
Council house sales.

1355 City University, Housing Research Group. *Could local authorities be better landlords? An assessment of how councils manage their housing*. London, The University, 1981.
Final report of research project into housing management in Brent, Coventry, Guildford and Manchester.

1356 Clapham, D. and Kintrea, K. 'Allocation systems and housing choice'. *Urban Studies* vol. 21 no. 3 (Aug. 1984) pp. 261–9.

1357 Corina, L. *Housing allocation policy and its effects*. Oldham Community Development Project, 1976. (University of York papers in community studies no. 7).

1358 Darke, J. 'Architects and user requirements in public sector housing'. *Environment and Planning B* vol. 11 no. 4 (1984) pp. 389–434.
In three parts: architects' assumptions about the users (pp. 389–404); the sources for architects' assumptions (pp. 405–16); towards an adequate understanding of user requirements in housing (pp. 417–34).

1359 Daunton, M. J. (ed.) *Councillors and tenants: local authority housing in English cities 1919–39*. Leicester University Press, 1984.
Case studies of inter-war council housing in Durham, Leeds and Bristol.

1360 Dugmore, K. 'Social patterns in GLC housing'. *Greater London Intelligence Quarterly* no. 35 (June 1976) pp. 26–33.

Historical development of GLC housing: physical characteristics of estates.

1361 Duncan, S. and Kirby, K. *Preventing rent arrears*. London, HMSO, 1983.

1362 Edwards, C. and Posnett, J. 'The opportunity cost of the sale of local authority rented accommodation'. *Urban Studies* vol. 17 no. 1 (Feb. 1980) pp. 45–52.

1363 English, J. 'Access and deprivation in local authority housing'. In C. Jones (ed.) *Urban deprivation and the inner city*. London, Croom Helm, 1979.

1364 English, J. (ed.) *The future of council housing*. London, Croom Helm, 1982.
Includes chapters devoted to the Housing Act 1980, housing management and council house sales.

1365 English, J. 'Housing allocation and a deprived Scottish estate'. *Urban Studies* vol. 13 no. 3 (Oct. 1976) pp. 319–24.

1366 Forrest, R. 'Council house sales and the private market'. *Policy and Politics* vol. 8 no. 2 (1980).

1367 Forrest, R. and Murie, A. 'Residualization and council housing: aspects of the changing social relations of housing tenure'. *Journal of Social Policy* vol. 12 no. 4 (Oct. 1983) pp. 453–68.

1368 Forrest, R and Murie, A. *Right to buy? Issues of need, equity and polarisation in the sale of council houses*. University of Bristol, School for Advanced Urban Studies, 1984. (Working paper 39).

1369 Foster, P. 'Access to public housing'. In P. Foster *Access to welfare: an introduction to welfare rationing*. London, Macmillan, 1983. pp. 131–44.

1370 Fox, D. 'Survey of rent collection, arrears and evictions: 1982–83'. *Housing* vol. 19 no. 9 (Sept. 1983) pp. 15–18.

Results of a survey of rent arrears problems in larger housing authorities.

1371   Garside, P. L. 'Intergovernmental relations and housing policy in London 1919–1970 with special reference to the density and location of council housing'. *London Journal* no. 9 (Summer 1983) pp. 39–57.

1372   Gilbert, J. and Rosenburg, L. *Housing investment strategies for difficult to let public sector housing estates.* Edinburgh, Scottish Development Department, 1980.

1373   Gray, F. 'Selection and allocation in council housing'. *Transactions of the Institute of British Geographers* new series vol. 1 no. 1 (1976) pp. 34–46.
The key decision makers determining residential differentiation are 'urban managers' who allocate housing: study of Hull.

1374   Greater London Council. *Sale of council houses.* 2nd ed. London, The Council, 1978. (Research Bibliography 75).

1375   Gregory, P. 'Council housing waiting lists'. *Policy and Politics* vol. 3 no. 4 (1975) pp. 71–87.
Preferences and housing need: study of Hull.

1376   Griffiths, P. *Homes fit for heroes: a Shelter report on council housing.* London, Shelter, 1975.
Critical of housing management.

1377   Henney, A. *Inside local government: a case for radical reform.* London, Sinclair Browne, 1984.
Radical critique of the size and inefficiency of local government which includes a discussion of local authority housing provision (pp. 178–219).

1378   Henney, A. *Trust the tenant — developing municipal housing.* London, Centre for Policy Studies, 1985.
Suggests devolution of municipal housing stock to new statutory bodies known as housing management trusts.

1379   Himsworth, C. M. G. 'The Lands Tribunal for Scotland

and the government of council house sales'. *Urban Law and Policy* vol. 6 no. 3 (June 1984) pp. 253–78.

1380   Himsworth, C. *Public sector housing law in Scotland.* 2nd ed. Glasgow, Planning Exchange, 1982.

1381   Hoath, D. *Council housing.* 2nd ed. London, Sweet and Maxwell, 1982. (Modern legal studies).

1382   Hole, W. V. and Black, F. W . *The role of existing records for the assessment by LAs of current housing needs and policies.* Watford, Building Research Establishment, 1975. (Current paper 5/75).

1383   Hole, W. V. and Brindley, T. S. 'Housing strategies in practice: problems and possibilities'. *Local Government Studies* vol. 9 no. 3 (May–June 1983) pp. 31–44.

1384   Hughes, D. *Public sector housing law.* London, Butterworth, 1981.

1385   Hughes, D. J. and Jones, S. R. 'Bias in the allocation and transfer of local authority housing: a study of the reports of the Commission for Local Administration in England'. *Journal of Social Welfare Law* July 1979 pp. 273–95.

1386   Ince, R. et al. *Tenant participation in the repair and maintenance of council houses: a study.* London, Department of the Environment, 1982.

1387   Jacobs, S. 'The sale of council houses: does it matter?' *Critical Social Policy* vol. 1 no. 2 (Autumn 1981) pp. 35–53.
   Provocative article including two rejoinders.

1388   Jennings, J. 'Geographical implications of the municipal housing programme in England and Wales 1919–39'. *Urban Studies* vol. 8 (1971) pp. 121–38.

1389   Judge, T. 'The problems of difficult estates'. *New Community* vol. 6 nos. 1–2 (Winter 1977–8) pp. 45–63.

1390   Karn, V. and Henderson, J. 'Housing atypical households: understanding the practices of local government housing departments'. In A. W. Franklin (ed.) *Family matters: perspectives on the family and social policy.* Oxford, Pergamon, 1983.

1391   Kilroy, B. 'The financial and economic implications of council house sales'. In J. English (ed.) *The future of council housing.* London, Croom Helm, 1982.

1392   Kirby, A. M. 'Managerialism and local authority housing: a review'. *Public Administration Bulletin* no. 30 (Aug. 1979) pp. 47–60.
Housing allocation and the role of management.

1393   Kirby, D. A. 'The inter-war council dwelling: a study of residential obsolescence and decay'. *Town Planning Review* vol. 42 no. 3 (July 1971) pp. 250–68.

1394   Kirwan, R. M. 'The demise of public housing'. In J. Le Grand and R. Robinson (eds.) *Privatisation and the welfare state.* London, Allen and Unwin, 1984. pp. 133–45.
The transfer of publicly owned housing to private owners and the movement of public housing towards the market.

1395   LAMSAC. *Rent arrears.* London, LAMSAC, 1978.
Wide ranging study of local authority housing practices.

1396   Lewis, N. and Livock, R. 'Council house allocation procedures: some problems of discretion and control'. *Urban Law and Policy* vol. 2 no. 2 (June 1979) pp. 133–74.

1397   Liell, P. *Council houses and the Housing Act 1980.* London, Butterworth, 1981.

1398   Liell, P. 'Housing Act 1980: the tenant's charter'. *New Law Journal* vol. 131 no. 6009 (9 July 1981) pp. 735–8.

1399   Low, N. 'Spatial equity and housing policy'. *Local Government Studies* vol. 9 no. 2 (Mar.–Apr. 1983) pp. 35–49.
Residential mobility of council tenants in England and proposals for improvement.

1400   Macey, J. P. and Baker, C. V. *Housing management.* 4th ed. London, Estates Gazette, 1982.

Standard text on management of housing.

1401   Matthews, R. *Restrictive practices*. London, Shelter, 1983. Criticizes imposition of restrictions on council waiting lists.

1402   Merrett, S. *State housing in Britain*. London, Routledge and Kegan Paul, 1979.
Structure of the British construction industry with particular reference to the provision of local authority housing.

1403   Murie, A. *The sale of council houses*. University of Birmingham, Centre for Urban and Regional Studies, 1975. (Occasional paper 35).
An early discussion of the issue before it became a major political issue.

1404   Murie, A. 'Selling council houses'. *Built Environment* vol. 8 no. 1 (1982) pp. 12–19.

1405   National Consumer Council. *Behind with the rent: a study of council tenants in rent arrears*. London, The Council, 1976.

1406   National Consumer Council. *Soonest mended: a review of the repair, maintenance and improvement of council housing*. London, The Council, 1979.

1407   National Consumer Council. *Tenancy agreements*. London, The Council, 1976.
Proposes a new model tenancy agreement.

1408   Niner, P. *Local authority housing policy and practice*. University of Birmingham, Centre for Urban and Regional Studies, 1975. (Occasional paper 31).
Includes case studies of housing authorities in the Midlands.

1409   Orbach, L. F. *Homes for heroes: a study of the evolution of British public housing 1915–1921*. London, Seeley Service, 1977.
Post First World War reconstruction and the 1919 Addison Acts as first example of state subsidized housing.

1410   Pettitt, R. *Computer aids to housing maintenance management*. London, HMSO, 1981.

1411   Pinch, S. P. 'Patterns of local authority housing allocation in Greater London between 1966 and 1973: an inter borough analysis'. *Transactions of the Institute of British Geographers* new series vol. 3 no. 1 (1978) pp. 35–54.

1412   Pinkus, C. E. and Dixson, A. *Solving local government problems: practical applications of operations research in cities and regions.* London, Allen and Unwin, 1981.
   Ch. 4 'Ranking applicants for local government housing' analyses a study made for Manchester housing department.

1413   Planning Exchange. *Local authority housing studies.* Glasgow, Planning Exchange, 1977? (Bibliography series no. 4).
   A comprehensive, well arranged and thoroughly annotated bibliography which concentrates largely on housing issues in Scotland.

1414   Popplestone, G. 'Managing rent arrears'. *CES Review* no. 8 (Jan. 1980) pp. 34–40.

1415   Popplestone, G. and Paris, C. *Managing difficult tenants.* London, Centre for Environmental Studies, 1979. (Research series 30).

1416   Power, A. *Local housing management: a priority estates project survey.* London, Department of the Environment, 1984.

1417   Power, A. *Priority estates project 1982: improving problem council estates: a summary of aims and progress.* London, Department of the Environment, 1982.
   Looks at experiments in Bolton and, in London, Brixton and Hackney.

1418   Radford, D. 'Rent arrears: how serious? how soluble?'. *Housing* vol. 16 no. 4 (Apr. 1980) pp.4–7.
   Outlines the main results of the National Survey of Rent Arrears completed in 1979 by the Institute of Housing.

1419   Radford, D. 'Rent arrears: a basis for comparison'. *Housing* vol. 16 no. 5 (May 1980) pp. 14–17.

1420   Radford, D. 'Rent arrears: comparing local control policies'. *Housing* vol. 16 no. 6 (June 1980) pp. 10–12.

1421   Randall, V. 'Housing policy-making in London boroughs: the role of paid officers'. *London Journal* vol. 7 no. 2 (Winter 1981) pp. 161–76.

1422   Ravetz, A. *Model estate: planned housing at Quarry Hill, Leeds.* London, Croom Helm, 1974.
Detailed case study of a housing estate built under the clearance legislation of the 1930s, heralded as the answer to the housing problem. Now demolished.

1423   *The right to buy handbook.* London, Butterworths, 1985.
Contains annotated texts of the Housing and Building Control Act 1984 and of the Housing Act 1980 as amended by the 1984 Act.

1424   Schifferes, S. *In distress over rent.* London, Shelter, 1978.
Use of distress warrants to remove tenants' belongings in lieu of rent arrears is counter-productive.

1425   Shelter. *The allocation of council housing.* London, Shelter, 1983.

1426   Shelter. *Facts on council house sales.* London, Shelter, 1979.

1427   Singleton, D. 'Housing allocation policy and practice in Northern Ireland'. *Housing Review* vol. 34 no. 1 (Jan.–Feb. 1985) pp. 9–12.

1428   Smith, G. C. and Ford, R. G. 'Migration decisions of transfer applicants in the council housing sector'. *Environment and Planning A* vol. 17 (1985) pp. 153–73.
Study of public housing in Birmingham.

1429   Sutton, J. and Whitehead, C. 'The sale of council houses: a cautionary note'. *Applied Economics* vol. 14 no. 3 (June 1982) pp. 295–303.

1430   Swenarton, M. C. *Homes fit for heroes: the politics and architecture of early state housing in Britain.* London, Heinemann, 1981.

Beginnings of state housing provision in Britain after the First World War.

1431   Taylor, P. J. *'Difficult to let', 'difficult to live in', and sometimes 'difficult to get out of': an essay on provision of council housing with special reference to Killingworth.* University of Newcastle upon Tyne, Centre for Urban and Regional Development Studies, 1978. (Discussion paper 16).

1432   United Kingdom, Audit Commission. *Bringing council tenants' arrears under control.* London, HMSO, 1984.
Latest in a series of reports on rent arrears.

1433   United Kingdom, Department of the Environment. *Appraisal of the financial effects of council house sales.* London, The Department, 1980.

1434   United Kingdom, Department of the Environment. *Council house sales: the Government's reply to the second report from the Environment Committee.* London, HMSO, 1981. (Cmnd. 8377).

1435   United Kingdom, Department of the Environment. *Local government financial statistics.* London, HMSO, annual.
Source for financial statistics of local authority housing.

1436   United Kingdom, Department of the Environment, Housing Development Directorate. *An investigation of difficult-to-let housing: a selection of strategies for improving estates.* London, The Department, 1979.

1437   United Kingdom, Department of the Environment, Housing Development Directorate. *An investigation of difficult to let housing, vol. 1, general findings.* London, HMSO, 1981. (Occasional paper 3/80).

1438   United Kingdom, Department of the Environment, Housing Development Directorate. *An investigation of difficult to let housing, vol. 2, case studies of post-war estates.* London, HMSO, 1981. (Occasional paper 4/80).

1439   United Kingdom, Department of the Environment,

Housing Development Directorate. *An investigation of difficult to let housing, vol. 3, case studies of pre-war estates.* London, HMSO, 1981. (Occasional paper 5/80).

1440 United Kingdom, Department of the Environment, Housing Development Directorate. *Priority estates project 1981: improving problem housing estates.* London, HMSO, 1981.
Looks at three experiments in Bolton and, in London, Brixton and Hackney.

1441 United Kingdom, Department of the Environment, Housing Development Directorate. *Rent arrears in local authority housing.* London, The Department, 1978. (HDD occasional paper 1/78).

1442 United Kingdom, Department of the Environment, Housing Services Advisory Group. *Allocation of council housing.* London, The Department, 1979.
Current practices and proposed reforms.

1443 United Kingdom, Department of the Environment, Housing Services Advisory Group. *Housing for people.* London, The Department, 1978.
Allocation of council housing.

1444 United Kingdom, Department of the Environment, Housing Services Advisory Group. *Organising a comprehensive housing service.* London, The Department, 1978.
Housing departments should have a much broader role than just providing housing to let.

1445 United Kingdom, Department of the Environment, Housing Services Advisory Group. *Organising an effective repairs and maintenance service.* London, Department of the Environment, 1980.

1446 United Kingdom, House of Commons, Environment Committee. *Council house sales: vol. 1, report; vol. 2, minutes of evidence; vol. 3, appendices.* London, HMSO, 1981. (Second report, Session 1980/81, HC 366).

1447   United Kingdom, Ministry of Housing and Local Government. *Report of the working party on the costing of management and maintenance of local authority housing.* London, HMSO, 1964.

1448   United Kingdom, Ministry of Housing and Local Government, Central Housing Advisory Committee. *Council housing: purposes, procedures and priorities.* London, HMSO, 1969.
The Cullingworth report. Important report which reviewed local authority activity in housing and highlighted areas of need.

1449   United Kingdom, Ministry of Housing and Local Government, Central Housing Advisory Committee. *Councils and their houses.* London, HMSO, 1959.

1450   United Kingdom, Scottish Development Department. *Appraisal of the financial effects of council house sales.* Edinburgh, The Department, 1980.

1451   United Kingdom, Scottish Housing Advisory Committee. *Housing management in Scotland.* Edinburgh, HMSO, 1967.

1452   United Kingdom, Scottish Office. *Scottish local government financial statistics.* Edinburgh, HMSO, annual.
Financial statistics of local authority housing in Scotland.

1453   Watson, C. J. 'Public housing in Britain: present and future'. In L.-J. Walden (ed.) *Housing policy: the just price and the role of the public housing sector: papers and discussions from two British–Scandinavian seminars.* Gavle, National Swedish Institute for Building Research, 1981. (Bulletin M81:24). pp. 127–34.

1454   Watson, P. S. 'Co-ordinating the housing service'. *Housing* vol. 16 no. 6 (June 1980) pp. 22–4.
Discusses the elusive concept of a comprehensive housing service.

1455   Wilkinson, D. *Rent arrears in public authority housing in Scotland.* Edinburgh, HMSO, 1980.
Scottish Office social research study.

9.4   North America

1456   Ahlbrandt, R. S. and Brophy, P. C. 'Management: an important element of the housing environment'. *Environment and Behavior* vol. 8 no. 4 (Dec. 1976) pp. 505–26.
Management in federally assisted housing and relationship with tenant satisfaction.

1457   Bingham, R. D. and Kirkpatrick, S. A. 'Providing social services for the urban poor: an analysis of public housing authorities in large American cities'. *Social Service Review* vol. 49 (Mar. 1975) pp. 64–78.
Surveys level of services provided by public housing authorities in 47 US cities.

1458   Canadian Council on Social Development. *A review of Canadian social housing policy.* Ottawa, The Council, 1977.

1459   Danielson, M. N. 'The politics of exclusionary zoning in suburbia'. *Political Science Quarterly* vol. 91 (Spring 1976) pp.1–18.
Factors accounting for local resistance to subsidized housing in the US.

1460   Farley, J. 'Has public housing gotten a bum rap? The incidence of crime in St. Louis public housing developments'. *Environment and Behavior* vol. 14 no. 4 (July 1982) pp. 443–77.
No evidence that crime rates in public housing schemes in St. Louis are higher than in rest of city.

1461   Fisher, R. M. *Twenty years of public housing.* New York, Harper, 1959.

1462   Freedman, L. *Public housing: the politics of poverty.* New York, Holt, Rinehart and Winston, 1969.

1463   Fuerst, J. S. and Petty, R. 'Public housing in the courts: pyrrhic victories for the poor'. *Urban Lawyer* vol. 9 no. 3 (Summer 1977) pp. 496–513.
Legal situation of poorer members of society in the US in eligibility to public housing and eviction.

1464   Gleeson, M. E. 'Application of a mortality model to subsidized housing'. *Environment and Planning A* vol. 16 no. 7 (July 1984) pp. 901–16.
Model of costs of construction and rehabilitation applied to public housing in the US.

1465   Isler, M. L. et al. *Housing management: a progress report.* Washington, DC, Urban Institute, 1971.

1466   Jones, R. *Problems affecting low-rent public housing projects: a field study.* Washington, DC, Department of Housing and Urban Development, 1979.

1467   Keyes, L. 'Turning around troubled estates in America'. *Roof* vol. 4 no. 4 (May 1979) pp. 91–3.
Projects by the US Department of Housing and Urban Development to improve life in public housing schemes.

1468   Kraft, J. and Kraft, A. 'Benefits and costs of low rent public housing'. *Journal of Regional Science* vol. 19 no. 3 (Aug. 1979) pp. 309–17.
Subsidies and benefits in US public housing and the costs of the programme.

1469   Lazin, F. A. 'Policy, perception and program failure: the politics of public housing in Chicago and New York'. *Urbanism Past and Present* no. 9 (Winter 1979–80) pp. 1–12.

1470   Macey, J. *Publicly provided and assisted housing in the USA: report on HUD's management policies and programs.* Washington, DC, Urban Institute, 1972. (Working paper 209-1-4).

1471   McGrew, J. L. 'Resistance to change continues to restrict public housing choices'. *Journal of Housing* vol. 38 (July 1981) pp. 375–81.
Location of public housing and implications for residential integration.

1472   Macmillan, J. A. and Nickel, E. 'An economic appraisal of urban housing assistance: rental supplements versus public housing'. *Canadian Public Administration* vol. 17 (Fall 1974) pp. 443–60.

1473   Macpherson, M. and Lipman, E. *Tenant selection criteria for public housing: a description and analysis.* Ottawa, Canada Mortgage and Housing Corporation, 1979.

1474   Meehan, E. J. 'Is there a future for public housing?' *Journal of Housing* vol. 40 no. 3 (May–June 1983) pp. 73–6.
Causes and consequences of the move away from public housing in the US.

1475   Meehan, E. J. *Public housing policy: convention versus reality.* New Brunswick, Rutgers University, Center for Urban Policy Research, 1975.
Contemporary US public housing crisis based on in-depth study of St. Louis.

1476   Meehan, E. J. *The quality of federal policy making: programmed failure in public housing.* Columbia, University of Missouri Press, 1979.
Public housing in St. Louis.

1477   Meyerson, M. and Banfield, E. C. *Politics, planning and the public interest: the case of public housing in Chicago.* Glencoe, Free Press, 1955.

1478   Muth, R. F. *Public housing.* Washington, DC, American Enterprise Institute, 1973.

1479   Olsen, E. O. and Barton, D. M. 'The benefits and costs of public housing in New York City'. *Journal of Public Economics* vol. 20 no. 3 (Apr. 1983) pp. 299–332.
Housing allowances would be more efficient and equitable than public production of housing services.

1480   Ostrowski, E. T. 'Managing public housing: the impact of the 1980s'. *Journal of Housing* vol. 41 no. 2 (Mar.–Apr. 1984) pp. 40–2.
History of public housing in the US and suggestions for the

future.

1481   Prescott, J. R. *Economic aspects of public housing*. Beverly Hills, Sage, 1974. (Sage library of social research vol. 8).

1482   *Public housing: a bibliography*. Monticello, Vance Bibliographies, 1982. (Architecture series A 823).
Mainly US sources.

1483   Sadacca, R. *Management performance in public housing*. Washington, DC, Urban Institute, 1974.

1484   Sadacca, R. et al. 'Effective subsidized housing management practices'. *Journal of Property Management* vol. 41 (Sept.–Oct. 1976) pp. 210–15.
Increasing reliance on the private sector for the management of housing for low and moderate income families.

1485   Sadacca, R. et al. *Ownership forms and management success in private, publicly assisted housing*. Washington, DC, Urban Institute, 1972.

1486   Sadacca, R. and Fong, J. *Change in the public housing management improvement program*. Washington, DC, Urban Institute, 1975.

1487   Scobie, R. S. *Problem tenants in public housing: who, where, and why are they?* New York, Praeger, 1975. (Praeger special studies).

1488   Struyk, R. J. *A new system for public housing: salvaging a national resource*. Washington, DC, Urban Institute, 1980.

1489   Struyk, R. J. 'Public housing modernization program: an analysis of problems and prospects'. *Journal of Housing* vol. 37 no. 9 (Oct. 1980) pp. 492–6.
US government plans to fund housing authorities in the modernization of housing projects.

1490   Sumka, H. J. 'An economic analysis of public housing in small cities'. *Journal of Regional Science* vol. 18 no. 3 (Dec. 1978) pp. 395–410.

Economics of public housing programmes in non-metropolitan areas of the US.

1491 United States, Congressional Budget Office. *Federal subsidies for public housing: issues and options.* Washington, DC, The Office, 1983.

1492 United States, Department of Housing and Urban Development. *Personnel administration in housing management: vol. 1, participant's workbook; vol. 2, instructor's manual.* Washington, DC, The Department, 1980.

1493 United States, Department of Housing and Urban Development. *Professional career systems in housing management: vol. 1, participant's workbook; vol. 2, instructor's guide.* Washington, DC, The Department, 1980.

1494 United States, Department of Housing and Urban Development. *Social and economic characteristics of residents of public housing: vol. 1, participant's workbook; vol. 2, instructor's manual.* Washington, DC, The Department, 1980.

1495 United States, Department of Housing and Urban Development. *Supervisory skills for housing managers: vol. 1, participant's workbook; vol. 2, instructor's manual.* Washington, DC, The Department, 1980.

1496 United States, House, Committee on Banking, Finance and Urban Affairs, Subcommittee on Housing and Community Development. *Public housing operating subsidies.* Washington, DC, Government Printing Office, 1981.

1497 United States, House, Committee on Government Operations, Manpower and Housing Subcommittee. *HUD support of local public housing authorities.* Washington, DC, Government Printing Office, 1981.

1498 Vogelsang, F. M. (ed.) *Public housing management in the seventies: readings.* Washington, DC, National Association of Housing and Redevelopment Officials, 1974.

9.5 Australasia

1499   Bradbrook, A. J. 'The state housing commission and their tenants: the need for legislative control'. *Melbourne University Law Review* vol. 10 (June 1976) pp. 409–41.

1500   Kemeny, J. 'Controlling public renting: structure and process in Australian public housing'. *Adelaide Law Review* vol. 8 (1982) pp. 1–28.

1501   Kemeny, J. 'Selling out in Australia'. *Roof* vol. 4 no. 5 (Sept. 1979) pp. 154–5.
Effects of the sale of public housing in Australia.

1502   Low, N. 'Victoria's reluctance to supply welfare housing'. *Royal Australian Planning Institute Journal* vol. 18 no. 4 (Nov. 1980) pp. 147–9.

1503   Wilson, P. R. *Public housing for Australia*. St Lucia, University of Queensland Press, 1976.

9.6 Africa, Asia and Latin America

1504   Friedman, B. S. 'Public housing in China: policies and practices'. *Journal of Housing* vol. 40 no. 3 (May–June 1983) pp. 82–5.

1505   Hollingshead, A. and Rogler, L. H. 'Attitudes towards slums and public housing in Puerto Rico'. In L. J. Duhl (ed.) *The urban condition: people and policy in the metropolis*. New York, Simon and Schuster, 1963.

1506   Hassan, R. 'Public housing'. In R. Hassan (ed.) *Singapore, society in transition*. Kuala Lumpur, Oxford University Press, 1976. pp. 240–68.

1507   Megbolugbe, I. F. 'The hopes and failures of public housing in Nigeria: a case study of Kulende and Adewale Housing Estates, Ilorin'. *Third World Planning Review* vol. 5 no. 4 (Nov. 1983) pp. 349–69.

1508   Pryor, E. G. 'Redeveloping public housing in Hong Kong'. *Ekistics* vol. 44 no. 261 (Aug. 1977) pp. 96–9.
Redevelopment of 1950s and 1960s estates.

1509   Sule, R. A. 'An assessment of the Nigerian housing allocation policy: the case of the ballot system'. *African Urban Studies* no. 1 (1978) pp. 67–85.

1510   Syagga, P. M. 'Maintenance management in local authority housing estates in Kenya'. *Build Kenya* vol. 3 no. 33 (Dec. 1978) pp. 34–43.

1511   Temple, F. T. and Temple, N W. 'The politics of public housing in Nairobi'. In M. S. Grindle (ed.) *Politics and policy implementation in the Third World.* Princeton University Press, 1980. pp. 224–49.

1512   Thambi, M. T. A. 'The administration of public housing'. In S. H. Tan and H. Sendut (eds.) *Public and private housing in Malaysia.* Kuala Lumpur, Heinemann, 1979. pp. 46–66.

1513   Western, J. S. et al. 'Poverty, urban renewal and public housing in Singapore'. *Environment and Planning* vol. 5 (1973) pp. 589–600.

1514   Yeh, A. G. O. and Fong, P. K. W. 'Public housing and urban development in Hong Kong'. *Third World Planning Review* vol. 6 no. 1 (Feb. 1984) pp. 79–94.

1515   Yeh, S. H. K. *Public housing in Singapore.* Singapore University Press, 1975.

1516   Yeung, Y.-M. and Drakakis-Smith, D. W. 'Comparative perspectives on public housing in Singapore and Hong Kong'. *Asian Survey* vol. 14 no. 8 (1974) pp. 763–75.

1517   Yeung, Y.-M. and Drakakis-Smith, D. W. 'Public housing in the city states of Hong Kong and Singapore'. In J. L. Taylor and D. G. Williams (eds.) *Urban planning practice in developing countries.* Oxford, Pergamon, 1982. pp. 217–38.

10

Private rental sector

Private rented housing, although perhaps of less significance now in housing policy than in earlier decades, still forms an important element in the housing market in many parts of the world. This section includes works on government policies towards rental housing, rent control, relations between landlord and tenant, legal remedies against exploitative landlords and prescriptions for the future health of the sector. Sections 2 'Housing market', 7 'Housing tenure' and 21 'Rural housing' also contain relevant references.

10.1 International and comparative

1518   Brenner, J. F. and Franklin, H. M. *Rent control in North America and four European countries.* New Brunswick, Transaction Books, 1980.

1519   Cullingworth, J. B. *A bibliography of rent control.* University of Toronto, Centre for Urban and Community Studies, 1982. (Bibliography series).
   Contains some 2,000 references from international sources, mainly UK, US and Canadian.

1520   Harloe, M. *Private rented housing in the United States and Europe.* London, Croom Helm, 1984.

1521   Institute of Economic Affairs. *Verdict on rent control.* London, The Institute, 1972.

Essays by F. Hayek et al. on the economic consequences of political action to restrict rents in five countries (Austria, UK, US, Sweden, France).

1522   Lindbeck, A. 'Rent control as an instrument of housing. policy'. In A. A. Nevitt (ed.) *The economic problems of housing.* London, Macmillan, 1967. pp. 53–72.

1523   Priemus, H. 'Rent control and housing tenure'. *Planning and Administration* vol. 9 no. 2 (Autumn 1982) pp. 29–46.
Reviews history of rent control in Western Europe and US, and link between rent control and housing tenure.

10.2   Europe

1524   De Moor, A. 'Landlord and tenant in French law: a recent statute'. *Oxford Journal of Legal Studies* vol. 3 no. 3 (1983) pp. 425–31.

1525   Kemeny, J. *The Swedish rental market: problems and policies.* University of Birmingham, Centre for Urban and Regional Studies, 1982. (Occasional paper 4 new series).

10.3   United Kingdom

1526   Aldridge, T. M. *Rent control and leasehold enfranchisement.* London, Oyez, 1967.

1527   Allen, J. 'Property relations and landlordism — a realist approach'. *Environment and Planning D* vol. 1 (1983) pp. 191–203.
Theoretical concepts of landlordism, applied to Britain.

1528   Arden, A. *Housing: security and rent control.* London, Sweet and Maxwell, 1978.
Explanation of complex legal issues.

1529   Arden, A. *The private tenant's handbook.* London, Allison and Busby, 1985.

1530   Awan, K. et al. 'Household attributes and the demand for private rental housing'. *Economics* vol. 49 no. 194 (May 1982) pp. 183–200.

1531   Banting, K. G. *Poverty, politics and policy*. London, Macmillan, 1979.
Includes a chapter on the formulation of the Rent Act 1965.

1532   Barnett, M. J. *The politics of legislation: the Rent Act 1957*. London, Weidenfeld and Nicolson, 1969.
Political study on the origins of legislation.

1533   Beirne, P. *Fair rent and legal fiction: housing rent legislation in a capitalist society*. London, Macmillan, 1977.
Looks at state regulation of rents up to the Housing Finance Act 1972 in context of a Marxist critique of the sociology of law.

1534   Bovaird, A. et al. 'Private rented housing: its current role'. *Journal of Social Policy* vol. 14 no. 1 (Jan. 1985) pp.1–23.

1535   Cannadine, D. *Lords and landlords: the aristocracy and the towns 1774–1967*. Leicester University Press, 1980.

1536   Clarke, D. N. and Adams, J. E. *Rent reviews and variable rents*. London, Oyez, 1981.
Reviews aims, limitations and methods of varying rent, especially rent review clauses.

1537   Constable, M. *Tied accommodation*. London, Shelter, 1974.
Rented accommodation dependent on employment by landlord.

1538   Cooper, M. C. and Stafford, D. C. 'The economic implications of "fair rents"'. In R. A. B. Leaper (ed.) *Health, wealth and housing*. Oxford, Blackwell, 1980. pp. 95–116.

1539   Crook, A. D. H. and Bryant, C. L. *Local authorities and private landlords: a case study of the impact of changes in the private rented sector on inner city housing*. University of Sheffield, Centre for Environmental Research, 1982.

1540   Cullingworth, J. B. *Housing in transition*. London, Heinemann, 1963.

1541   Doling, J. 'How much protection do the Rent Acts provide?' *Journal of Planning and Environment Law* Nov. 1983 pp. 713–23.

1542   Doling, J. and Davies, E. M. *Public control of privately rented housing*. Aldershot, Gower, 1984. (Studies in urban and regional policy 2).
Historical account of government legislation in the private rented sector.

1543   Elliott, B. A. and McCrone, D. 'Property relations in the city: the fortunes of landlordism'. In M. Harloe (ed.) *Proceedings of the conference on urban change and conflict*. London, Centre for Environmental Studies, 1975. pp. 31–61.

1544   Englander, D. *Landlord and tenant in urban Britain 1838–1918*. Oxford, Clarendon Press, 1983.

1545   Farrand, J. *The Rent Act 1977 and the Protection from Eviction Act 1977*. London, Sweet and Maxwell, 1978.

1546   Farrand, J. T. and Arden, A. *Rent Acts and regulations amended and annotated*. 2nd ed. London, Sweet and Maxwell, 1981.

1547   Gasson, R. *Provision of tied cottages*. University of Cambridge, Department of Land Economy, 1975. (Occasional paper no. 4).
Tied accommodation in agricultural areas.

1548   Gray, P. G. and Parr, E. *The Rent Act 1957 report of enquiry*. London, HMSO, 1960. (Cmnd. 1246).

1549   Green, S. *Rachman*. London, Michael Joseph, 1979.
Portrait of notorious exploiter of private rented sector in 1960s London.

1550   Greve, J. *Private landlords in England*. London, Bell, 1965.

Important early study of landlords containing useful information on motivations for renting.

1551   Hamnett, C. 'The flat break-up market in London: a case-study of large scale disinvestment — its causes and consequences'. In M. Boddy (ed.) *Land, property and finance*. University of Bristol, School for Advanced Urban Studies, 1979. (Working paper 2).

1552   Hamnett, C. and Randolph, W. 'The role of landlord disinvestment in housing market transformation: an analysis of the flat break-up in central London'. *Institute of British Geographers Transactions* vol. 9 no. 3 (1984) pp. 259–79.
Sale of privately rented flats to individual owner occupiers in central London housing market.

1553   Harloe, M. 'Decline and fall of private renting'. *CES Review* no. 9 (Apr. 1980) pp. 30–4.

1554   Hill, H. A. and Redman, J. H. *Law of landlord and tenant*. 17th ed. London, Butterworth, 1982.
Textbook, including updating service, on all aspects of the law.

1555   Kemp, P. *House property as capital: private rental housing in the late Victorian city*. Brighton, University of Sussex, 1982. (Urban and regional studies working paper 29).

1556   Kemp, P. 'Housing landlordism in late nineteenth-century Britain'. *Environment and Planning A* vol. 14 no. 11 (Nov. 1982) pp. 1437–47.

1557   Kemp, P. *Housing production and the decline of the privately rented sector: some preliminary remarks*. Brighton, University of Sussex, 1980. (Urban and regional studies working paper no. 20).

1558   Kleinman, M. and Whitehead, C. 'The geography of private renting'. *Housing Review* vol. 34 no. 1 (Jan.–Feb. 1985) pp. 13–16.
Spatial distribution of private renting in the UK.

1559   Krimgoltz, M. and Good, B. J. C. *Renting and letting a home: a practical guide for landlord and tenant*. London, Godwin, 1976.

1560   Maclennan, D. 'An economic approach to rent controls: tenants and the 1974 Rent Act'. *Social Policy and Administration* vol. 15 no. 2 (Summer 1981) pp. 181–97.

1561   Maclennan, D. 'Information networks in a local housing market'. *Scottish Journal of Political Economy* vol. 26 no. 1 (Feb. 1979) pp. 73–88.
   Students in furnished rented accommodation in Glasgow and sources of information used to find such lettings.

1562   Magnus, S. W. *The Rent Act 1977.* London, Butterworth, 1978.
   Text of the Act and annotations; the Act consolidates earlier legislation.

1563   Martin, G. *Landlord improvement activity since 1980. A study of the effects of local and national initiatives towards the private rented sector.* University of Sheffield, Department of Town and Regional Planning, 1983. (Occasional paper 43).

1564   Nelken, D. *The limits of the legal process: a study of landlords, law and crime.* London, Academic Press, 1983. (Law, state and society).
   Private sector landlord malpractices and criminal activities in London.

1565   Nevitt, A. A. 'The nature of rent-controlling legislation in the UK'. *Environment and Planning* vol. 2 (1970) pp. 127–36.

1566   Newton, L. K. (ed.) *The Rent Act 1977 revised.* London, Oyez Longman, 1981.
   Includes amendments made in the Housing Act 1980.

1567   Paley, B. *Attitudes to letting in 1976: a survey of private landlords, private tenants and owner occupiers in areas of England and Wales which in 1971 were predominantly rented in the private sector.* London, HMSO, 1978.
   Useful data in an OPCS study.

1568   Partington, M. *Landlord and tenant: text and materials on housing and law.* London, Weidenfeld and Nicolson, 1980.

1569   Pettit, P. H. *Landlord and tenant under the Rent Act 1977*. London, Butterworth, 1978.

1570   Pettit, P. H. *Private sector tenancies*. London, Butterworth, 1981.
   Legal text.

1571   Prophet, J. *Fair rents: a practical guide to the statutory regulation of rents of residential tenancies: including the work of rent officers, rent assessment committees and rent tribunals*. London, Shaw, 1979.

1572   Ramsay, E. *Caught in the housing trap: employees in tied housing*. London, SHAC, 1979. (Research paper 1).

1573   Ricketts, M. 'A model of the furnished rental housing market under regulation'. *Scottish Journal of Political Economy* vol. 29 no. 1 (Feb. 1982) pp. 1–21.

1574   Schifferes, S. *The forgotten problem: a study of tied accommodation and the cycle of insecurity*. London, Shelter, 1980.

1575   Seward, G. and Stewart-Smith, W. R. *The Leasehold Reform Act 1967*. Croydon, Knight, 1968.

1576   SHAC. *Private tenants: protection from eviction*. Rev. ed. London, SHAC, 1981.

1577   SHAC. *Your rights to repairs: a guide for private and housing association tenants*. London, SHAC, 1981.

1578   Short, J. R. 'Landlords and the private rented sector: a case study'. In M. Boddy (ed.) *Land, property and finance*. University of Bristol, School for Advanced Urban Studies, 1979. (Working paper no. 2).

1579   Stafford, B. and Doling, J. *Rent control and rent regulation in England and Wales 1915–80*. University of Birmingham, Centre for Urban and Regional Studies, 1981. (Occasional paper no. 2).

1580   Stafford, D. C. 'The final economic demise of the private landlord?' *Social and Economic Administration* vol. 10 (Spring 1976) pp. 3–14.

1581   Todd, J. E. *The privately rented sector in 1978: the report of a follow-up survey carried out among a sample of private renters who had been interviewed in the National Dwelling and Household Survey.* London, HMSO, 1982.
Updates no. 1567.

1582   United Kingdom, Committee on Housing in Greater London. *Report.* London, HMSO, 1965. (Cmnd. 2605).
The Milner Holland report which documented the problems of London's private rented sector and which resulted in the Rent Act 1965 with its security of tenure and fair rent legislation.

1583   United Kingdom, Committee on the Rent Acts. *Report.* London, HMSO, 1971. (Cmnd. 4609)
The Francis report.

1584   United Kingdom, Department of the Environment. *Report of the working party on rent assessment panel procedures.* London, The Department, 1981.

1585   United Kingdom, House of Commons, Environment Committee. *The private rented sector: vol. 1, report; vol. 2, minutes of evidence; vol. 3, appendices.* London, HMSO, 1982. (Session 1981–82 HC 40).

1586   United Kingdom, Ministry of Housing and Local Government. *Rent Act 1957: report of inquiry.* London, HMSO, 1960. (Cmnd. 1246).

1587   University of Birmingham, Centre for Urban and Regional Studies, Housing Monitoring Team. *Landlords in Dudley.* Birmingham, The Centre, 1980. (Research memorandum 85).
Rare study of private landlords in a particular locality.

1588   Widdowson, R. *Agricultural tied cottages.* London, Shelter, 1975.

1589   Yates, D. and Hawkins, A. J. *Landlord and tenant law.* London, Sweet and Maxwell, 1981.

10.4 North America

1590 Appelbaum, R. P. and Gilderbloom, J. I. 'Housing supply and regulation: a study of the rental housing market'. *Journal of Applied Behavioural Science* vol. 19 no. 1 (1983) pp. 1–18.

1591 Blumberg, R. and Grow, J. R. *The rights of tenants.* New York, Avon Books, 1978.

1592 Cain, T. J. and Scott, M. W. 'New rental housing: confronting the investment gap'. *Urban Land* vol. 40 no. 5 (May 1981) pp. 3–7.

1593 Chin, F. *Rent control: a selected bibliography 1975–1980.* Monticello, Vance Bibliographies, 1980. (Public administration series bibliography no. P-519).

1594 Clark, W. A. V. and Heskin, A. D. 'The impact of rent control on tenure discounts and residential mobility'. *Land Economics* vol. 58 no. 1 (Feb. 1982) pp. 109–17.
Impact of moderate rent control on tenants.

1595 Clayton, F. A. and Lampert, G. 'The Canadian experience with rent controls'. *Habitat* vol. 25 no. 2 (1982) pp. 8–13.
Rent controls have had a bad effect on housing in Canada.

1596 Downs, A. *Rental housing in the 1980s.* Washington, DC, Brookings Institution, 1983.

1597 Drury, M. et al. *Lower income housing assistance program (section 8): nationwide evaluation of the existing housing program.* Washington, DC, Department of Housing and Urban Development, 1978.
Technical supplement by L. Yap published separately.

1598 Duensing, E. *Rental housing: programs and trends.* Monticello, Vance Bibliographies, 1981. (Public administration series bibliography P-750).
Mainly US sources.

1599 Einhorn, D. *Federal tax incentives and rental housing.* Washington, DC, Department of Housing and Urban Development, 1983.

1600   Friedman, J. and Weinberg, D. H. 'The demand for rental housing: evidence from the housing allowance demand experiment'. *Journal of Urban Economics* vol. 9 no. 3 (May 1981) pp. 311–31.

1601   Gilderbloom, J. I. 'The impact of moderate rent control in New Jersey: an empirical study of 26 rent controlled cities'. *Urban Analysis* vol. 7 no. 2 (Feb. 1983) pp. 135–54.
Moderate rent controls had no significant effects on construction, demolitions or tax values.

1602   Gilderbloom, J. I. 'Moderate rent control: its impact on the quality and quantity of the housing stock'. *Urban Affairs Quarterly* vol. 17 no. 2 (Dec. 1981) pp. 123–42.

1603   Gilderbloom, J. (ed.) *Rent control: a source book.* Santa Barbara, Foundation for National Progress Housing Information Center, 1981.

1604   Goodman, A. C. and Kawai, M. 'Estimation and policy implications of rental housing demand'. *Journal of Urban Economics* vol. 16 no. 1 (July 1984) pp. 76–90.
Method of estimating housing and welfare effects of subsidy.

1605   Gruen, N. J. and Gruen, C. 'The evolution of rent control: and a strategy for its defeat'. *Urban Land* vol. 39 no. 7 (July–Aug. 1980) pp. 5–10.
Examines stages in, and arguments for and against, the introduction of rent control in the US.

1606   Hayek, F. A. et al. *Rent control: a popular paradox: evidence on the economic effects of rent control.* Vancouver, Fraser Institute, 1975.
Collections of essays on rent control in Canada.

1607   Hirsch, W. Z. and Cheung-Kwok, L. 'Habitability laws and the shrinkage of substandard rental housing'. *Urban Studies* vol. 16 no. 1 (Feb. 1979) pp. 19–28.

Laws controlling the relationship between landlord and tenant in the US.

1608   Johnson, M. L. 'Kicking the poor: the impact of rent control in Washington, DC'. *Journal of Contemporary Studies* vol. 4 (Spring 1981) pp. 23–30.

1609   Keating, W. D. *Rent and eviction controls: a selected annotated bibliography.* Monticello, Council of Planning Librarians, 1976. (Exchange bibliography no. 1136).

1610   Krohn, R. G. and Tiller, R. 'Landlord–tenant relations in a declining Montreal neighborhood'. *Sociological Review Monographs* vol. 14 (1969) pp. 5–32.

1611   Lebowitz, N. H. '"Above party, class or creed": rent control in the United States 1940–47'. *Journal of Urban History* vol. 7 (1981) pp. 207–49.

1612   Lett, M. R. *Rent control: concepts, realities and mechanisms.* New Brunswick, Transaction Books, 1976.

1613   Lowry, I. S. (ed.) *Rental housing in New York City: confronting the crisis.* New York, Rand Corporation, 1970.

1614   Lowry, I. S. *Rental housing in the seventies: searching for the crisis.* Santa Monica, Rand Corporation, 1981.
   Research undertaken for the US Department of Housing and Urban Development.

1615   Marans, R. W. et al. *Measuring restrictive rental practices affecting families with children: a national survey: a report.* Washington, DC, Department of Housing and Urban Development, 1980.

1616   Marshall, R. C. and Guasch, J. L. 'Occupancy discounts in the US rental housing market'. *Oxford Bulletin of Economics and Statistics* vol. 45 no. 4 (Nov. 1983) pp. 357–78.
   Private landlords offering lower rents to existing tenants than new tenants.

1617   Mayer, N. S. 'Conserving rental housing: a policy analysis'. *Journal of the American Planning Association* vol. 50 no. 3 (Summer 1984) pp. 311–25.

1618   Miron, J. R. and Cullingworth, J. B. *Rent control: impacts on income distribution, affordability and security of tenure.* University of Toronto, Centre for Urban and Community Studies, 1983.

1619   O'Mara, W. P. 'The future of rental housing'. *Urban Land* vol. 38 no. 11 (Dec. 1979) pp. 19–22.
Report of Urban Land Institute seminar.

1620   O'Mara, W. P. and Zimmerman, T. V. 'Rental housing on the comeback'. *Urban Land* vol. 42 no. 2 (Feb. 1983) pp. 8–13.
US rental housing.

1621   Patterson, J. and Watson, K. *Rent stabilization: a review of current policies in Canada.* Ottawa, Canadian Council on Social Development, 1976.

1622   Rose, J. *Landlords and tenants.* New Brunswick, Transaction Books, 1973.

1623   Schechter, H. B. 'Economic squeeze pinches the future of housing'. *Journal of Housing* vol. 37 no. 4 (Apr . 1980) pp. 192–6.
Rental market in the US, especially for low and moderate rental housing.

1624   Selesnick, H. L. *Rent control.* Lexington, Mass., Lexington Books, 1976.

1625   Smith, L. B. 'The crisis in rental housing: a Canadian perspective'. *Annals of American Academy of Political and Social Science* vol. 465 (Jan. 1983) pp. 58–75.

1626   Starr, R. 'Controlling rents, razing cities'. *Property Journal* vol. 5 no. 3 (Sept. 1979) pp. 76–81.
Effects of rent controls on the private rented sector in New York.

1627   Sternlieb, G. *Residential abandonment: the tenement landlord revisited.* New Brunswick, Rutgers University, Center for Urban Policy Research, 1974.

1628 Sternlieb, G. *The tenement landlord.* New Brunswick, Rutgers University Press, 1969.
Housing investment and management in declining urban areas.

1629 Sternlieb, G. and Hughes, J. W. *The future of rental housing.* New Brunswick, Center for Urban Policy Research, 1981.
Long term changes in US private rental housing.

1630 Straszheim, M. R. 'The section 8 rental assistance program: costs and policy options'. *Policy Studies Journal* vol. 8 no. 2 (1979) pp. 307–23.
Effects of subsidies paid under section 8 of the US Housing and Urban Development Act 1974.

1631 Streich, P. and Clarke, L. *Multi-family federal rental assistance programs in Canada and the United States.* Washington, DC, Department of Housing and Urban Development, 1980.

1632 United States, Department of Housing and Urban Development. *Landlord–tenant relationships: a selected bibliography.* Washington, DC, The Department, 1971.

1633 United States, Department of Housing and Urban Development. *Rental housing: condition and outlook.* Washington, DC, The Department, 1981.

1634 United States, Department of Housing and Urban Development. *Rental housing for lower income families.* Washington, DC, Government Printing Office, 1971.

1635 United States, General Accounting Office. *Rental housing: a national problem that needs immediate attention.* Washington, DC, Government Printing Office, 1979.
Report to Congress.

1636 United States, General Accounting Office. *Section 236 rental housing–an evaluation with lessons for the future.* Washington, DC, The Office, 1978.

Report to Congress by the Comptroller General.

1637   *Urban Law Annual* vol. 17 (1979).
Special issue on methods of dealing with landlord–tenant problems through housing courts in the US.

1638   Welfeld, I. 'Right rents and arbitrary subsidies: a table for the current US mess'. *Urban Law and Policy* vol. 1 no. 2 (Apr. 1978) pp. 161–89.
Subsidized rental housing in the US. Problems lie in the rent and subsidy structure of housing assistance programmes.

10.5   Australasia

1639   Badcock, B. A. and Cloher, D. U. U. 'The contribution of housing displacement to the decline of the boarding and lodging population in Adelaide 1947–77'. *Institute of British Geographers Transactions* vol. 5 no. 2 (1980) pp. 151–69.
Pressures affecting the rented housing market in Adelaide.

1640   Grant, J. *Rental housing in the Auckland region.* Wellington, New Zealand National Housing Commission, 1982. (Research paper 82/3).

1641   Holmes, A. 'Strata title'. *Housing and Planning Review* vol. 39 no. 4 (Aug.–Sept. 1984) pp. 10–11.
Reviews the strata title system for leasehold pioneered in New South Wales, and problems of introducing it to the UK.

1642   Paris, C. *Affordable and available housing: the role of the private rental sector.* Canberra, Australian Institute of Urban Studies, 1984. (AIUS publication 117).

1643   Paris, C. 'Private rental housing in Australia'. *Environment and Planning A* vol. 16 no. 8 (Aug. 1984) pp. 1079–98.

1644   Thorns, D. C. *Rental housing: choices and constraints.* Wellington, New Zealand National Housing Commission, 1980. (Research paper 80/3).

1645   Whiteley, S. *Private rented housing in New Zealand*. Wellington, New Zealand National Housing Commission, 1979. (Commission paper 79/2).

1646   Yates, J. *Landlords and rental property in Melbourne*. Canberra, Australian Housing Research Council, 1982.

10.6   Africa, Asia and Latin America

1647   Amis, P. 'Squatters or tenants: the commercialization of unauthorised housing in Nairobi'. *World Development* vol. 12 no. 1 (Jan. 1984) pp. 87–96.
   As an unauthorized private rental sector develops, low income shelter becomes a commercial activity.

1648   Edwards, M. A. 'Cities of tenants: renting among the urban poor in Latin America'. In A. G. Gilbert et al. (eds.) *Urbanisation in contemporary Latin America*. Chichester, Wiley, 1982. pp. 129–58.

1649   Maunder, W. F. *Hong Kong urban rents and housing*. Hong Kong University Press, 1969.

1650   United Nations, Department of International Economic and Social Affairs. *Review of rent control in developing countries*. New York, United Nations, 1979.

11

Alternative tenures

General works on housing tenure and the main types of tenure have been covered in earlier sections. Intermediate or alternative tenures are, however, becoming more important sources of housing for an increasing proportion of the population unable or unwilling to commit themselves to home ownership or public housing. This section therefore covers references to examples of alternative tenures such as housing associations, co-operatives, condominiums, self-help housing groups and various other forms increasingly featured in the literature of housing. Reference should of course also be made to section 7 'Housing tenures' as well as sections 14 'Special needs' and 18 'Improvement and urban renewal'.

11.1   International and comparative

1651   Barnes, K. 'Housing associations: European ideas, American applications'. *Journal of Housing* vol. 39 no. 1 (Jan.–Feb. 1982) pp. 10–13.
   Functions and organization of housing associations in Britain and West Germany, and applications of the German model in Baltimore, Maryland, US.

1652   Cahill, W. D. *Co-operative housing: a selective and partially annotated bibliography*. Monticello, Vance Bibliographies, 1979. (Public administration series bibliography no. P.271).

1653   Digby, M. *Co-operative housing*. Plunkett Foundation for

Co-operative Studies, 1978. (Occasional paper no. 42). Includes case studies from over 30 countries.

1654   Hands, J. *Housing co-operatives.* Society for Co-operative Dwellings, 1975.
International review, advice for British co-operatives, and discussion of future developments.

1655   Heinen, B. *Contribution of co-operative housing societies to the solution of technical and social problems of urbanization.* New York, United Nations, 1969.

1656   Hetzel, O. and Szymanski, M. *Housing associations in England: a model for success in America.* New Brunswick, Transaction Books, 1981. (Learning from abroad vol. 3).

1657   Howenstine, E. J. *Converting public housing to individual and co-operative ownership: lessons from foreign experience.* Washington, DC, Department of Housing and Urban Development, 1983.

1658   International Federation for Housing and Planning. *The 1983 social/non-profit housing seminar/ideas market: report of the IFHP seminar in Haraldskaer, Denmark, 13–17 March.* The Hague, The Federation, 1983.

1659   International Federation for Housing and Planning. *The special role of non-profit housing in urban revitalisation: report of the IFHP seminar in Haraldskaer, Denmark, 11–14 May.* The Hague, The Federation, 1980.

1660   Johnson, J. J. *Housing co-operatives and associations: a selective bibliography.* Adelaide, South Australia Housing Trust, 1978. (Library bibliography no. 22).

1661   Lane, F. S. 'Condominiums and co-ownership: 1'. *Journal of Planning and Environment Law* Aug. 1979 pp. 505–17.
Discussion of US and English ideas of shared residential tenure, and definition of condominium.

1662   Stead, P. *Self-build housing groups and co-operatives: ideas in practice.* London, Anglo-German Foundation for the Study of Industrial Society, 1980.

1663   United Nations, Department of Economic and Social Affairs. *Non-profit housing associations. Organisation, financing and structural integration.* New York, United Nations, 1975.
   Proceedings of the inter-regional seminar on housing through co-operatives and other non-profit associations, Holte, Denmark, Sept. 1973.

1664   United Nations, Department of Economic and Social Affairs. *Self-help practices in housing: selected case studies.* New York, United Nations, 1974.

1665   United States, Department of Housing and Urban Development. *Co-operative housing.* Washington, DC, The Department, 1971.
   Prepared for the US Agency for International Development.

11.2   Europe

1666   Gorst, T. 'The Amsterdam School: housing associations and the municipality'. *Architectural Association Quarterly* vol. 11 no. 4 (1979) pp. 4–13.

1667   Greve, J. *Voluntary housing in Scandinavia: a study of Denmark, Norway and Sweden.* University of Birmingham, Centre for Urban and Regional Studies, 1971. (Occasional paper 21).
   Housing associations and co-operatives in Scandinavia and their relevance to Britain.

1668   Gulbrandsen, L. and Torgersen, U. 'Private sentiments in a public context: aspects of co-operative housing in Oslo'. *Scandinavian Political Studies* 1978 pp. 255–83.

1669   Umraith, H. 'European approaches to co-operative and non-profit housing'. In M. Wheeler (ed.) *The right to housing.* Montreal, Harvest House, 1969. pp. 286–94.

1670   Walker, K. 'Social housing in Denmark'. *Voluntary Housing* vol. 10 no. 2 (Mar. 1978) pp. 11–13.

Finance and organization of co-operatives and housing associations in Denmark.

1671 Weesep, J. Van. 'Condominium conversion in Amsterdam: boon or burden?' *Urban Geography* vol. 5 no. 2 (Apr.–June 1984) pp. 165–77.

1672 Weesep, J. Van and Maas, M. W. A. 'Housing policy and conversions to condominiums in the Netherlands'. *Environment and Planning A* vol. 16 no. 9 (Sept. 1984) pp. 1149–61.
Examines the origins of condominiums in the Netherlands, current housing policies and the conversion of rental housing.

1673 Woltemade, U. J. 'Social housing and non-profits in West Germany'. *Habitat* vol. 26 no. 1 (1983) pp. 37–43.
Development of non-profit housing associations in Germany since the 1860s. Includes case studies and a comparison with Canada.

11.3 United Kingdom

1674 Alder, J. 'Housing associations: the Third World of housing policy'. *Journal of Social Welfare Law* Jan. 1983 pp. 22–38.
Law of housing associations from the tenants' point of view.

1675 Baker, C. V. *Housing associations.* London, Estates Gazette, 1976.

1676 Berry, S. J. C. 'Managing by ourselves: the development of housing co-operatives in Scotland'. *Housing Review* vol. 30 no. 4 (July–Aug. 1981) pp. 116–19.

1677 Bird, B. E. I. and Palmer, J. A. D. *Housing association tenants.* London, Housing Corporation, 1979.

1678 Brown, W. J. et al. *Housing associations and older housing: the rehabilitation process.* University of Birmingham, Centre for Urban and Regional Studies, 1984. (Research memorandum 96).

1679 Eno, S. and Treanor, D. *Collective housing handbook.* Castle Douglas, Laurieston Hall Publications, 1982.

1680   Holmes, C. 'Self help housing'. In P. Hain (ed.) *Community politics*. London, Calder, 1976.

1681   Institute of Housing. *Working together: report of an Institute Working Party on local authorities and housing associations*. London, The Institute, 1985. (Professional practice series no. 1).

1682   Jelfs, M. *Mortgage finance for housing co-operatives*. 2nd ed. London, Empty Property Unit, 1984.

1683   Jones, P. 'The Housing Corporation'. *Housing and Planning Review* vol. 39 no. 6 (Dec. 1983) pp. 19–21.
Brief review of activities.

1684   Jones, P. 'How the housing associations have improved Scotland'. *Housing and Planning Review* vol. 37 no. 2 (Summer 1981) pp. 16–19.
Work of housing associations in Scotland.

1685   Kirby, A. 'The Housing Corporation 1974–1979: an example of state housing policy in Britain'. *Environment and Planning A* vol. 13 no. 10 (Oct. 1981) pp. 1295–1303.

1686   Kirby, A. 'Voluntarism and the state funding of housing — political explanations and geographic outcomes in Britain'. *Tijdschrift voor Economische en Sociale Geografie* vol. 76 no. 1 (1985) pp. 53–62.

1687   M'Kenzie-Hall, J. E. *Low cost homes to rent or buy*. London, Hale, 1971.
Dated but interesting account of housing associations.

1688   Maclennan, D. et al. *The rehabilitation activities and effectiveness of housing associations in Scotland*. Edinburgh, Scottish Office, Central Research Unit, 1983.

1689   Mason, T. and Courtenay, G. *Improved homes: a survey of tenants for MIH*. Liverpool, Merseyside Improved Houses, 1980.
Work of a Liverpool housing association.

1690   Merseyside Improved Houses. *50 years: the story of a housing association from 1928 to 1978.* Liverpool, Merseyside Improved Houses, 1979.

1691　National Federation of Housing Associations. *Co-ownership housing associations.* London, The Federation, 1975.

1692　National Federation of Housing Associations. *Financing a hostel.* London, The Federation, 1984.

1693　National Federation of Housing Associations. *A guide to housing associations.* London, The Federation, 1975.

1694　National Federation of Housing Associations. *The Housing Act 1980: a guide for housing associations.* London, The Federation, 1980.

1695　National Federation of Housing Associations. *Housing association yearbook.* London, The Federation, annual.
　　Reference guide to the housing association movement.

1696　National Federation of Housing Associations. *Housing associations: their part in Britain's housing.* London, The Federation, 1982?

1697　National Federation of Housing Associations. *Minimum standards for housing rehabilitation.* London, The Federation, 1980.
　　Final edition.

1698　National Federation of Housing Associations. *Special projects: a guide for voluntary organisations working with housing associations.* Rev. ed. London, 1981. (Special project guide no. 1).

1699　National Federation of Housing Associations and Chartered Institute of Public Finance and Accountancy. *A manual of housing association finance.* London, The Institute, 1981.

1700　Noble, D. 'From rules to discretion: the Housing Corporation'. In M. Adler and S. Asquith (eds.) *Discretion and welfare.* London, Heinemann, 1981. (Studies in social policy and welfare 15). pp. 171–84.

Discusses the suitability of legal techniques in resolving problems of procedure in housing associations.

1701 Raynsford, N. 'The role of voluntary organisations in housing'. *Housing and Planning Review* vol. 35 no. 1 (Spring 1980) pp. 13–15.

1702 Tarn, J. N. *Five per cent philanthropy: an account of housing in urban areas between 1840 and 1914.* Cambridge University Press, 1973.
Early work of charitable housing associations.

1703 Thompson, A. *The role of housing associations in major urban areas.* University of Birmingham, Centre for Urban and Regional Studies, 1977. (Research memorandum 60).
Case study of Merseyside Improved Houses.

1704 Turney, J. *Improvement for sale by housing associations.* London, Housing Corporation, 1982.

1705 United Kingdom, Department of the Environment. *Final report of the working party on housing co-operatives.* London, HMSO, 1975.
Report of the Campbell Working Party.

1706 United Kingdom, Department of the Environment. *Housing Act 1974: Housing Corporation and housing associations.* London, HMSO, 1974. (Circular 170/74).

1707 United Kingdom, Department of the Environment. *Housing co-operatives.* London, HMSO, 1976. (Circular 8/76).
Reaction to the Campbell report.

1708 United Kingdom, Department of the Environment, Housing Services Advisory Group. *Housing action areas and the role of housing associations.* London, The Department, 1981.

1709 United Kingdom, Department of the Environment, Housing Services Advisory Group. *Housing associations and their part in current housing strategies.* London, The Department, 1978.

1710   United Kingdom, House of Commons, Committee of Public Accounts. *Department of the Environment and Housing Corporation: duplication in the administration of housing association grants: duality of interest in housing association transactions.* London, HMSO, 1981. (11th report, Session 1980–81, HC 328).

1711   United Kingdom, House of Commons, Committee of Public Accounts. *Housing associations and the Housing Corporation.* London, HMSO, 1979. (Fifth report, Session 1978–79, HC 327).

1712   United Kingdom, House of Commons, Committee of Public Accounts. *Housing associations and the Housing Corporation: advances to the Housing Corporation and to housing associations.* London, HMSO, 1980. (Session 1979–80, HC 741).
Official scrutiny of administrative procedure.

1713   United Kingdom, Housing Corporation. *Annual report.* London, The Corporation, annual.
Useful overview of the work of housing associations. Includes statistical tables.

1714   United Kingdom, Housing Corporation. *Directory of housing co-operatives.* London, The Corporation, 1981.
Valuable list of housing co-operatives.

1715   United Kingdom, Housing Corporation. *Liverpool housing associations rehabilitation survey final report.* Housing Corporation/Liverpool City Council/Merseyside Voluntary Housing Group, 1978?

1716   United Kingdom, Housing Corporation. *Recommended form of published accounts for housing associations.* 3rd ed. London, The Corporation, 1983.

1717   United Kingdom, Ministry of Housing and Local Government, Central Housing Advisory committee. *Housing associations.* London, HMSO, 1971.
Summary of evidence to the Cohen Committee.

1718   United Kingdom, National Building Agency. *Maintenance procedures for housing associations.* London, The Agency, 1977.

1719   United Kingdom, National Building Agency. *Self-build: a manual for self-build housing associations.* London, The Agency, 1978.

1720   United Kingdom, Scottish Development Department. *Housing Act 1974: Housing Corporation, housing associations and housing authorities in Scotland.* Edinburgh, HMSO, 1975. (Circular 10/75).

1721   United Kingdom, Scottish Office. *Options for housing co-operatives in Scotland: a review of the role of housing co-operatives and an examination of some of the issues which arise in their development and operations.* Edinburgh, The Office, 1979.

1722   Williamson, J. M. and Kirwan, M. R. *Housing associations: accounting and audit guide.* London, Deloitte, Haskins and Sells and National Federation of Housing Associations, 1984.

1723   Wood, D. 'Condominiums and co-ownership: 2'. *Journal of Planning and Environment Law* Sept. 1979 pp. 601–8.
Co-ownership in England and Wales; asks if condominiums should be introduced.

11.4   North America

1724   Allen, C. 'A triumph for third sector housing'. *Habitat* vol. 25 no. 1 (1982).
Housing associations in Ottawa.

1725   Barash, S. (ed.) *Complete guide to appraising condominiums and co-operatives.* Englewood Cliffs, Prentice-Hall, 1981.

1726   Casazza, J. A. 'The condominium conversion phenomenon'. *Urban Land* vol. 39 no. 10 (Nov. 1980) pp.4–6.
Conversion of rental housing units into condominiums.

1727   Clurman, D. and Hebard, E. *Condominiums and co-operatives.* New York, Wiley, 1970.

1728   Day, C. C. and Fogel, M. I. 'The condominium crisis: a problem unresolved'. *Urban Law Annual* vol. 21 (1981) pp. 3–85.

Supply of rental housing and legislative responses.

1729   Dinkelspiel, J. R. *Condominiums: the effects of conversion on a community*. Boston, Auburn House, 1981.
Study of Brookline, Massachusetts.

1730   Franklin, S. B. 'Housing co-operatives: a viable means of home ownership for low-income families'. *Journal of Housing* vol. 38 (July 1981) pp. 392–8.

1731   Goliger, G. 'How the people of Milton-Parc saved their neighbourhood'. *Habitat* vol. 25 no. 3 (1982) pp. 2–9.
Non-profit housing co-operatives renovating part of Montreal.

1732   Haire, C. P. *In want of a policy: a survey of the needs of non-profit housing companies and co-operative housing societies*. Ottawa, Canadian Council on Social Development, 1975.
Co-operative housing in Canada.

1733   Hamnett, C. 'North Americans opt for the "condo"'. *Geographical Magazine* vol. 55 no. 9 (Sept. 1983) pp. 458–9.
Development of condominiums as trend towards home ownership in the US.

1734   Hetzel, O. J. and Szymanski, M. A. 'Providing low and moderate income housing through non-profit housing associations'. *Urban Law Annual* vol. 21 (1981) pp. 87–140.

1735   Kunze, C. 'Public housing co-operatives reduce dependence on operating subsidies, modernization funding'. *Journal of Housing* vol. 38 (Oct. 1981) pp. 489–93.

1736   Le Croissette, D. *Condominium living: your guide to buying and living in a condominium*. Montrose, Calif., Younghusband Co., 1980.

1737   Navarro, P. 'Rent control and the landlords' loophole: condominium conversions in Cambridge, Mass.'. *Urban Land* vol. 39 no. 10 (Nov. 1980) pp. 6–9.

1738   Teaford, S. D. 'Home ownership for low income families: the condominium'. *Hastings Law Journal* vol. 21 (1970) pp. 243–86.

1739   United States, Department of Housing and Urban Development. *Aided self help housing: its history and potential.* Washington, DC, The Department, 1976.

1740   United States, Department of Housing and Urban Development. *The conversion of rental housing to condominiums and co-operatives: a national study of scope, causes and impacts.* Washington, DC, The Department, 1980.

1741   United States, Department of Housing and Urban Development. *The conversion of rental housing to condominiums and co-operatives: annotated bibliography.* Washington, DC, The Department, 1980.

1742   United States, Department of Housing and Urban Development. *HUD condominium/co-operative study: vol. 1, national evaluation; vols. 2 and 3, appendices.* Washington, DC, The Department, 1975.

1743   United States, Department of Housing and Urban Development. *HUD–FHA condominiums: their future: a staff paper.* Washington, DC, The Department, 1975.

1744   United States, House, Committee on Government Operations, Commercial, Consumer and Monetary Affairs Subcommittee. *Condominium and co-operative conversion: the federal response.* Washington, DC, Government Printing Office, 1981.
In three hearings.

1745   Weston, J. 'The co-op solution'. *Habitat* vol. 22 no. 2 (1979) pp. 26–33.
Housing co-operatives in Canada.

1746   Zimmer, J. E. *From rental to co-operative: improving low and moderate income housing.* Beverly Hills, Sage, 1977. (Sage professional papers in administrative and political studies vol. 4).

11.5 Africa, Asia and Latin America

1747   Altmann, J. 'Planning and implementing self-help projects in developing countries: the case of housing'. *Planning and Administration* vol. 6 no. 1 (Spring 1979) pp. 13–24.
Guidelines to co-operative housing in developing countries.

1748   Altmann, J. 'Self-help housing in urban squatter settlements'. *Habitat International* vol. 6 no. 4 (1982) pp. 417–24.

1749   Altmann, J. and Baldeaux, D. 'Co-operative housing in Lesotho'. *Planning and Administration* vol. 7 no. 2 (Autumn 1980) pp. 26–32.

1750   Bamberger, M. 'The role of self-help housing in low-cost shelter programmes for the Third World'. *Built Environment* vol. 8 no. 2 (1982) pp. 95–107.

1751   Burgess, R. 'Petty commodity housing or dweller control?' *World Development* vol. 6 nos. 9–10 (1978) pp. 1105–33.
A critique of J. F. C. Turner's views on housing policy in developing countries.

1752   Burgess, R. 'Self-help housing: a new imperialist strategy? A critique of the Turner school'. *Antipode* vol. 9 (1977) pp. 50–9.

1753   Burgess, R. 'Self-help housing advocacy: a curious form of radicalism: a critique of the work of J. F. C. Turner'. In P. M. Ward (ed.) *Self-help housing: a critique.* London, Mansell, 1982. pp. 56–98.

1754   Burns, L. S. 'Self-help housing: an evaluation of outcomes'. *Urban Studies* vol. 20 part 3 (Aug. 1983) pp. 299–309.
Survey of the attitudes of participants in a self-help housing project in El Salvador.

1755   Burns, L. S. and Shoup, D. C. 'Effects of resident control and ownership in self-help housing'. *Land Economics* vol. 57 (1981) pp. 106–14.

1756   Clinard, M. B. *Slums and community development: experiments in self-help.* London, Collier Macmillan, 1966.

1757   Harms, H. 'Historical perspectives on the practice and purpose of self-help housing'. In P. M. Ward (ed.) *Self-help housing: a critique.* London, Mansell, 1982. pp. 17–55.

1758   Huque, A. *The myth of self-help housing: a critical analysis of the conventional depiction of shanty towns.* Stockholm, Royal Institute of Technology, Department for Building Function Analysis, 1982.

1759   Hyland, B. 'Constraints to housing the poor'. *Mazingira* no. 12 (1979) pp. 6–15.
Governments in developing countries should follow principles listed to help the poor to house themselves.

1760   Lewin, A. C. *Housing co-operatives in developing countries: a manual for self-help in low cost housing schemes.* Chichester, Wiley, 1981.
Practical manual looking at the organization, construction and legal processes of self help housing groups.

1761   Lewin, A. C. *Self-help housing through co-operatives: prospects and problems for urban Africa.* Cologne, The Author, 1976.

1762   Muller, M. S. *Housing co-operative societies in Kenya: performance and potential.* University of Nairobi, Housing Research and Development Unit, 1978.
Recommends formation of building groups among low income workers and a non-profit housing development agency.

1763   Payne, G. K. 'Self-help housing: a critique of the Gecekondus of Ankara'. In P. M. Ward (ed.) *Self-help housing: a critique.* London, Mansell, 1982. pp. 117–40.

1764   Skinner, R. J. and Rodell, M. J. (eds.) *People, poverty and shelter: problems of self-help housing in the Third World.* London, Methuen, 1983.

1765   Sudra, T. 'Self-help housing: towards the support of a popular process and the role of government intervention'. *Openhouse* vol. 4 no. 4 (1979) pp. 28–43.

1766 Turner, J. F. C. 'Issues in self-help and self-managed housing'. In P. M. Ward (ed.) *Self-help housing: a critique*. London, Mansell, 1982. pp. 99–114.

1767 United Nations, Department of Economic and Social Affairs. *Self-help practices in housing: selected case studies*. New York, United Nations, 1973.
  Five case studies from Colombia, Senegal, El Salvador, Ethiopia and Sudan.

1768 University of Birmingham, Institute of Local Government Studies, Development Administration Group. *Report of an evaluation of the self-help housing agencies in Botswana*. Birmingham, The Institute, 1983.

1769 Ward, P. M. (ed.) *Self-help housing: a critique*. London, Mansell, 1982.

1770 Ward, P. M. 'Self-help housing in Mexico City: social and economic determination of success'. *Town Planning Review* vol. 49 no. 1 (Jan. 1978) pp. 38–50.

1771 Widstrand, C. G. (ed.) *Co-operatives and rural development in East Africa*. New York, Africana Publishing Co., 1970.

12
Social aspects

This section features references on the social aspects of housing provision, in particular the ways in which housing policy may be modified or changed as a response to social considerations or pressure groups as well as the ways in which social attitudes and activities may be influenced by housing policy. Topics covered here include public participation in housing policy making and management, social and psychological aspects of housing design, the prevention of criminal behaviour in housing developments, housing satisfaction, housing aid and advice, community action, housing protest movements and sociological studies of households.

12.1 International and comparative

1772 Becker, F. D. *Housing messages*. Stroudsberg, Dowden, Hutchinson and Ross, 1977. (Community development series no. 30).
Ways of matching residential demand and preference and the social consequences of people living in environments not reflecting their values and life-styles.

1773 Belcher, J. C. and Vazquez-Calcerrada, P. B. 'A cross-cultural approach to the social functions of housing'. *Journal of Marriage and the Family* 1972 pp. 750–61.

1774 Brindley, T. S. and Raine, J. W. 'Social area analysis and planning research'. *Urban Studies* vol. 16 no. 3 (Oct. 1979) pp.

273–89.
Reviews the history and appraises the potential of social area analysis for policy research.

1775   Canter, D. and Lee, T. (eds.) *Psychology and the built environment.* London, Architectural Press, 1974.

1776   Carmon, N. 'Social planning of housing'. *Journal of Social Policy* vol. 5 (Jan. 1976) pp. 49–59.
Surveys sociological studies which define factors in the social planning of housing.

1777   Castells, M. *The city and the grass roots.* London, Edward Arnold, 1983.
Popular urban social movements including case studies on the Glasgow rent strike and Latin American squatter movements.

1778   Duncan, J. S. (ed.) *Housing and identity: cross-cultural perspectives.* London, Croom Helm, 1981.
A social–psychological perspective on housing and its role in the social order.

1779   Green, N. 'The sociological approach to planning for housing and urban renewal'. *Planning and Building Developments* no. 18 (Jan.–Feb. 1976) pp. 33–9.

1780   Habraken, N. J. *Supports: an alternative to mass housing.* London, Architectural Press, 1972.
Translated from the 1961 Dutch edition. Social and psychological expression in housing through community involvement.

1781   'Housing in neighborhoods'. *Ekistics* vol. 50 no. 298 (Jan.–Feb. 1983) pp. 1–81.
Studies from US, Japan and the Third World.

1782   'Human habitats: from tradition to modernism'. *International Social Science Journal* vol. 30 no. 3 (1978) pp. 449–603.
Special issue.

1783   International Federation for Housing and Planning. *Community planning and development: the effectiveness of housing and*

other socio-economic development programmes at various planning levels. The Hague, The Federation, 1980.
Papers and proceedings of the 35th World Congress, Jerusalem, Nov. 1980.

1784 International Federation for Housing and Planning. *Equal opportunities in urban life: towards a redistribution of available resources to improve urban living conditions for the under-privileged.* 2 vols. The Hague, The Federation, 1982.
Papers and proceedings of the 36th World Congress, Oslo.

1785 Katz, S. and Mayer, M. 'Gimme shelter: self-help housing struggles within and against the state in New York City and West Berlin'. *International Journal of Urban and Regional Research* vol. 9 no. 1 (Mar. 1985) pp. 15–46.

1786 Keiser, M. B. *Housing: an environment for living.* New York, Macmillan, 1978.

1787 King, A. (ed.) *Buildings and society: essays on the social development of the built environment.* London, Routledge and Kegan Paul, 1980.

1788 Lawrence, R. J. 'Understanding the home environment: spatial and temporal perspectives'. *International Journal for Housing Science and its Applications* vol. 7 no. 1 (1983) pp. 13–25.
Relationship between people and the environment. Architecture should be more relevant.

1789 Mackay, D. *Multiple family housing: from aggregation to integration.* London, Thames and Hudson, 1977.
Community housing projects from all over the world.

1790 Mendelsohn, R. 'The sociology of housing'. *Shelter* (Canberra) no. 19 (June 1975) pp. 4–8.

1791 National Swedish Institute for Building Research. *Social aspects of housing and urban development: a bibliography.* Stockholm, The Institute, 1969.
Compiled and published with the United Nations Centre for Housing, Building and Planning, Department of Economics and Social Affairs.

1792 Newman, O. *Defensible space: people and design in the violent city.* London, Architectural Press, 1973.
Environments which reduce the risk of a criminal encounter and help create a sense of identity among residents.

1793 Newmark, N. L. et al. 'Housing: a variable in upward mobility?' *International Journal for Housing Science and its Applications* vol. 3 no. 3 (1979) pp. 205–13.
Values and life-style are as important to housing satisfaction as physical aspects.

1794 Olivegren, J. 'Better sociopsychological climates for housing estates'. *Ekistics* vol. 41 no. 245 (Apr. 1976) pp. 216–23.

1795 Peattie, L. R. 'Social issues in housing'. In B. Frieden and W. Nash (eds.) *Shaping an urban future.* Cambridge, Mass., MIT Press, 1969. pp. 15–34.

1796 Rapoport, A. *The meaning of the built environment: a non verbal communication approach.* Beverly Hills, Sage, 1983.

1797 Rimlinger, G. *Welfare policy and industrialization in Europe, America and Russia.* New York, Wiley, 1971.
Study of differential development of welfare policies from an economic viewpoint.

1798 Schoor, A. 'Housing policy and poverty'. In P. Townsend (ed.) *The concept of poverty.* London, Heinemann, 1970. pp. 113–23.
Ways in which society determines housing need and the effects of poor housing on residents.

1799 Soen, D. 'Habitability: occupants' needs and dwelling satisfaction'. *Ekistics* vol. 46 no. 275 (Mar.–Apr. 1979) pp. 129–34.

1800 Thorns, D. C. *The quest for community: social aspects of residential growth.* London, Allen and Unwin, 1976.
International perspective, reviewing a selection of studies of new residential areas.

1801 Tremblay, K. *Toward a sociology of housing: a working biblio-*

graphy. Chicago, Council of Planning Librarians, 1978. (Exchange bibliography 1485).
Contains over 300 references on the attempt to define housing sociology. Mainly US material from the 1970s.

1802 Turner, J. F. C. *Housing by people: towards autonomy in building environment.* London, Boyars, 1976.
Argues for self-help and deprofessionalization in housing and participation by people who live in houses.

1803 Turner, J. F. C. and Fichter, R. *Freedom to build.* London, Collier Macmillan, 1972.
World wide study of costs and quality of housing where dwellers are involved.

1804 Ungerson, C. and Karn, V. (eds.) *The consumer experience of housing: cross-national perspectives.* Farnborough, Gower Press, 1980.
Papers presented at the 9th World Congress of Sociology, Uppsala, 1978.

1805 United Nations, Department of Economic and Social Affairs. *The role of housing in promoting social integration.* New York, United Nations, 1978.
Includes studies of US, Israel, Colombia and Sri Lanka.

1806 United Nations, Department of Economic and Social Affairs. *Social aspects of housing and urban development.* New York, United Nations, 1967.

1807 United Nations, Department of Economic and Social Affairs. *The social impact of housing: goals, standards, social indicators and popular participation.* New York, United Nations, 1977.
Proceedings of the inter-regional seminar on the social aspects of housing, Holte, Denmark, 14–27 Sept. 1975.

1808 United States, Department of Housing and Urban Development. *Post-occupancy evaluations of residential environments: an international bibliography.* Washington, DC, The Department, 1977.

1809 Vapnarsky, C. A. 'An approach to the sociology of housing'. *Ekistics* vol. 22 no. 129 (1966) pp. 127–35.

12.2 Europe

1810 Ceccarelli, P. 'Politics, parties and urban movements: Western Europe'. In N. and S. Fainstein (eds.) *Urban policy under capitalism.* Beverly Hills, Sage, 1982. pp. 261–76.

1811 Davis, E. E. and Fine-Davis, M. 'Predictors of satisfaction with housing and neighbourhood: a nationwide study in the Republic of Ireland'. *Social Indicators Research* Dec. 1981 pp. 477–94.

1812 European Communities Commission. *Report on social developments.* Luxembourg, The Commission, annual.
Includes sections on housing.

1813 Hjarne, L. 'Aims and forms of tenant influence: some preliminary considerations'. *Acta Sociologica* vol. 24 no. 4 (1981) pp. 251–64.
Participation in Sweden.

1814 Hogberg, A.-L. *Housing estate management for tenants: programme for real-estate management 1978–1981: part 1.* Stockholm, Swedish Council for Building Research, 1982.

1815 Madge, C. and Willmott, P. *Inner city poverty in Paris and London.* London, Routledge and Kegan Paul, 1981.
Ch. 4 'Inner city housing problems' (pp. 55–72).

1816 Moore, N. C. 'Social aspects of flat dwelling'. *Public Health* vol. 89 (Mar. 1975) pp. 109–15.
Matched study of low rise flat dwellers and house dwellers in West Germany: general dissatisfaction by flat dwellers.

1817 Petonnet, C. *Those people: subculture of a housing project.* London, Greenwood Press, 1973. (Contributions in sociology).
Translated from the French.

1818   Read, J. T. 'Housing and social reform in France 1894–1935'. *Martin Centre for Architectural and Urban Studies Transactions* vol. 1 (1976) pp. 297–315.

1819   Savill, D. 'Tenant participation in housing management in Sweden'. *Housing Review* vol. 31 no. 6 (Nov.–Dec. 1982) pp. 209–12.
Tenant organizations' participation in public, private and co-operative housing sectors in Sweden.

1820   Supik, A. 'Social amenities and housing in Scandinavian countries'. *Institution of Civil Engineers Proceedings, Part 1, Design and Construction* vol. 68 (Aug. 1980) pp. 349–68.
Provision of public and co-operative housing with emphasis on social facilities on housing estates and quality of the residential environment. Case studies.

1821   Szelenyi, I. 'Housing system and social structure'. *Sociological Review Monograph* no. 17 (1972) pp. 269–98.
Special issue entitled 'Hungarian social studies'.

1822   United Nations, Economic Commission for Europe. *Quality of life and human settlements: examples of protection and improvement in South European countries.* New York, 1981.
Based on papers prepared for the 8th and 9th meetings of the Group of Experts on Housing, Building and Planning Problems and Policies in the countries of Southern Europe held in 1977 and 1979.

12.3   United Kingdom

1823   Andrews, C. L. *Tenants and town hall.* London, HMSO, 1979.
Detailed study of relations between tenants and housing department in an inner London borough.

1824   Association of Housing Aid. *Housing aid in crisis.* London, The Association, 1982.

1825   Association of Housing Aid. *National directory of housing aid centres.* 2nd ed. London, The Association, 1984.

1826 Baldwin, J. *The urban criminal.* London, Tavistock, 1976.
How problem estates are made, and the issue of criminality:
study of Sheffield.

1827 Barker, A. *Public participation in Britain: a classified bibliography.* London, Bedford Square Press, 1979.
Contains several references on housing issues.

1828 Bentham, C. G. 'Urban problems and public dissatisfaction in the metropolitan areas of England'. *Regional Studies* vol. 17
no. 5 (Oct. 1983) pp. 339–46.
Uses data from NDHS to compare dissatisfaction with residential areas with economic indicators.

1829 Berthoud, R. and Brown, J. C. *Poverty and the development
of anti-poverty policy in the United Kingdom.* London, Heinemann,
1981.
Ch. 6 'Housing and poverty' (pp. 177–98).

1830 Blowers, A. T. 'Council housing: the social implications of
layout and design in an urban fringe estate'. *Town Planning Review*
vol. 41 (1970) pp. 80–92.

1831 Borrie, G. *Advice agencies: what they do and who uses them.*
London, National Consumer Council, 1983.
Includes housing aid centres, based on a survey of callers to
advice centres.

1832 Bottoms, A. E. and Xanthos, P. 'Housing policy and crime
in the British public sector'. In P. J. Brantingham and P. L.
Brantingham (eds.) *Environmental criminology.* London, Sage,
1981. pp. 203–25.

1833 Bryan, M. 'Domestic violence: a question of housing?'
Journal of Social Welfare Law July 1984 pp. 195–207.
Considers relationship between housing aid and domestic
violence and problems of existing legislation.

1834 Burke, G. *Housing and social justice.* Harlow, Longman,
1981.

Housing from the social policy perspective.

1835   Burnett, J. *A social history of housing 1815–1970*. Newton Abbot, David and Charles, 1978.

1836   Butcher, H. 'Neighbourhood information centres — access or advocacy?' *Journal of Social Policy* vol. 5 no. 4 (1976) pp. 375–88.
Considers what advice centres should be doing for users and how other agencies view advice/advocacy. Includes housing.

1837   Carmon, N. 'Social planning of housing'. *Journal of Social Policy* vol. 5 (1975) pp. 49–59.
Planners should be aware of social goals, involving value judgements.

1838   CES. *The outer estates in Britain: preliminary comparison of four estates, interim report*. London, CES, 1984. (CES Paper 23).
Estates in Glasgow, Middlesbrough, Knowsley, Hull.

1839   Clarke, R. V. G. (ed.) *Tackling vandalism*. London, HMSO, 1978. (Home Office research study 47).
Ch. 4 on London housing estates examines defensible space theory.

1840   Craven, E. 'Housing'. In R. Klein (ed.) *Social policy and public expenditure: inflation and priorities*. London, Centre for Studies in Social Policy, 1975.

1841   Cutting, M. *A housing rights handbook*. London, Penguin, 1979.
A little dated now, but contains valuable information and practical advice on housing issues.

1842   Damer, S. 'Wine alley: the sociology of a dreadful enclosure'. *Sociological Review* vol. 22 no. 2 (1974) pp. 221–48.

1843   Downey, P. et al. *Management co-operatives: tenant responsibility in practice*. London, HMSO, 1982.

1844   Durant, R. *Watling: a survey of social life on a new housing estate*. London, King and Son, 1939.

Early study of social effects of estate life.

1845   Dyos, H. and Wolff, M. (eds.) *The Victorian city.* 3 vols. London, Routledge and Kegan Paul, 1974.
Discusses the creation of industrial cities and the perception of them by their inhabitants.

1846   Fraser, D. *The evolution of the British welfare state.* London, Macmillan, 1973.
Historical study of social administration in Britain featuring the development of housing policy.

1847   Gilbert, B. B. *British social policy 1914–1939.* London, Batsford, 1970.
Includes discussion of housing policies and their implementation. See pp. 137–61 and 197–203.

1848   Gill, O. *Luke Street: housing policy, conflict and the creation of a delinquent area.* London, Macmillan, 1977.
Creation of a delinquent area and its maintenance through housing policy and practice.

1849   Harloe, M. et al. *Housing advice centres.* London, Shelter/ CES, 1976.
Study of selected centres in the UK.

1850   Harloe, M. et al. 'Housing aid: how does it help?' *Housing Review* vol. 25 no. 5 (Oct. 1976) pp. 111–14.

1851   Harrison, P. *Inside the inner city: life under the cutting edge.* London, Penguin, 1983.
Chapters on housing conditons, dump estates and council housing.

1852   Hillier, B. and Hanson, J. *The social logic of space.* Cambridge University Press, 1984.
Report of a research project at the Bartlett School of Architecture, London, examining the relationship between architecture and community and the limitation of anti-social behaviour.

1853   Hole, V. 'Social effects of planned rehousing'. *Town Planning Review* vol. 30 no. 2 (July 1959) pp. 161–73.

1854   Holtermann, S. *Census indicators of urban deprivation.* London, Department of the Environment, 1975.

1855   Holtermann, S. 'The welfare economics of priority area policies'. *Journal of Social Policy* vol. 7 no. 1 (Jan. 1978) pp. 23–40.

1856   Hooper, D. et al. 'Social work intervention on a new housing estate'. *British Journal of Social Work* vol. 8 no. 4 (1978) pp. 453–64.
Controlled experiment whereby half families moving onto a new housing estate got social work and half not.

1857   Jacobs, S. *The right to a decent house.* London, Routledge and Kegan Paul, 1976.
Community action in Glasgow against local authority rehousing.

1858   Kohn, P. *Community information and advice services.* Greater London Council, 1977. (Bibliography no. 84).
213 annotated references on items such as housing advice centres and legal aid.

1859   Lambert, J. 'Housing class and community action in a redevelopment area'. In C. Lambert and D. Weir (eds.) *Cities in modern Britain.* London, Collins, 1975.

1860   Lambert, J. et al. 'Neighbourhood politics and housing opportunities'. *Community Development Journal* vol. 10 no. 2 (Apr. 1975) pp. 95–112.

1861   Legal Action Group. *Directory of legal advice and law centres.* Rev. ed. London, The Group, 1983.
Details of leading housing advice centres.

1862   Le Grand, J. *The strategy of equality: redistribution and the social services.* London, Allen and Unwin, 1982.
Ch. 5 (pp. 82–105) discusses housing.

1863   Local Government Training Board. *Housing and matrimonial disputes.* Luton, The Board, 1983.
Law of marriage, separation and divorce applied to housing in Britain.

1864   McCarthy, J. *Some social implications of improvement policy in London.* London, Department of the Environment, 1975.

1865   McCormick, B. 'Housing and unemployment in the UK'. *Oxford Economic Papers* vol. 35 no. 3 (Nov. 1983) pp. 283–305.
Special supplement.

1866   McDonnell, K. 'Struggles in the welfare state: working in housing aid'. *Critical Social Policy* vol. 2 no. 1 (Summer 1982) pp. 63–77.

1867   McDowell, L. M. 'Measuring housing deprivation in postwar Britain'. *Area* vol. 11 no. 3 (1979) pp. 264–9.

1868   Matthews, R. *Housing and campaigning: a Shelter guide.* London, Shelter, 1983.

1869   Means, R. *Social work and the 'undeserving' poor.* University of Birmingham, Centre for Urban and Regional Studies, 1977. (Occasional paper 37).
Work of a family advice centre with council housing tenants and poor families in Birmingham.

1870   Melling, J. *Rent strikes: people's struggle for housing in West Central Scotland.* Edinburgh, Polygon Books, 1983.
Rent strikes in the period 1890–1916.

1871   Morby, G. *Knowhow: a guide to information, training and campaigning materials for information and advice workers.* Rev. ed. London, Library Association and Pluto Press, 1982.
Contains useful community information on issues such as housing, race relations and social security.

1872   Murie, A. *Housing inequality and deprivation.* London, Heinemann, 1983. (Studies in deprivation and disadvantage no. 7).

Published as part of the SSRC/DHSS research programme on transmitted deprivation.

1873   Mylan, D. *Housing aid and advice centres*. London, Association of Housing Aid, 1979.
Comments on training, salaries and administration; influence on policy and client representation.

1874   National Consumer Council. *Information and advice services in the United Kingdom*. London, The Council, 1983.
Includes a review of housing aid and advice centres.

1875   Pacione, M. 'Evaluating the quality of the residential environment in a deprived council estate'. *Geoforum* vol. 13 no. 1 (1982) pp. 45–55.
Research on an estate in Clydebank, Scotland.

1876   Parker, T. *The people of Providence: a housing estate and some of its inhabitants*. London, Hutchinson, 1983.
Social conditions and attitudes on a London housing estate seen through the words of its inhabitants.

1877   Planning Exchange. *Multiple deprivation/community development*. Glasgow, The Exchange, 1976? (Bibliography series no. 2).
Contains many references on community development projects, problem estates, homelessness and improvement areas with a large proportion of material on Scotland.

1878   Purkis, A. and Hodson, P. *Housing and community care*. London, Bedford Square Press, 1982.

1879   Raynsford, N. 'Housing aid and advice'. *Housing* vol. 15 no. 1 (Jan. 1979) pp. 14–18.
Account by the director of SHAC of history of advice centres: key issues developed.

1880   Richardson, A. 'Tenant participation in council house management'. In R. Darke and R. Walker (eds.) *Local government and the public*. London, Leonard Hill, 1977. pp. 198–214.

1881   Robinson, R. 'Inequality and housing'. *Urban Studies* vol. 22 no. 3 (June 1985) pp. 249–56.

Devises a measure of housing equality across the UK.

1882   Scottish Council of Social Service. *Tenant management co-operatives: a guide for landlords and tenants.* Edinburgh, The Council, 1981.

1883   Seabrook, J. *The idea of neighbourhood.* London, Pluto Press, 1984.
Includes discussion of decentralization of local government services, especially housing management, in Walsall.

1884   SHAC. *A decade of housing aid, SHAC 1970–80.* London, SHAC, 1980.

1885   SHAC. *Housing rights guide.* London, SHAC, 1985.
Details practical advice on how to find, pay for and keep a home.

1886   Shelter National Housing Aid Trust. *Housing aid facts and figures.* London, The Trust, 1983.

1887   Socialist Housing Activists Workshop. *Socialism and housing action: the red paper on housing.* Gateshead, Tyne and Wear Resource Centre, 1979?

1888   Stewart, A. *Housing action in an industrial suburb.* London, Academic Press, 1981.
Tenants' ambitions towards owner occupation and improved housing conditions in Saltley, Birmingham.

1889   Townsend P. *Poverty in the United Kingdom: a survey of household resources and standards of living.* London, Penguin, 1979.
Ch. 13 'Deprivation in housing' (pp. 476–528).

1890   Tunnard, J. and Whately, C. *Rights guide for home owners.* 5th ed. London, Child Poverty Action Group/SHAC, 1985.
Valuable guide for low income owner occupiers.

1891   United Kingdom, Central Policy Review Staff. *Housing and social policies.* London, HMSO, 1978.

Relationships between housing and DHSS, education, health, police and employment.

1892 United Kingdom, Central Policy Review Staff. *Vandalism.* London, HMSO, 1978.
Recommendations for design features on estates to combat vandalism with local case studies.

1893 United Kingdom, Committee on Local Authority and Allied Personal Social Services. *Report of the committee on local authority and allied personal social services.* London, HMSO, 1968. (Cmnd. 3703).
The Seebohm report, which recommended the formation of housing advice centres and the importance of social need in allocation of housing.

1894 United Kingdom Department of the Environment. *The estate outside the dwelling. Reactions of residents to aspects of housing layout.* London, HMSO, 1972. (Design bulletin 25).

1895 United Kingdom, Department of the Environment, Housing Development Directorate. *Getting tenants involved: a handbook on systems for tenant participation in housing management.* London, The Department, 1977. (Occasional paper 2/77).

1896 United Kingdom, Department of the Environment, Housing Development Directorate. *Reducing vandalism on public housing estates.* London, HMSO, 1981. (Occasional paper 1/81).

1897 United Kingdom, Department of the Environment, Housing Development Directorate. *A survey of tenants' attitudes to recently completed estates.* London, HMSO, 1981. (Occasional paper 2/81).

1898 United Kingdom, Department of the Environment, Housing Development Directorate. *Tenant participation in council housing management.* London, The Department, 1977. (Occasional paper 2/77).

1899 United Kingdom, Department of the Environment, Housing Services Advisory Group. *Tenancy agreements.* London, The Department, 1977.

1900 United Kingdom, Scottish Development Department. *Housing and social work: a joint approach.* Edinburgh, HMSO, 1975.
The Morris report, which recommended that housing welfare work should properly be part of a social work department.

1901 United Kingdom, Scottish Housing Advisory Committee. *Council house communities: a policy for progress.* Edinburgh, HMSO, 1970.
Report of the Subcommittee on Amenity and Social Character of Local Authority Housing Schemes.

1902 Ward, C. *Tenants take over.* London, Architectural Press, 1974.
Tenants should directly control their own housing, especially council estates, through co-operatives.

1903 Ward, C. *Vandalism.* London, Architectural Press, 1973.

1904 White, J. *Rothschild Buildings: life in an east end tenement block 1887–1920.* London, Routledge and Kegan Paul, 1981.
First hand account of life in philanthropic housing.

1905 Wilkinson, R. K. and Talbot, V. 'An investigation of the attitudes of re-housed families from slums and twilight areas in Batley, Leeds and York'. *Social and Economic Administration* vol. 5 no. 4 (Oct. 1971) pp. 236–62.

1906 Wilson, R. *Difficult housing estates.* London, Tavistock, 1963.
Early sociological study of a troubled housing estate.

1907 Wohl, A. S. *The eternal slum: housing and social policy in Victorian London.* London, Edward Arnold, 1977.

1908 Wordsall, F. *The tenement, a way of life: a social, historical and architectural study of housing in Glasgow.* Edinburgh, Chambers, 1979.

1909 Young, M. and Willmott, P. *Family and kinship in East London.* London, Routledge and Kegan Paul, 1957.

Social life and attitudes in a redeveloped area of East London.

12.4 North America

1910 American Public Health Association. *Planning the neighborhood.* Chicago, The Association, 1948.

1911 Atlas, J. and Dreier, P. 'The housing crisis and the tenants' revolt'. *Social Policy* vol. 10 no. 4 (Jan.–Feb. 1980) pp. 13–24.
Tenant consciousness and the potential for tenants' organizations in the US.

1912 Baar, K. 'Rent control in the 1970s: the case of the New Jersey tenants' movement'. *Hastings Law Journal* vol. 28 (1977) pp. 631–83.

1913 Baldwin, P. 'How small grants make a difference'. *Ekistics* vol. 48 no. 287 (Mar.–Apr. 1981) pp. 108–11.
Tenant involvement in decision making in the US.

1914 Beyer, G. H. *Housing and society.* New York, Macmillan, 1965.
Economic and social aspects of housing.

1915 Birenbaum, R. 'Crime prevention through environmental design'. *Habitat* vol. 26 no. 2 (1983) pp. 2–8.
New environmental design and management approach to crime prevention in residential areas in Canada based on defensible space.

1916 Booth, A. *Urban crowding and its consequences.* New York, Praeger, 1976.
Research in Toronto: conclusion that overcrowding has little social effect.

1917 Burghart, S. (ed.) *Tenants and the urban housing crisis.* Dexter, Mich., New Press, 1972.

1918 Case, F. E. and Gale, J. *Environmental impact review and housing: process lessons from the California experience.* New York, Praeger, 1982.

1919   Downs, A. *Neighborhoods and urban development.* Washington, DC, Brookings Institution, 1982.

1920   Downs, A. *Opening up the suburbs.* Yale University Press, 1973.

1921   Dreier, P. 'The tenants' movement in the United States'. *International Journal of Urban and Regional Research* vol. 8 no. 2 (1984) pp. 255–79.

1922   Eager, R. C. and Hyatt, W. S. 'Neighborhood revival through community associations'. *Urban Land* vol. 37 no. 9 (Oct. 1978) pp. 4–11.

1923   Fallis, G. *Housing programs and income distribution in Canada.* University of Toronto Press, 1980. (Ontario Economic Council research studies).

1924   Gans, H. J. *The Levittowners: ways of life and politics in a suburban community.* New York, Random House, 1967.

1925   Goetze, R. *Building neighborhood confidence: a humanistic strategy for urban housing.* Cambridge, Mass., Ballinger, 1976.

1926   Goliger, G. 'The changing Canadian suburb'. *Habitat* vol. 26 no. 2 (1983) pp. 20–3.
How the Canadian suburb is changing and adapting.

1927   Gulati, P. 'Consumer participation in administrative decision making'. *Social Service Review* vol. 56 (Mar. 1982) pp. 72–84.
Report of a HUD survey into the impact of tenant participation in 750 public housing projects in the US.

1928   Healy, R. G. 'Effects of improved housing on worker performance'. *Journal of Human Resources* vol. 6 (1971) pp. 297–308.

1929   Heskin, A. 'The history of tenants in the United States, struggle and ideology'. *International Journal of Urban and Regional Research* vol. 5 no. 2 (1981) pp. 178–203.

1930   Heskin, A. D. *Tenants and the American dream: ideology and the tenant movement.* New York, Praeger, 1983.
Tenant attitudes in California and trends towards political organization.

1931   Holleb, D. B. 'A decent home and suitable living environment'. *Ekistics* vol. 46 no. 275 (Mar.–Apr. 1979) pp. 106–9.
Housing deprivation in the US.

1932   Holleb, D. B. 'Housing and the environment: shooting at moving targets'. *Annals of the American Academy of Political and Social Science* vol. 453 (Jan. 1981) pp. 180–221.

1933   Hovinen, G. R. 'Leapfrog developments in Lancaster county: a study of residents' perceptions and attitudes'. *Professional Geographer* vol. 29 no. 2 (May 1977) pp. 194–9.
Residents' attitudes to urban sprawl caused by leapfrog development.

1934   Hoyt, H. *The structure and growth of residential neighborhoods in American cities.* Washington, DC, Government Printing Office, 1939.

1935   Kalt, N. C. and Zalkind, S. S. *Urban problems: psychological inquiries readings and text.* New York, Oxford University Press, 1976.
'Housing' (pp. 143–203) contains five readings on social aspects of housing in American cities.

1936   Lawson, R. 'Tenant mobilization in New York'. *Social Policy* vol. 10 no. 5 (Mar.–Apr. 1980) pp. 30–40.
Work of the New York State Tenants Coalition in uniting neighbourhood tenants' organizations and relations with the government.

1937   Le Gates, R. T. and Murphy, K. 'Austerity, shelter and social conflict in the United States'. *International Journal of Urban and Regional Research* vol. 5 (June 1981) pp. 255–74.
Effects of fiscal crisis on US housing policy and which groups will be most affected.

221

1938 Lindamood, S. and Hanna, S. D. *Housing, society and consumers: an introduction.* St. Paul, West Publishing Co., 1980.

1939 Lipsky, M. *Protest in city politics: rent strikes, housing and the power of the poor.* Chicago, Rand McNally, 1970.

1940 Lynch, K. *Image of the city.* Cambridge, Mass., MIT Press and Harvard University Press, 1960.
Social aspects of city life.

1941 Merry, S. E. 'Defensible space undefended: social factors in crime control through environmental design'. *Urban Affairs Quarterly* vol. 16 no. 4 (June 1981) pp. 397–422.

1942 Morris, E. W. and Winter, M. *Housing, family and society.* New York, Wiley, 1978.

1943 Newman, O. *Community of interest.* Garden City, Anchor Press, 1980.
Discussion of creation of small community housing developments in cities through physical design and social mix.

1944 Newman, O. and Franck, K. A. *Factors influencing crime and instability in urban housing developments.* Washington, DC, National Institute of Justice, 1980.

1945 Onibukon, A. G. 'Social system correlates of residential satisfaction'. *Environment and Behavior* vol. 8 (Sept. 1976) pp. 323–44.
Influences of social characteristics on residential satisfaction: research in Canada.

1946 Rein, M. *Welfare and housing.* Cambridge, Mass., MIT Press and Harvard University Press, 1972.

1947 Rouse, W. V. and Rubenstein, H. *Crime in public housing: a review of major issues and selected crime reduction strategies.* 2 vols. Washington, DC, Department of Housing and Urban Development, 1979.
Volume 1: report and volume 2: a review of two conferences and an annotated bibliography.

1948 Saltman, J. *Open housing: dynamics of a social movement.* New York, Praeger, 1978. (Praeger special studies).
Includes an analysis of the activities of a fair housing group in Akron, Ohio.

1949 Schoor, A. L. *Slums and social insecurity.* Washington, DC, Government Printing Office, 1963.

1950 Smith, R. T. *Welfare reform and housing assistance.* New York, Rand Corporation, 1979.

1951 Smith, W. F. *Housing: the social and economic elements.* Los Angeles, University of California Press, 1970. (Studies in urbanization and environmental design).

1952 Sternlieb, G. and Hughes, J. W. 'The evolution of housing and its social compact'. *Urban Land* vol. 41 no. 12 (Dec. 1982) pp. 17–20.
Social history of housing and need to find less costly forms.

1953 United States, Department of Housing and Urban Development. *Housing our families.* Washington, DC, Government Printing Office, 1980.

1954 United States, Department of Housing and Urban Development. *The manager and social service: vol. 1, participant's workbook; vol. 2, instructor's manual.* Washington, DC, The Department, 1980.

1955 United States, Department of Housing and Urban Development. *Resident participation in the housing management process: vol. 1, participant's workbook; vol. 2, instructor's guide.* Washington, DC, The Department, 1980.

1956 Varady, D. P. 'Indirect benefits of subsidized housing programs'. *Journal of the American Planning Association* vol. 48 no.4 (Autumn 1982) pp. 432–40.
Little evidence of neighbourhood benefits from housing programmes.

1957 Wilbur, D. E. *Housing expectations and realities.* Birmingham, Ala., Gryphon House, 1971.

1958   Wilner, D. M. et al. *The housing environment and family life.* Baltimore, Johns Hopkins University Press, 1962.

1959   Wright, G. *Building the dream: a social history of housing in America.* Cambridge, Mass., MIT Press, 1983.

12.5   Australasia

1960   Australia, Commission of Enquiry into Poverty in Australia. *Poverty in Australia: first main report of the commission.* Canberra, The Commission, 1975.
   The Henderson report.

1961   Davey, J. A. *Social factors and housing need in New Zealand.* Wellington, New Zealand National Housing Commission, 1977. (Research paper 1/77).

1962   Easton, B. *Social policy and the welfare state in New Zealand.* Sydney, Allen and Unwin, 1980.

1963   Milligan, V. 'The state of housing: questions of social policy and social change'. In A. Greycar (ed.) *Retreat from the welfare state.* Sydney, Allen and Unwin, 1983.

12.6   Africa, Asia and Latin America

1964   Bryant, C. 'Squatters, collective action and participation: learning from Lusaka'. *World Development* vol. 8 no. 1 (Jan. 1980) pp. 73–86.

1965   Butterworth, D. C. *The people of Buena Ventura: relocation of slum dwellers in post-revolutionary Cuba.* Urbana, University of Illinois Press, 1980.

1966   Casasco, J. A. 'The social function of the slum in Latin America: some positive aspects'. *America Latina* vol. 87 (1969) pp. 87–112.

1967   Castells, M. 'Squatters and politics in Latin America: a comparative analysis of urban social movements in Chile, Peru and Mexico'. In H. I. Safa (ed.) *Towards a political economy of urbanization in Third World countries.* Oxford University Press, 1982.

1968   Dias, H. D. *The legal framework for public participation in the management of human settlements in Thailand.* Bangkok, Asian Institute of Technology, Division of Human Settlements Development, 1981. (Working paper 7).

1969   Dwyer, D. J. 'Attitudes towards spontaneous settlement in Third World countries'. In D. J. Dwyer (ed.) *The city as a centre of change in Asia.* University of Hong Kong Press, 1972. pp. 168–78.

1970   Finlayson, K. A. 'The role of community involvement in low-income housing'. *ITCC Review* vol. 9 no. 1 (Jan. 1980) pp. 44–60.
    Public participation in low income housing in South Africa.

1971   Gilbert, A. G. and Ward, P. 'Community action by the urban poor: democratic involvement, community self help or a means of social control'. *World Development* vol. 12 no. 8 (Aug. 1984) pp. 769–82.
    First of 2 articles to examine popular participation in squatter upgrading in 3 Latin American cities.

1972   Gilbert, A. and Ward, P. 'Community participation in upgrading irregular settlements: the community response'. *World Development* vol. 12 no. 9 (Sept. 1984) pp. 913–22.
    Community involvement in improving squatter settlements in Bogotá, Mexico City and Valencia (Venezuela).

1973   Hassan, R. *Families in flats: a study of low-income families in public housing.* Singapore University Press, 1977.
    The life of over 400 low income families in public housing estates in Singapore.

1974   'Housing policies part 2: tenants' reactions to government projects'. *Ekistics* vol. 48 no. 287 (Mar.–Apr. 1982) pp. 95–176.
    Special issue containing several articles.

1975   Leeds, A. 'Housing settlement types, arrangements for living, proletarianization and the social structure of the city'. In J.

Abu-Lughod and R. Hay (eds.) *Third World urbanization*. Chicago, Maaroufa Press, 1977. pp. 330–7.

1976   Leeds, A. and Leeds, E. 'Accounting for behavioral differences: three political systems and the responses of squatters in Brazil, Peru and Chile'. In L. Walton and L. H. Masotti (eds.) *The city in comparative perspective*. New York, Wiley, 1976. pp. 193–248.

1977   Lobo, S. *A house of my own: social organization in the squatter settlements of Lima, Peru*. Tucson, University of Arizona Press, 1982.

1978   Macpherson, S. *Social policy in the Third World: the social dilemmas of underdevelopment*. Brighton, Wheatsheaf, 1982.
'Urbanisation and housing' (pp. 115–42).

1979   Menezes, L. 'Slums are people'. *Town and Country Planning* vol. 48 no. 4 (July 1979) pp. 121–3.
World Bank programme in Madras aims to improve slums by providing services and accessibility to amenities.

1980   Nishiyama, U. 'Changes in Japanese life style and housing in the past thirty-five years'. *Japan Architect* vol. 56 no. 294 (Oct. 1981) pp. 61–8.

1981   Peil, M. *African urban society*. Chichester, Wiley, 1984.
'Housing' (pp. 279–323).

1982   Perlman, J. E. *The myth of marginality: urban poverty and politics in Rio de Janeiro*. Berkeley, University of California Press, 1976.

1983   Ray, T. F. *The politics of the barrios of Venezuela*. Berkeley, University of Los Angeles Press, 1969.
Political, social behaviour and attitudes of squatters.

1984   Richards, P. J. 'Housing and employment'. *International Labour Review* vol. 118 no. 1 (Jan.–Feb. 1979) pp. 13–26.
Situation in developing countries.

1985   Ross, M. H. *The political integration of urban squatters*. Evan-

ston, Northwestern University Press, 1973. (African urban studies).
Factors affecting community formation in urban squatter areas in the Mathara Valley, Nairobi.

1986 Rubbo, A. 'Cauca Valley, Colombia: changing traditions in housing'. *Ekistics* vol. 43 no. 257 (Apr. 1977) pp. 212–20.
Changing systems of agriculture and housing.

1987 Salua, A.T. 'Toward a reappraisal of social indicators for housing in developing countries'. *Social Indicators Research* vol. 6 (July 1979) pp. 293–9.

1988 Schlyter, A. and Chanda, J. *Bibliography on human settlements with emphasis on households and residential environment — Zambia.* Stockholm, Swedish Council for Building Research, 1982.

1989 Shrivastav, P. P. '"City for the citizen" or "citizen for the city"?' *Habitat International* vol. 6 nos. 1–2 (1982) pp. 197–207.
Housing of the urban poor in Delhi.

1990 Smith, D. L. 'Housing design and family needs in Nairobi-Kenya'. *Ekistics* vol. 48 no. 287 (Mar.–Apr. 1981) pp. 145–51.

1991 Wee, A. 'Some social implications of rehousing programmes in Singapore'. In D. J. Dwyer (ed.) *The city as a centre of change in Asia.* Hong Kong University Press, 1972. pp. 216–30.

1992 Yi, C.-C. 'Urban housing satisfaction in a transitional society: a case study in Taichung, Taiwan'. *Urban Studies* vol. 22 no. 1 (Feb. 1985) pp. 1–12.

13

Homelessness and squatting

The emphasis in this section is on references to the inter-related issues of homelessness, empty property and squatting, and the policy responses made to them. Much of the material cited refers to Third World countries, reflecting the enormous amount of literature published on the problems of squatter settlements in these parts of the world in recent years. That the problem is by no means solved in the industrialized world can, however, be seen by the references to squatting and homelessness in Europe and North America. Reference should also be made to sections 12 'Social aspects' for the responses of popular movements to homelessness; 17 'Housing conditions and standards'; and 18 'Improvement and urban renewal' for sources on poor quality housing and policy responses to it, including references to the effect on the housing stock of redevelopment, clearance and residential upgrading.

13.1 Europe

1993   Anderiesen, G. 'Tanks in the streets: the growing conflict over housing in Amsterdam'. *International Journal for Urban and Regional Research* vol. 5 (Mar. 1981) pp. 83–95.
   Reaction to an organized squatter movement.

1994   Draaisma, J. and Van Hoogstraten, P. 'The squatter movement in Amsterdam'. *International Journal of Urban and Regional Research* vol. 7 no. 3 (1983) pp. 406–16.

1995   Priemus, H. 'Squatters in Amsterdam: urban social movement, urban managers or something else?' *International Journal of Urban and Regional Research* vol. 7 no. 3 (1983) pp. 417–27.

1996   Røe, B. 'Settlements without planning: Athens'. *Ekistics* vol. 46 no. 275 (Mar.–Apr. 1979) pp. 82–100.

1997   Tsalavouta, V. 'Legal aspects of planning for site and services projects in Greece'. *Ekistics* vol. 49 no. 292 (Jan.–Feb. 1982) pp. 48–57.

1998   Williams, A. 'Portugal's illegal housing'. *Planning Outlook* vol. 23 no. 3 (1981) pp. 110–14.
Origins, description and remedies for bairros clandestinos.

13.2   United Kingdom

1999   Advisory Service for Squatters. *Squatters handbook.* 7th ed. London, The Service, 1981.

2000   Arden, A. *The Homeless Persons Act.* London, Legal Action Group, 1982. (Law and practice guide no. 5).

2001   Austerberry, H. et al. *Homeless in London 1971–81.* London School of Economics and Political Science, International Centre for Economics and Related Disciplines, 1984. (Occasional paper no. 4).

2002   Bailey, R. *The homeless and empty houses.* London, Penguin, 1977.
Empty, short life, substandard municipal property could be used by single homeless. Describes establishment of Housing Emergency Office.

2003   Bailey, R. *The squatters.* London, Penguin, 1973.
History of squatting in Britain.

2004   Birkinshaw, P. 'Homelessness and the law — the effects and response to legislation'. *Urban Law and Policy* vol. 5 no. 3 (Sept. 1982) pp. 255–95.

2005   Bone, M. and Mason, V. *Empty housing in England: a report on the 1977 Vacant Property Survey carried out on behalf of the Department of the Environment.* London, HMSO, 1980.

2006   Brandon, D. et al. *The survivors: a study of homeless young newcomers to London and the responses made to them.* London, Routledge and Kegan Paul, 1980.

2007   Campaign for Single Homeless People. *Housing and supplementary benefits: a rights guide for single homeless people, boarders and hostel residents.* London, The Campaign, annual.
Review of benefit regulations for homeless people and their advisers.

2008   Campaign for Single Homeless People. *Single and homeless: the facts.* London, The Campaign, 1983.

2009   Cant, D. H. 'Squatting and private property rights'. *International Journal of Urban and Regional Research* vol. 3 no. 3 (Sept. 1979) pp. 404–17.

2010   Carnwath, R. *A guide to the Housing (Homeless Persons) Act 1977.* Croydon, Knight, 1978.

2011   Chartered Institute of Public Finance and Accountancy. *Homelessness statistics.* London, The Institute, annual.

2012   Conway, J. and Kemp, P. *Bed and breakfast: slum housing of the eighties.* London, SHAC, 1985.

2013   Corden, J. 'Accommodation and homelessness on release from prison'. *British Journal of Social Work* vol. 9 no. 1 (Spring 1979) pp. 75–86.

2014   Digby, P. W. *Hostels and lodgings for single people: a survey of hostels and lodging houses carried out on behalf of the DHSS.* London, HMSO, 1976.
Wide ranging OPCS survey of 700 hostels and interviews with over 2,000 residents.

2015   Drake, M. et al. *Single and homeless.* London, HMSO, 1981.

2016   Drake, M. and Francis, C. *A study of the records of a national referral agency.* London, Department of the Environment, 1982. (Single and homeless working paper no. 1).

2017   Duncan, S. et al. *A home of their own — a survey of rehoused hostel residents.* London, Department of the Environment, 1983.

2018   Duncan, S. and Downey, P. *Settling down: a study of the rehousing of users of DHSS Resettlement Units.* London, HMSO, 1985.
DOE report on the monitoring of the Joint Assessment and Resettlement Team housing initiative.

2019   Fletcher, A. *Homes wasted.* London, Shelter, 1982.
Empty housing.

2020   Franklin, A. *Squatting in England 1969–79: a case study of social conflict in advanced industrial capitalism.* University of Bristol, School for Advanced Urban Studies, 1984. (Working paper no. 37).

2021   Glastonbury, B. *Homeless near a thousand homes.* London, Allen and Unwin, 1971.
Study of the causes of, and provision for, homeless families in South Wales and the West of England.

2022   Goss, S. *Working the Act: the Homeless Persons Act in practice.* London, SHAC, 1983. (Research report 6).

2023   Greve, J. *London's homeless.* Welwyn, Codicote Press, 1964.
One of the earliest works to consider the scale of the homelessness problem in Britain.

2024   Greve, J. et al. *Homelessness in London.* Edinburgh, Scottish Academic Press, 1971.
Causes of homelessness and provisions made for homeless families.

2025   Hoath, D. *Homelessness.* London, Sweet and Maxwell, 1983. (Modern legal studies).

2026 Kearns, K. C. 'Intraurban squatting in London'. *Annals of the Association of American Geographers* vol. 69 no. 4 (Dec. 1979) pp. 589–98.
Squatting fills a gap in an increasingly polarized housing market.

2027 Kearns, K. C. 'Urban squatting: social activism in the housing sector'. *Social Policy* vol. 11 no. 2 (Sept.–Oct. 1980) pp. 21–9.

2028 Kingham, M. *Squatters in London.* London, Shelter, 1977.
Looks at who squats and why.

2029 McIntosh, N. 'Homelessness: four big gaps in the new Act'. *New Society* vol. 46 no. 483 (30 Nov. 1978) pp. 516–18.
Reviews the first year of the Housing (Homeless Persons) Act 1977 and evaluates its success.

2030 Maitra, A. K. 'Dealing with the disadvantaged single homeless: are we doing enough?' *Public Health* vol. 96 no. 3 (May 1982) pp. 141–4.

2031 Morrison, H. 'New system of statistics on homelessness'. *Statistical News* no. 35 (Nov. 1976) pp. 6–9.

2032 Paris, C. and Popplestone, G. *Squatting: a bibliography.* London, Centre for Environmental Studies, 1978.

2033 Partington, M. *The Housing (Homeless Persons) Act 1977.* London, Sweet and Maxwell, 1978.
The Act in context, with background.

2034 Prichard, A. M. *Squatting.* London, Sweet and Maxwell, 1981. (Modern legal studies).

2035 Randall, G. et al. *A place for the family: homeless families in London.* London, SHAC, 1982. (Research report no. 5).

2036 Raynsford, N. 'Homelessness and the implementation of the Housing (Homeless Persons) Act 1977'. *Housing* vol. 14 no. 10 (Oct. 1978) pp. 14–17.

2037   Richards, J. *The Housing (Homeless Persons) Act 1977: a study in policymaking.* University of Bristol, School for Advanced Urban Studies, 1981. (Working paper 22).

2038   Robson, P. W. and Watchman, P. 'The Homeless Person's obstacle race: parts 1 and 2'. *Journal of Social Welfare Law* Jan.–Feb, Mar. 1981 pp. 1–15, 65–82.

2039   SHAC. *Homelessness: prospects for the 1980s.* London, SHAC, 1981. (Policy paper 5).

2040   Shelter. *Another empty home — 7,000 empty houses.* London, Shelter, 1976.

2041   Shelter. *Ordinary people: homeless in the housing crisis.* London, Shelter, 1982.

2042   Smith, P. F. 'The Housing (Homeless Persons) Act 1977 — four years on'. *Journal of Planning and Environment Law* Mar. 1982 pp. 143–57.

2043   United Kingdom, Department of the Environment. *Better use of vacant and under-occupied housing.* London, HMSO, 1977. (Circular 76/77).

2044   United Kingdom, Department of the Environment. *Homelessness.* London, HMSO, 1974. (Circular 18/74).
Proposes that responsibility for homeless people should be with local housing authorities, not social services departments. Preceded the Housing (Homeless Persons) Act 1977.

2045   United Kingdom, Department of the Environment. *The Housing (Homeless Persons) Act 1977.* London, HMSO, 1977. (Circular 90/77).
Guide to the Act.

2046   United Kingdom, Department of the Environment. *Housing (Homeless Persons) Act 1977.* London, HMSO, 1977. (Circular 116/77).
Notes on the code of guidance.

2047   United   Kingdom,   Department   of   the   Environment.
*Housing (Homeless Persons) Act 1977: Code of Guidance (England and
Wales)*. 2nd ed. London, HMSO, 1983.

2048   United   Kingdom,   Department   of   the   Environment,
Housing Services Advisory Group. *Hostels, common lodging houses
and houses in multiple occupation*. London, The Department, 1980.

2049   United   Kingdom,   Department   of   Health   and   Social
Security. *Final report of the working party on homelessness in London*.
London, HMSO, 1972.
   Led to DHSS Circular 37/72, *Homeless single persons in need of
   care and support*.

2050   United   Kingdom,   Department   of   Health   and   Social
Security. *Hostels for young people*. London, HMSO, 1975.

2051   United   Kingdom,   Department   of   Health   and   Social
Security. *Working group on homeless young people*. *Report*. London,
The Department, 1976.

2052   Ward,   C.   *Housing: an   anarchist   approach*.   London,
Freedom Press, 1976.
   Discusses squatting within a critique of the professionalization
   of architecture and planning.

2053   Watchman, P. Q. and Robson, P. *Homelessness and the law*.
Glasgow, Planning Exchange, 1983.

2054   Wates, N. *The battle for Tolmers Square*. London, Routledge
and Kegan Paul, 1976.
   Squatting in London in the mid-1970s.

2055   Wates, N. and Wolmar, C. (eds.) *Squatting: the real story*.
London, Bay Leaf Books, 1980.
   Introduction   to   the   law   and   case   studies   of   successful
   campaigns.

2056   Widdowson, B. *Intentional homelessness*. London, Shelter,
1981.
   Study of how some local authorities have used loopholes in the
   Housing (Homeless Persons) Act 1977.

2057   Women's National Commission. *Homelessness amongst women: report of an ad hoc working group.* London, Cabinet Office, 1983.

2058   Woodward, P. J. and Davidge, E. M. 'Homelessness four years on'. *Journal of Planning and Environment Law* Mar. 1982 pp. 158–67.

13.3   North America

2059   Bahr, H. M. *Skid row.* Oxford University Press, 1973.
Résumé of research on disaffection among single homeless people in the US.

2060   Borgos, S. 'The ACORN squatters' campaign'. *Social Policy* vol. 15 no. 1 (Summer 1984) pp. 17–26.
Account of a squatters' campaign in Philadelphia and how it has affected federal housing policy.

2061   Collin, R. W. 'Homelessness: the policy and the law'. *Urban Lawyer* vol. 16 no. 2 (Spring 1984) pp. 317–29.
Homelessness in the US and the role of the courts.

2062   Fabricant, M. and Epstein, I. 'Legal and welfare rights advocacy: complementary approaches in organising on behalf of the homeless'. *Urban and Social Change Review* vol. 17 no. 1 (Winter 1984) pp. 15–19.
American policy initiatives against homelessness.

2063   Glazer, N. 'The urban dilemma: New York'. *Ekistics* vol. 46 no. 275 (Mar.–Apr. 1979) pp. 72–6.
Problem of abandoned housing in New York.

2064   Kasinitz, P. 'Gentrification and homelessness: the single room occupant and the inner city revival'. *Urban and Social Change Review* vol. 17 no. 1 (Winter 1984) pp. 9–15.
US situation.

2065   Kaufman, N. K. 'Homelessness: a comprehensive policy approach'. *Urban and Social Change Review* vol. 17 no. 1 (Winter 1984) pp. 27–9.

US policy solutions to homelessness.

2066 Morgan, D. J. 'Residential housing abandonment in the United States: the effects on those who remain'. *Environment and Planning A* vol. 12 no. 12 (Dec. 1980) pp. 1343–56.
Abandoned housing has adverse effects on residents remaining in the neighbourhood.

2067 Siegal, H. A. *Outposts of the forgotten: socially terminal people in slum hotels and single room occupancy tenements.* New Brunswick, Transaction Books, 1978.
Study of New York.

2068 Stoner, M.R. 'An analysis of public and private sector provisions for homeless people'. *Urban and Social Change Review* vol. 17 no. 1 (Winter 1984) pp. 3–8.
Homelessness in the US.

2069 United States, Department of Housing and Urban Development. *Abandoned housing research: a compendium.* Washington, DC, Government Printing Office, 1973.

2070 United States, General Accounting Office. *Housing abandonment: a national problem needing new approaches: report to the Congress by the Comptroller General of the United States.* Washington, DC, The Office, 1978.

13.4 Australasia

2071 Australian Capital Territory, Department of Territories and Local Government. *Homelessness: a capital problem. Report of a committee of inquiry into homelessness and inadequate housing in the ACT and surrounding regions.* Canberra, The Department, 1984.

13.5 Africa, Asia and Latin America

2072 Abrams, C. 'Squatting and squatters'. In J. Abu-Lughod and R. Hay (eds.) *Third World urbanization.* Chicago, Maaroufa Press, 1977. pp. 293–9.

2073   Aksoy, S. 'The housing problems of Istanbul and the Gecekondu phenomenon'. *Planning and Administration* vol. 7 no. 1 (Spring 1980) pp. 39–48.
History, role and future of squatter settlements in Istanbul.

2074   Angel, S. and Benjamin, S. 'Seventeen reasons why the squatter problem can't be solved'. *Ekistics* vol. 41 no. 242 (Jan. 1976) pp. 20–6.

2075   Anthony, H. A. *The challenge of squatter settlements, with special reference to the cities of Latin America.* Vancouver, University of British Columbia Press, 1979. (Human settlement issues 3).

2076   Bukhari, M. S. 'Squatting and the use of Islamic law'. *Habitat International* vol. 6 nos. 5–6 (1982) pp. 555–63.

2077   Butterworth, D. 'Squatters or suburbanites? The growth of shanty towns in Oaxaca, Mexico'. In R. Scott (ed.) *Latin American modernization problems: case studies in the crisis of change.* Urbana, University of Illinois Press, 1973. pp. 208–32.

2078   Collier, D. *Squatters and oligarchs.* Baltimore, Johns Hopkins University Press, 1976.

2079   Drakakis-Smith, D. W. 'Slums and squatters in Ankara'. *Town Planning Review* vol. 47 no. 3 (1976) pp. 225–40.

2080   Eke, E. F. 'Changing views on urbanisation, migration and squatters'. *Habitat International* vol. 6 nos. 1–2 (1982) pp. 143–63.
Changing attitudes to squatters in developing countries.

2081   Finlayson, K. A. 'Squatting and the role of informal housing in incremental growth and self-improvement'. *ITCC Review* vol. 7 no. 4 (Oct. 1978) pp. 42–52.

2082   Grose, R. N. *Squatting and the geography of class conflict: limits to housing autonomy in Jamaica.* Ithaca, Cornell University, Program on International Studies in Planning, 1979.

2083   'Housing policies: part 1: positive aspects of squatter settlements'. *Ekistics* vol. 48 no. 286 (Jan.–Feb. 1981) pp. 1–88.

Case studies of Third World squatter settlements.

2084   Johnstone, M. 'The evolution of squatter settlements in peninsular Malaysian cities'. *Journal of Southeast Asian Studies* vol. 12 (1981) pp. 364–80.

2085   Juppenlatz, M. *Cities in transformation: the urban squatter problem of the developing world.* St. Lucia, University of Queensland Press, 1970.

2086   Leeds, A. 'The significant variables determining the character of squatter settlements'. *America Latina* vol. 12 no. 3 (1969) pp. 44–84.

2087   Lloyd, P. *Slums of hope.* London, Penguin, 1979.
Migration processes, shanty town development and attitudes of squatters in Third World cities.

2088   Lloyd, P. *The young towns of Lima.* Cambridge University Press, 1980.
Squatter settlements in Peru.

2089   Mangin, W. 'Latin American squatter settlements: a problem and a solution'. *Latin American Research Review* vol. 2 no. 3 (1967) pp. 65–98.

2090   Mangin, W. (ed.) *Peasants in cities: readings in the anthropology of urbanization.* Boston, Houghton Mifflin, 1970.

2091   Marris, P. 'The meaning of slums and patterns of change'. *International Journal of Urban and Regional Research* vol. 3 (1979) pp. 419–41.

2092   Memon, P. A. 'The growth of low-income settlements: planning response in the Peri urban zone of Nairobi'. *Third World Planning Review* vol. 4 no. 2 (May 1982) pp. 145–58.

2093   Michl, S. 'Urban squatter organisation as a national government tool: the case of Lima, Peru'. In F. Rabinowitz and F. Trueblood (eds.) *Latin American urban research vol. 3.* Beverly Hills, Sage, 1971. pp. 155–78.

2094   Morrish, M. *Squatter settlement in the Third World*. York, Longman Group Resources Unit, 1984.
Written for 16–19 year old geography students; concentrates on squatter growth and development in Lima.

2095   Moser, C. O. N. 'A home of one's own: squatter housing strategies in Guayaquil, Ecuador'. In A. Gilbert (ed.) *Urbanization in contemporary Latin America*. Chichester, Wiley, 1982. pp. 159–90.

2096   Norwood, H. C. 'Squatters compared'. *African Urban Notes* series B no. 2 (1975) pp. 119–32.

2097   Peil, M. 'African squatter settlements: a comparative study'. *Urban Studies* vol. 13 no. 2 (June 1976) pp. 155–66.

2098   Philippines, National Housing Council. 'Squatting and slum dwelling in metropolitan Manila'. *Ekistics* vol. 27 (1969) pp. 29–36.

2099   Poethig, R. P. 'The squatters of Southeast Asia'. *Ekistics* vol. 31 (1971) pp. 121–5.

2100   Portes, A. 'Housing policy, urban poverty and the state: the favelas of Rio de Janeiro 1972–76'. *Latin American Research Review* vol. 14 (1979) pp. 3–24.

2101   Redclift, M. R. 'Squatter settlements in Latin American cities: the response from government'. *Journal of Development Studies* vol. 10 (1973) pp. 92–109.

2102   Sarin, M. 'Urban planning, petty trading and squatter settlements in Chandigarh, India'. In R. Bromley and C. Gerry (eds.) *Casual work and poverty in Third World cities*. Chichester, Wiley, 1979. pp. 133–60.

2103   Sudra, T. 'Mexican shanty towns: costs, benefits and policy options'. *Habitat International* vol. 6 nos. 1–2 (1982) pp. 189–96.

2104   Turner, J. F. C. 'Uncontrolled urban settlements: problems and policies'. In G. Breese (ed.) *The city in newly developing countries: readings on urbanism and urbanization.* Englewood Cliffs, Prentice-Hall, 1972. pp. 507–34.

2105   United Nations, Centre for Human Settlements. *Survey of slum and squatter settlements.* Dublin, Tycooly International, 1982. (Development studies series no. 1).

2106   Van der Linden, J. 'Squatting by organised invasion in Karachi: a new reply to a failing housing policy?' *Third World Planning Review* vol. 4 no. 4 (Nov. 1982) pp. 400–12.

2107   Ward, P. M. 'Intra-city migration to squatter settlements in Mexico City'. *Geoforum* vol. 7 nos. 5–6 (1976) pp. 369–82.

2108   Weisner, T. S. 'Kariobangi: the case history of a squatter resettlement scheme in Kenya'. In W. Arens (ed.) *A century of change in East and Central Africa.* Leiden, Mouton, 1976. pp. 77–97.

14
Special needs

This section is concerned with references to housing provision for groups of people who have been perceived to have special, well-defined housing needs, either through mental or physical disability, age or discrimination. Included, therefore, are works on housing policies for the elderly, disabled, students, single people, single parent families and women. No attempt has been made to divide the section into categories of special need because many of the works referred to are interdisciplinary in nature and refer to more than one category of need. Reference should also be made to sections 11 'Alternative tenures' and 12 'Social aspects'.

14.1 International and comparative

2109 Beyer, G. H. and Nierstrasz, F. H. J. *Housing the aged in western countries*. New York, Elsevier, 1967.

2110 Gillisen, A. *Some aspects of housing and accommodation for the elderly, based on studies in selected overseas countries*. Adelaide, South Australian Housing Trust, 1978.

2111 Heumann, L. and Boldy, D. *Housing for the elderly. Planning and policy formulation in Western Europe and North America*. London, Croom Helm, 1982.

2112 *Housing the aging*. Westport, Conn., Greenwood, 1976.
Reprint of 5th Conference of Aging, University of Michigan, published in 1954.

2113   Klodawsky, F. et al. *Housing and single parents: an overview of the literature*. University of Toronto Press, 1984. (Bibliographic series no. 5).

2114   Lawton, M. P. and Nahemow, L. 'Social science methods for evaluating the quality of housing for the elderly'. *Journal of Architectural Research* vol. 7 no. 1 (Mar. 1979) pp. 5–11.

2115   Rostron, J. 'The physically disabled — an international audit of housing policies'. *Public Health* vol. 98 no. 4 (July 1984) pp. 247–55.
   Assessment of housing policies towards the disabled in Britain, Sweden, Canada and the Netherlands.

2116   Spagnoletti, C. D. *Women and planning: an annotated bibliography*. Adelaide, South Australian Housing Trust, 1977. (Library bibliography no. 20).

2117   Steinfeld, E. 'The place of old age: the meaning of housing for old people'. In J. S. Duncan (ed.) *Housing and identity*. London, Croom Helm, 1981. pp. 198–246.

2118   United Nations, Department of Economic and Social Affairs. *The aging in slums and uncontrolled settlements*. New York, United Nations, 1977.

2119   United Nations, Economic Commission for Europe. *Housing for special groups: proceedings of an international seminar held in The Hague, 8–13 Nov. 1976*. Oxford, Pergamon, 1977?
   Published as a supplement to *Habitat International*.

2120   United States, Department of Housing and Urban Development. *The built environment for the elderly and the handicapped: a selective bibliography*. 2nd ed. Washington, DC, The Department, 1979.
   Selective, partially annotated list of periodical articles and publications since 1970.

2121   United States, Department of Housing and Urban Development. *Children in the built environment: a bibliography*. Washington, DC, The Department, 1979.

2122 World Health Organization. *The effects of the indoor housing climate on the health of the elderly: report of a WHO Working Group, Graz, Austria, 20–24 September 1982.* Copenhagen, The Organization, 1984.

14.2 Europe

2123 Goldenberg, L. *Housing for the elderly: new trends in Europe.* New York, Garland, 1981.

2124 Millard, P. H. 'Services for the elderly, with particular reference to services provided in fifteen European countries'. *World Hospitals* vol. 15 no. 1 (Feb. 1979) pp. 15–68.
Special issue, including housing provision.

2125 Netherlands, Ministry of Housing and Physical Planning. *Special housing needs in the Netherlands.* The Hague, The Ministry, 1976.

2126 Pringle, B. M. 'Housing living arrangements for the elderly: some ideas from northern Europe'. *Journal of Property Management* vol. 44 (Mar.–Apr. 1979) pp. 74–8.

2127 Wiktorin, M. 'Housing policy and disadvantaged groups in Sweden'. *International Journal of Urban and Regional Research* vol. 6 (1982) pp. 246–55.

14.3 United Kingdom

2128 Abrams, M. *Beyond three-score and ten: a first report on a survey of the elderly.* London, Age Concern, 1978.

2129 Age Concern. *Profiles of the elderly: vol. 5, their housing.* London, Age Concern, 1980.

2130 Age Concern and Help the Aged Housing Trust. *Housing for ethnic elders.* London, Age Concern, 1984.
Report of a working party into the housing difficulties of older members of the ethnic minority community.

2131 Aldous, G. *Housing law for the elderly*. London, Oyez Longman, 1982. (Oyez Longman practice notes 72).

2132 Armitage, J. *Barriers: a survey of housing, physical disability and the role of local authorities*. London, Shelter, 1983.

2133 Austerberry, H. and Watson, S. 'A woman's place: a feminist approach to housing in Britain'. *Feminist Review* no. 8 (Summer 1981) pp. 49–62.

2134 Austerberry, H. and Watson, S. *Women on the margins: a study of single women's housing problems*. London, City University, Housing Research Group, 1983.

2135 Binney, V. 'Refuges and housing for battered women'. In J. Pahl (ed.) *Private violence and public policy: the needs of battered women and the response of the public services*. London, Routledge and Kegan Paul, 1985. pp. 166–78.

2136 Binney, V. et al. *Leaving violent men: a study of refuges and housing for battered women*. London, Women's Aid Federation England, 1981.

2137 Borsay, A. 'Housing and the disabled consumer'. *Housing Review* vol. 33 no. 6 (Nov.–Dec. 1984) pp. 247–9.
Results of research into the attitudes of physically disabled people towards their housing.

2138 Brion, M. and Tinker, A. *Women in housing: access and influence*. London, Housing Centre Trust, 1980.

2139 Buckle, J. R. *Work and housing of impaired persons in Great Britain*. London, HMSO, 1971.

2140 Butler, A. et al. *Sheltered housing for the elderly: policy, practice and the consumer*. London, Allen and Unwin, 1983. (National Institute Social Services Library no. 44).
Culmination of years of research at Leeds University.

2141 Bytheway, B. and James, L. *The allocation of sheltered housing: a study of theory, practice and liaison*. University of Swansea, Medical Sociology Research Centre, 1978.

Survey of the attitudes in, and liaison between, the different agencies involved in sheltered housing provision.

2142 Campaign for the Homeless and Rootless. *Access to permanent housing for single people.* London, CHAR/Cyrenians/NACRO, 1980

2143 Campaign for the Homeless and Rootless. *Local housing policies for single people: the CHAR blueprint.* London, The Campaign, 1982.

2144 Campaign for the Homeless and Rootless. *Needs and provision for young single homeless people: a review of information and literature.* London, The Campaign, 1976.

2145 Casey, J. *Your housing in retirement.* London, Age Concern, 1983.

2146 Central Council for the Disabled. 'Interim report of the working party on housing for disabled people'. *Clearing House for Local Authority Social Services Research* no. 6 (1975) pp. 1–72.

2147 Chippindale, A. *Housing for single young people.* University of York, Institute of Advanced Architectural Studies, 1976.

2148 Clark, D. *Sheltered housing for the elderly in Scotland.* Edinburgh, Scottish Federation of Housing Associations, 1981.

2149 Currie, H. *Single initiatives I: a study of single person and special needs housing by housing associations.* Edinburgh, Scottish Council for Single Homeless, 1980.

2150 Currie, H. *Single initiatives II: a discussion paper on planning approval and definition problems in single person housing.* Edinburgh, Scottish Council for Single Homeless, 1980.

2151 Edmonds, J. *Housing for single young people.* University of York, Institute of Advanced Architectural Studies, 1977.

2152 Edmonds, J. et al. *Housing for single young people: cluster dwellings for housing association tenants: a development project using existing buildings.* University of York, Institute of Advanced Architectural Studies, 1981. (Research paper 18).

2153   Etherington, S. *Housing and mental health: a guide for housing workers.* London, Mind and Circle 33, 1983.

2154   Fox, D. 'Housing and the elderly'. In D. Holman (ed.) *The impact of ageing: strategies for care.* London, Croom Helm, 1981. pp. 86–108.

2155   Goldsmith, S. *Designing for the disabled.* 3rd rev. ed. London, Architectural Press, 1984.

2156   Goldsmith, S. *Wheelchair housing.* London, Department of the Environment, 1975. (HDD occasional paper 2/75).

2157   Harris, A. I. et al. *Handicapped and impaired in Great Britain.* London, HMSO, 1971.
OPCS study including discussion of housing problems.

2158   Hawes, D. 'New initiatives in housing the mentally handicapped'. *Housing and Planning Review* vol. 37 no. 4 (Winter 1981) pp. 7–10.

2159   Hearnden, D. *Co-ordinating housing and social services: from good intentions to good practice.* London, Centre for Policy on Ageing, 1984.

2160   Heginbotham, C. *Housing for mentally handicapped people.* London, Centre on Environment for the Handicapped, 1981.

2161   Heginbotham, C. *Housing projects for mentally handicapped people.* London, Centre on Environment for the Handicapped, 1981.

2162   Heumann, L. F. 'The function of different sheltered housing categories for the semi-independent elderly'. *Social Policy and Administration* vol. 15 no. 2 (Summer 1981) pp. 164–80.

2163   Hole, W. V. and Taylor, J. R. B. *The housing needs of single young people and the use of older properties.* Watford, Building Research Establishment, 1978. (Current paper 43/78).

2164 Holmes, C. 'Housing for the single'. *Housing and Planning Review* vol. 39 no. 5 (Oct. 1984) pp. 16–17.
Problems for single people in council housing and owner occupation, and the need for improvement in private rented accommodation.

2165 Hunt, A. *The elderly at home*. London, HMSO, 1978.
OPCS study of people aged 65 and over living in the community in England in 1976.

2166 Hunt, J. and Hoyes, L. *Housing the disabled*. Torfaen Borough Council (with support of Cwmbran Development Corporation), 1980.
Reports a project designed to identify and meet the housing needs of disabled people within Torfaen, Wales.

2167 Ineichen, B. *Mental illness*. Harlow, Longman, 1979. (Social structure of modern Britain series).
Includes survey of literature on mental health in relation to housing, high rise flats and new towns (pp. 33–40).

2168 Institution of Environmental Health Officers. *Housing problems of the elderly owner occupier: a report of a working party*. London, The Institution, 1983.

2169 *Integrating the disabled*. Horsham, National Fund for Research into Crippling Diseases, 1976.
Final report of the working party chaired by Lord Snowdon.

2170 Karn, V. A. *Retiring to the seaside*. London, Routledge and Kegan Paul, 1977.

2171 Knapp, M. R. J. 'The design of residential homes for the elderly: an examination of variations with census data'. *Socio-economic Planning Sciences* vol. 11 no. 4 (1977) pp. 205–12.

2172 Lambert, C. M. *Housing for the elderly: a select list of material in the DOE/DTp Library*. London, Departments of the Environment and Transport Library, 1983. (Bibliography no. 209).

2173 Law, C. M. and Warnes, A. M. 'The changing geography

of the elderly in England and Wales'. *Institute of British Geographers Transactions* vol. 1 no. 4 (1976) pp. 453–71.
The elderly are becoming increasingly concentrated in particular parts, especially the South Coast of England.

2174   Law, C. M. and Warnes, A. M. 'The movement of retired people to seaside resorts: a study of Morecambe and Llandudno'. *Town Planning Review* vol. 44 (1973) pp. 373–90.

2175   Lemon, A. 'Retirement and its effect on small towns: the example of Norfolk and Suffolk'. *Town Planning Review* vol. 44 (1973) pp. 254–62.

2176   Lockhart, T. *Housing adaptions for disabled people.* London, Architectural Press, 1981.

2177   Lomas, S. 'A guide to sources of information on housing for disabled people'. *Housing* vol. 17 no. 10 (Oct. 1981) pp. 18–19.

2178   McDowell, L. 'Students and the 1974 Rent Act'. *Social and Economic Administration* vol. 10 (Spring 1976) pp. 15–31.

2179   McDowell, L. 'Towards an understanding of the gender division of urban space'. *Environment and Planning D* vol. 1 no. 1 (Mar. 1983) pp. 59–72.
Nature of changing relationships can add to the analysis of housing policy in post-war Britain.

2180   *Making space: women and the man-made environment.* London, Pluto Press, 1984.

2181   Malin, N. *Group homes for mentally handicapped people.* London, HMSO, 1983.
DHSS study of various schemes for the housing of the mentally handicapped.

2182   Morgan, D. and McDowell, L. *Patterns of residence: costs and options in student housing.* Guildford, University of Surrey, Society for Research into Higher Education, 1979.

2183   Morton, J. *Ferndale: a caring repair service for elderly home owners.* London, Shelter, 1982.

2184 Murray, J. *Special housing? The role of local authority housing departments in accommodating mentally ill and mentally handicapped people.* London, MIND, 1978.

2185 National Federation of Housing Associations. *Single person shared housing: planning permission and environmental health standards for homes and hostels.* London, The Federation, 1980. (NFHA special project guide no. 4).

2186 Nicholson, J. *Mother and baby homes: a survey of homes for unmarried women.* London, Allen and Unwin, 1968.

2187 Pahl, J. *A refuge for battered women.* London, HMSO, 1978.

2188 Penton, J. and Barlow, A. *A handbook of housing for disabled people.* 2nd ed. London, Royal Association for Disability and Rehabilitation, 1981.

2189 Pomeroy, D. M. 'Housing for handicapped children'. *Housing* vol. 14 no. 8 (Aug. 1978) pp. 15–19.

2190 Prescott-Clarke, P. *Organising house adaptations for disabled people: a research study.* London, HMSO, 1982.
    Report of a study commissioned jointly by the DOE, DHSS and Welsh Office and undertaken by Social and Community Planning Research.

2191 Raper, M. *Housing for single young people: a study related to the demand for existing housing stock.* University of York, Institute of Advanced Architectural Studies, 1974. (Research paper 7).

2192 Ritchie, J. and Keegan, J. *Housing for mentally ill and mentally handicapped people: a research study of housing provision in England and Wales.* London, HMSO, 1983.

2193 Rose, E. A. *Housing for the aged.* Farnborough, Saxon House, 1978.

2194 Rose, E. A. *Housing needs and the elderly.* Aldershot, Gower, 1982.

Case study of a Birmingham suburb, but short and over-priced.

2195 Rose, E. and Bozeat, N. *Communal facilities in sheltered housing.* Aldershot, Gower, 1980.

2196 Rostron, J. 'Housing the physically disabled: a synopsis of government policy and legislation'. *Journal of Planning and Environment Law* (Nov. 1984) pp. 791–3.

2197 Rostron, J. 'Housing the physically handicapped'. *Town and Country Planning* vol. 44 no. 12 (Dec. 1976) pp. 538–41.

2198 Royal Association for Disability and Rehabilitation. *Housing grants and allowances for disabled people: a guide for disabled individuals to assistance with home improvements and housing costs.* London, The Association, 1981.

2199 Royal Association for Disability and Rehabilitation. *Towards a housing policy for disabled people.* London, The Association, 1976.
Report of the results of a two year research study carried out by the Central Council for the Disabled into provision for the disabled by local authorities, new towns, housing associations and the private sector.

2200 Scottish Council for Single Homeless. *Think single: an assessment of the accommodation experiences, needs and preferences of single people.* Edinburgh, The Council, 1981.

2201 Scottish Council on Disability. *Accommodation for disabled people in Scotland: survey of provision, needs and resources.* Edinburgh, The Council, 1978.

2202 Shennan, V. *A home of their own.* London, Souvenir Press Educational and Academic, 1983.
Housing provision for the mentally handicapped, arguing particularly for group homes without resident staff.

2203 Tester, S. *Housing for disabled people.* London, Department of the Environment, 1978. (HDD occasional paper 3/78).

2204   Thompson, C. and West, P. 'The public appeal of sheltered housing'. *Ageing and Society* vol. 4 part 3 (Sept. 1984) pp. 305–26.
Popularity of sheltered housing among a survey of old people in the UK, and policy implications.

2205   Tinker, A. 'The elderly at home: the housing implications of the 1978 study by OPCS'. *Housing Review* vol. 27 no. 5 (Sept.–Oct. 1978) pp. 114–16.

2206   Tinker, A. *Housing the elderly near relatives: moving and other options.* London, Department of the Environment, 1980. (HDD occasional paper 1/80).

2207   Tinker, A. *Staying at home: helping elderly people.* London, HMSO, 1984.

2208   Townsend, P. *The last refuge: a survey of residential institutions and homes for the aged in England and Wales.* London, Routledge and Kegan Paul, 1962.
Early work on the housing problems of old people.

2209   Troop, R. A. 'Housing needs of people in wheelchairs'. *Public Health* vol. 95 no. 1 (Jan. 1981) pp. 48–51.

2210   United Kingdom, Department of the Environment. *Housing for one-parent families.* London, HMSO, 1977. (Circular 78/77).

2211   United Kingdom, Department of the Environment. *Housing for people who are physically handicapped.* London, HMSO, 1974. (Joint circular 74/74).

2212   United Kingdom, Department of the Environment. *Housing for single working people: standards and costs.* London, HMSO, 1976. (Circular 12/76).

2213   United Kingdom, Department of the Environment. *Housing initiatives for single people of working age.* London, The Department, 1982.

2214 United Kingdom, Department of the Environment. *Report on a survey of housing for old people provided by local authorities and housing associations in England and Wales.* London, The Department, 1980.
Based on two reports prepared for the DOE by the Social Services Building Research Team, Oxford Polytechnic.

2215 United Kingdom, Department of the Environment, Housing Development Directorate. *Housing single people 1.* London, The Department, 1971. (Design bulletin 23).

2216 United Kingdom, Department of the Environment, Housing Development Directorate. *Housing single people 2.* London, The Department, 1974. (Design bulletin 29).

2217 United Kingdom, Department of the Environment, Housing Development Directorate. *Housing single people: an appraisal of a purpose-built scheme.* London, The Department, 1979. (Design bulletin 33).

2218 United Kingdom, Department of the Environment, Housing Development Directorate. *Mobility housing.* London, The Department, 1974. (Occasional paper 2/74).

2219 United Kingdom, Department of the Environment, Housing Services Advisory Group. *The housing of one-parent families.* London, The Department, 1978.

2220 United Kingdom, Department of Health and Social Security. *Report of the committee on one-parent families.* London, HMSO, 1974. (Cmnd. 5629).
The Finer report, which made recommendations on housing.

2221 United Kingdom, Scottish Development Department. *Housing for the disabled.* Edinburgh, HMSO, 1979. (Scottish housing handbook 6).

2222 United Kingdom, Scottish Development Department. *Housing for the elderly.* Edinburgh, HMSO, 1980. (Scottish housing handbook 5).

2223   United Kingdom, Scottish Development Department. *Housing for single people, shared accommodation and hostels.* Edinburgh, HMSO, 1984. (Scottish housing handbook 7).

2224   Wirz, H. et al. *Sheltered housing in Scotland — a research report.* Edinburgh, Scottish Office, Central Research Unit, 1982.

14.4   North America

2225   Andreae, A. E. *Senior citizens' housing: locational considerations and social implications.* University of Toronto, Centre for Urban and Community Studies, 1978. (Major report no. 14).

2226   Birch, E. L. 'Woman-made America: the case of early public housing policy'. *American Institute of Planners Journal* vol. 44 no. 2 (Apr. 1978) pp. 130–44.
   Housing reform movement, especially the role of women, leading to the 1937 Wagner-Steagall Act which first saw federal government subsidizing public housing in the US.

2227   Broder, J. N. 'Non profit housing for the elderly in highly urban settings: using a federal housing program to meet urban renewal goals'. *Urban Lawyer* vol. 13 no. 1 (Winter 1981) pp. 107–11.
   The US Department of Housing and Urban Development provides cheap loans to non-profit housing bodies for provision of housing for the elderly.

2228   Burstein, J. 'Housing ownership by low-income families: elderly could pave the way'. *Journal of Housing* vol. 40 no. 4 (July–Aug. 1983) pp. 104–7.
   Use of intermediate housing tenure schemes such as co-operatives and lease purchasing for housing the elderly in the US.

2229   Canada Mortgage and Housing Corporation. *Housing the elderly.* 2nd ed. Ottawa, The Corporation, 1972.

2230   Case, F. D. 'Dormitory architecture influences: patterns of student social relations over time'. *Environment and Behavior* vol. 13 no. 1 (Jan. 1981) pp. 23–41.

Influence of accommodation facilities on student relations.

2231   Castro, M. D. and Savannah, S. D. *Housing for the elderly —
designs, economics, legislation and socio-psychological aspects.* Monticello, Council of Planning Librarians, 1976. (Exchange bibliography no. 1028).

2232   Chellis, R. D. et al. *Congregate housing for older people: a
solution for the 1980s.* Lexington, Mass., Heath, 1982.

2233   Chevan, A. 'Age, housing choice and neighborhood age
structure'. *American Journal of Sociology* vol. 87 no. 5 (Mar. 1982)
pp. 1133–49.
Process by which age segregation occurs in residential areas.

2234   Clarke, C. D. 'Security for elderly public housing tenants'.
Journal of Housing vol. 35 no. 6 (June 1978) pp. 281–3.
Employment by Los Angeles Housing Authority of security
officers to look after elderly residents. Personal contact
important.

2235   Davis, R. H. (ed.) *Housing for the elderly.* Los Angeles,
University of California Press, 1973.

2236   De Vise, P. 'The expanding singles housing market in
Chicago: implications for reviving city neighbourhoods'. *Urbanism Past and Present* no. 9 (Winter 1979–80) pp. 30–9.

2237   Goliger, G. 'Constance Hamilton Co-op: housing by
women for women'. *Habitat* vol. 26 no. 1 (1983) pp. 22–6.
Description of a co-operative in Toronto designed to meet the
housing needs of women.

2238   Goodman, J. L. 'The future's poor: projecting the population eligible for federal housing assistance'. *Socio-economic Planning Sciences* vol. 13 no. 3 (1979) pp. 117–25.
Federal assistance to elderly households in the future.

2239   Green, I. et al. *Housing for the elderly: development and design
process.* New York, Van Nostrand Reinhold, 1975.

2240 Grier, G. W. (ed.) *Housing the aging: research needs.* Washington, DC, Brookings Institution, 1963.

2241 Grier, G. W. and Heifitz, J. *Housing older people: their needs, the federal programs.* Washington, DC, The President's Council on Aging, 1964.

2242 Gutowski, M. and Field, T. *The graying of suburbia.* Washington, DC, Urban Institute, 1979.

2243 Horrobin, P. J. *Housing the elderly.* Boston, Herman Publishing, 1974.

2244 Howell, S. C. *Designing for aging: patterns of use.* Cambridge, Mass., MIT Press, 1980.

2245 Hunter, J. A. *Housing for the visually impaired: research based design.* Madison, University of Wisconsin, Centre for Architecture, 1981.

2246 Huttman, E. D. *Housing and social services for the elderly: social policy trends.* New York, Praeger, 1977. (Praeger special studies in US economic, social and political issues).

2247 Kowal, C. et al. 'Housing needs of single persons'. *Journal of Housing* vol. 33 (June 1976) pp. 277–81.
Situation in three US cities.

2248 Lawton, M. P. 'Housing characteristics and the well-being of elderly tenants in federally assisted housing'. *Journal of Gerontology* vol. 30 (Sept. 1975) pp. 601–7.

2249 Lawton, M. P. *Planning and managing housing for the elderly.* New York, Wiley, 1975.

2250 Lawton, M. P. and Hoover, S. L. (eds.) *Community housing choices for older Americans.* New York, Springer, 1981.
Based on papers at a conference sponsored by the Philadelphia Geriatric Center, Apr. 1978.

2251 Leavitt, J. and Saegert, S. 'Women and abandoned buildings: a feminist approach to housing'. *Social Policy* vol. 15 no. 1 (Summer 1984) pp. 32–9.

Role of women in co-operatives in New York and the Tenant Interim Lease Program.

2252   Malozemoff, I. K. et al. *Housing for the elderly: evaluation of the effectiveness of congregate residences: an urban systems approach.* Boulder, Westview Press, 1978.
Group housing for the elderly in the US.

2253   Manard, B. B. et al. *Better homes for the old.* Lexington, Mass., Heath, 1977.

2254   Mayer, N. S. 'Grants, loans and housing repair for the elderly'. *Journal of the American Planning Association* vol. 47 no. 1 (Jan. 1981) pp. 25–34.
Grants are better than loans to help elderly home owners repair their homes.

2255   Mercer, J. 'Locational consequences of housing policies for the low-income elderly: the case of Vancouver, BC'. In S. M. Golant *Location and environment of the elderly population.* Washington, DC, Winston, 1979.

2256   National Association of Housing and Redevelopment Officials. *Management of public housing for the elderly.* Washington, DC, The Association, 1965.

2257   Parker, R. E. 'The future of elderly housing'. *Journal of Property Management* vol. 49 no. 3 (May–June 1984) pp. 12–16.
Implications of the changing needs for low cost housing for the elderly, mainly in the US.

2258   Parker, R. E. *Housing for the elderly: the handbook for managers.* Chicago, Institute of Real Estate Management, 1984. (Institute of Real Estate Management monographs: series on specific property types).

2259   Rabizadeh, M. *Housing for the elderly.* Eugene, University of Oregon Books, 1982.

2260   Raschko, B. B. *Housing interiors for the disabled and elderly.* New York, Van Nostrand Reinhold, 1982.

2261 Reizenstein, J. E. and Ostrander, E. R. 'Design for independence: housing for the severely disabled'. *Environment and Behavior* vol. 13 no. 5 (Sept. 1981) pp. 633–47.
Flats for the severely disabled built by non-profit organizations in the US.

2262 Rose, A. and MacDonald, J. G. *Factors influencing the quality of life of community-based elderly: housing conditions of the elderly in Ontario.* 2 vols. University of Toronto Press, 1984.

2263 Samuelson, D. S. 'Accommodating the graying of America: a competitive viewpoint'. *Urban Land* vol. 40 no. 1 (Jan. 1981) pp. 4–10.
Problems of housing the US's growing elderly population.

2264 Schmertz, M. F 'Housing and community design for changing family needs'. *Architectural Record* no. 10 (Oct. 1979) pp. 97–104.
Changing family patterns and housing requirements of women in the US.

2265 Scholen, K. and Yung-Ping, C. (eds.) *Unlocking home equity for the elderly.* Cambridge, Mass., Ballinger, 1980.
Means by which elderly home owners can continue to live in their homes, based on using their equity.

2266 Shilling, B. A. *Exclusionary zoning: restrictive definitions of family: an annotated bibliography.* Chicago, Council of Planning Librarians, 1980. (CPL bibliography no. 31)
Regulation of housing for non-traditional households in the US and Canada.

2267 Silverman, J. A. 'Housing the still-independent if not so active elderly'. *Housing* (New York) vol. 60 no. 5 (Nov. 1981) pp. 64–9.

2268 Skinner, A. J. 'Women consumers: women professionals: their roles and problems in housing and community development are concerns of special HUD office'. *Journal of Housing* vol. 35 (May 1978) pp. 228–30.

2269 Smart, E. J. (ed.) *Housing for a maturing population*. Washington, DC, Urban Land Institute, 1983.

2270 Smith, B. and Hiltner, J. 'Multifactor uniform areas of elderly housing'. *Professional Geographer* vol. 29 no. 4 (Nov. 1977) pp. 366–73.
Variations in housing elderly population between US states.

2271 Spaeth, D. A. *Housing for the elderly: a selected bibliography*. Monticello, Vance Bibliographies, 1980. (Architecture series bibliography no. A-308).

2272 Struyk, R. J. and Soldo, B. J. *Improving the elderly's housing: a key to preserving the nation's housing stock and neighborhoods*. Cambridge, Mass., Ballinger, 1980.
Outline of alternatives to US government housing programmes for the elderly.

2273 'Symposium on housing policy'. *The Gerontologist* vol. 25 no. 1 (Feb. 1985) pp. 30–46.
Four articles on housing for older US citizens.

2274 United States, Department of Housing and Urban Development. *An evaluation of housing for the severely disabled: in the context of a service delivery system: a report*. Washington, DC, The Department, 1979.
Evaluation of a development in Columbus, Ohio.

2275 United States, Department of Housing and Urban Development. *Housing for the elderly and handicapped: the experience of the section 202 program from 1959 to 1977*. Washington, DC, The Department, 1979.
First evaluation of the programme established under the Housing Act 1959.

2276 United States, Department of Housing and Urban Development. *Management of congregate housing: a HUD guide*. Washington, DC, Government Printing Office, 1972.

2277 United States, Department of Housing and Urban Development. *Management of housing for the elderly: a HUD guide*. Washington, DC, Government Printing Office, 1972.

2278   United States, Department of Housing and Urban Development. *Minimum housing standards for the elderly.* Washington, DC, Government Printing Office, 1966.

2279   United States, Department of Housing and Urban Development. *US housing developments for the elderly or handicapped.* Washington, DC, The Department, 1979.

2280   United States, Department of Housing and Urban Development. *Women and housing: a report on sex discrimination in five American cities.* Washington, DC, The Department, 1976.
Prepared by the National Council of Negro Women, containing evidence from St. Louis, Atlanta, San Francisco, New York and San Antonio.

2281   United States, Department of Housing and Urban Development. *Women in the mortgage market.* Washington, DC, The Department, 1976.

2282   United States, General Accounting Office. *Weaknesses in the planning and utilization of rental housing for persons in wheelchairs: report to Congress.* Washington, DC, The Office, 1981.

2283   United States, House, Committee on Aging, Subcommittee on Housing and Consumer Interests. *Elderly housing overview: HUD's inaction: report.* Washington, DC, Government Printing Office, 1976.

2284   United States, House, Select Committee on Aging, Subcommittee on Housing and Consumer Interests. *Congregate housing services.* Washington, DC, Government Printing Office, 1981.
Federally funded services for the elderly living in public housing.

2285   United States, House, Select Committee on Aging, Subcommittee on Housing and Consumer Interests. *Housing the elderly: present problems and future considerations.* Washington, DC, Government Printing Office, 1981.

2286   United States, Senate, Special Committee on Aging.

Adequacy of federal response to housing. Washington, DC, Government Printing Office, 1971.
Hearing before the Subcommittee on Housing for the Aging.

2287 United States, Senate, Special Committee on Aging. *Housing problems of the elderly.* Washington, DC, Government Printing Office, 1964.

2288 Varady, D. P. 'Housing problems and mobility plans among the elderly'. *Journal of the American Planning Association* vol. 46 no. 3 (July 1980) pp. 301–14.
Factors in residential mobility among the elderly.

2289 Varady, D.P. and Sutton, B. 'The utilization of housing cost assistance and social service programs by the community resident elderly'. *Journal of the American Planning Association* vol. 47 no. 4 (Oct. 1982) pp. 421–33.
Factors influencing participation by the elderly in housing programmes in Cincinnati.

2290 Volgeslang, F. *Training needs in managing housing for the elderly.* Washington, DC, National Association of Housing and Redevelopment Officials, 1968.

2291 Welfeld, I. and Struyk, R. J. *Housing options for the elderly.* Washington, DC, Department of Housing and Urban Development, 1979. (Occasional papers in housing and community affairs vol. 3).

2292 White House Conference on Aging. *Housing.* Washington, DC, Government Printing Office, 1971.

2293 Zais, J. P. et al. *Housing assistance for older Americans: the Reagan prescription.* Washington, DC, Urban Institute, 1982. (Changing domestic priorities series).

2294 Zais, J. and Thisbodeau, T. *The elderly and urban housing.* Baltimore, Urban Institute Press, 1983.
Effects of inner city housing rehabilitation on the elderly in US cities.

14.5 Australasia

2295 Allport, C. 'Women and suburban housing: post-war planning in Sydney 1943–61'. In P. Williams (ed.) *Social process and the city.* Sydney, Allen & Unwin, 1983. pp. 64–87.

2296 Davey, J. A. *Special housing needs in New Zealand.* Wellington, New Zealand National Housing Commission, 1980. (Research paper 80/2).

2297 Davey, J. A. and Barrington, R. *Special housing needs in New Zealand: an overview of the housing situation of minority groups.* Wellington, New Zealand National Housing Commission, 1979.

2298 Hancock, L. and Burke, T. *Youth housing policy.* Canberra, Australian Housing Research Council, 1983.
Youth accommodation problems in Australia, supply and demand.

2299 Kendig, H. 'The culmination of inequality: housing costs and income support in old age'. *Australian Journal of Ageing* vol. 3 part 1 (1984) pp. 8–15.
Australian policies towards housing for the aged and recommendations for action.

2300 Kendig, H. 'Housing and living arrangements'. In A. Howe (ed.) *Towards an older Australia: readings in social gerontology.* St. Lucia, University of Queensland Press, 1981. pp. 84–101.
Housing the aged in Australia.

2301 Lee, T. 'Public housing, relocation and dislocation: a case study of one-parent families in Hobart, Tasmania'. *Town Planning Review* vol. 49 no. 1 (Jan. 1978) pp. 84–92.
Rehousing of fatherless families in Hobart.

2302 Lee, T. R. 'Single parents need social mix'. *Royal Australian Planning Institute Journal* vol. 15 no. 3 (Aug. 1977) pp. 91–3.
Views of single female parents in the Hobart area of Australia.

2303 Milne, P. *Housing single parent families: a problem on the increase.* Adelaide, South Australia Housing Trust, 1976.

Examines the situation of single parent families in South
Australia and their housing requirements.

15

Race and housing

Continuing on from the previous section with the theme of discrimination in housing provision and the evolution of policies to ensure equal opportunities in access to adequate housing, this section examines the vexed theme of race in housing. References are included on racial discrimination in housing issues such as allocation, mortgage lending, segregation and residential location. Much of the literature deals with racial problems in industrialized societies because little has so far been written on problems of racial discrimination in developing countries.

15.1   International and comparative

2304   McKay, D. H. *Housing and race in industrial society.* London, Croom Helm, 1977.
   Comparative study of UK and US.

15.2   Europe

2305   Blanc, M. 'Immigrant housing in France: from hovel to hostel to low cost flats'. *New Community* vol. 11 no. 3 (Spring 1984) pp. 225–34.

2306   Kunst, F. (ed.) *Housing and labour immigrants: problems and policies in West German metropolitan areas.* Berlin Technical University, 1982. (Working paper 21).

Papers from a conference on integration of immigrants and housing problems. English text.

15.3   United Kingdom

2307   Akinsanya, J. and Dada, L. *A bibliography of race and race relations*. London, New Dimension Publications, 1984.
Contains over 4,500 sources on the British race situation: includes a section on housing.

2308   Banton, M. 'Two theories of racial discrimination in housing'. *Ethnic and Racial Studies* vol. 2 no. 4 (Oct. 1979) pp. 416–27.

2309   Burney, E. *Housing on trial*. Oxford University Press, 1967.
Examination of local authority allocation policies.

2310   Cater, J. 'The impact of Asian estate agents on patterns of ethnic residence: a case study of Bradford'. In P. Jackson and S. J. Smith (eds.) *Social interaction and ethnic segregation*. London, Academic Press, 1981. pp. 163–83.

2311   City University. *Housing work in multi-racial areas: a review of training approaches and resources*. London, The University, 1980.

2312   Commission for Racial Equality. *Local authorities and the housing implications of section 71 of the Race Relations Act 1976*. London,The Commission, 1980.

2313   Commission for Racial Equality. *Race and housing in Liverpool: a research report*. London, The Commission, 1984.

2314   Commission for Racial Equality. *Race relations in Britain: a register of current research*. 2nd ed. London, The Commission, 1983.

2315   Commission for Racial Equality. *Racial harassment on local authority housing estates*. London, The Commission, 1981.

2316   Davies, J. *Asian housing in Britain*. London, Social Affairs Unit, 1985.
Discrimination in housing has been exaggerated. Critique of no. 2342.

2317   Duncan, S. S. *Housing disadvantage and residential mobility (immigrants and institutions in a northern town)*. Brighton, University of Sussex, 1977. (Urban and regional studies no. 5).

2318   Fields, S. et al. *Ethnic minorities in Britain: a study of trends in their position since 1961*. London, HMSO, 1981. (Home Office research study no. 68).

2319   Flett, H. *Council housing and the location of ethnic minorities*. Birmingham, University of Aston, SSRC Research Unit on Ethnic Relations, 1977. (Working paper on ethnic relations no. 5).
Study in Manchester.

2320   Flett, H. 'Dispersal policies in council housing: arguments and evidence'. *New Community* vol. 7 no. 2 (Summer 1979) pp. 184–93.

2321   Flett, H. et al. 'The practice of racial dispersal in Birmingham 1969–1975'. *Journal of Social Policy* vol. 8 no. 3 (July 1979) pp. 289–309.
Racial dispersal in public housing in Birmingham.

2322   Gallagher, P. *The role of housing policy advisers*. London, Commission for Racial Equality, 1981.

2323   Haddon, R. 'A minority in a welfare state society: the location of West Indians in the London housing market'. *New Atlantis* vol. 2 no. 1 (1970) pp. 80–133.
Critique of the theory of housing classes.

2324   Hann, C. 'Public housing in Hackney'. *New Community* vol. 11 no. 3 (Spring 1984) pp. 249–55.
Reviews CRE report on racial discrimination in housing in the London Borough of Hackney.

2325   Harrison, M. L. and Stevens, L. *Ethnic minorities and the availability of mortgages.* University of Leeds, Department of Social Policy and Administration, 1981. (Social policy research monograph 5).

2326   Henderson, J. and Karn, V. 'Race, class and the allocation of public housing in Britain'. *Urban Studies* vol. 21 no. 2 (May 1984) pp. 115–28.
   Uses survey data to argue that racial discrimination is built into the allocation practices of local authority housing departments.

2327   Ineichen, B. 'Ethnic variation in housing decision making and attitudes to property in early marriage'. *Plural Societies* vol. 9 no. 4 (1978) pp. 23–34.

2328   Karn, V. A. 'The financing of owner-occupation and its impact on ethnic minorities'. *New Community* vol. 6 nos. 1–2 (Winter 1977–8) pp. 49–65.

2329   Karn, V. 'Race and housing in Britain: the role of major institutions'. In K. Young and N. Glazer (eds.) *Ethnic pluralism and public policy.* London, Heinemann, 1983.

2330   Kornalijnslijper, N. and Ward, R. *The housing position and residential distribution of ethnic minorities in Britain: a bibliography.* Birmingham, SSRC Research Unit on Ethnic Relations, 1982.

2331   Lee, T. R. 'Ethnic and social class factors in residential segregation: some implications for dispersal'. *Environment and Planning* vol. 5 (1973) pp. 477–90.

2332   Lee, T. R. *Race and residence: the concentration and dispersal of immigrants in London.* Oxford University Press, 1977.

2333   London Race and Housing Forum. *Racial harassment on local authority housing estates.* London, Commission for Racial Equality, 1981.

2334   Madan, R. *Coloured minorities in Great Britain: a comprehensive bibliography 1970–77.* London, Aldwych Press, 1979.

Covers housing (pp. 129–36).

2335 Niner, P. 'Housing associations and ethnic minorities'. *New Community* vol. 11 no. 3 (Spring 1984) pp. 238–48.

2336 Parker, J. and Dugmore, K. *Colour and allocation of GLC housing: the report of the GLC lettings survey 1974–75.* Greater London Council, 1976. (Research report 21).

2337 Peach, C. and Shah, S. 'The contribution of council house allocation to West Indian desegregation in London 1961–71'. *Urban Studies* vol. 17 no. 3 (Oct. 1980) pp. 333–41.

2338 Ratcliffe, P. *Racism and reaction: a profile of Handsworth.* London, Routledge and Kegan Paul, 1981. Ch. 4 (pp. 139–99) covers housing.

2339 Rex, J. 'The concept of housing class and the sociology of race relations'. *Race* vol. 12 (1971) pp. 293–301.

2340 Rex, J. *Race, colonialism and the city.* London, Routledge and Kegan Paul, 1973.

2341 Rex, J. 'Urban segregation and inner city policy in Great Britain'. In C. Peach et al. (eds.) *Ethnic segregation in cities.* London, Croom Helm, 1981. pp. 25–42.

2342 Rex, J. and Moore, R. *Race, community and conflict.* Oxford University Press, 1967.
Develops the theory of housing classes based on housing tenure in which ethnic minorities occupy the lower levels.

2343 Rex, J. and Tomlinson, S. *Colonial immigrants in a British city.* London, Routledge and Kegan Paul, 1979.

2344 Richmond, A. H. *Migration and race relations in an English city.* Oxford University Press, 1973.

2345 Ridoutt, T. 'Ethnic monitoring in housing departments: a necessary beginning'. *New Community* vol. 11 no. 3 (Spring 1984) pp. 234–7.

2346   Robinson, V. 'Contrasts between Asian and white housing choice'. *New Community* vol. 7 no. 2 (Summer 1979) pp. 195–202.

2347   Robinson, V. 'The development of South Asian settlement in Britain and the myth of return'. In C. Peach et al. (eds.) *Ethnic segregation in cities*. London, Croom Helm, 1981. pp. 149–69.

2348   Schwartz, N. H. 'Race and the allocation of public housing in Great Britain: the autonomy of the local state'. *Comparative Politics* vol. 16 no. 2 (Jan. 1984) pp. 205–22.

2349   Schwartz, N. H. 'Race and council housing in Britain: the structure of administration and policy'. *Local Government Studies* vol. 5 no. 6 (Nov.–Dec. 1979) pp. 69–83.

2350   Simmons, I. 'Contrasts in Asian residential segregation'. In P. Jackson and S. J. Smith (eds.) *Social interaction and ethnic segregation*. London, Academic Press, 1981. pp. 81–99.

2351   Smith, D. J. 'The housing of racial minorities: its unusual nature'. *New Community* vol. 6 nos. 1–2 (Winter 1977–8) pp. 18–26.

2352   Smith, D. J. and Whalley, A. *Racial minorities and public housing*. London, Political and Economic Planning, 1975. (Broadsheet 556).
Considers whether housing management procedures of local authorities work against racial minorities.

2353   United Kingdom, Community Relations Commission. *Urban deprivation, racial inequality and social policy*. London, HMSO, 1977.

2354   United Kingdom, Department of the Environment. *Race relations and housing: observations on the report on housing of the Select Committee on Race Relations and Immigration*. London, HMSO, 1975. (Cmnd. 6232).

2355   United Kingdom, House of Commons, Home Affairs Committee. *Racial disadvantage*. London, HMSO, 1981. (Session 1980/81, HC 424).

2356 United Kingdom, House of Commons, Select Committee on Race Relations and Immigration. *Housing: vol. 1, report; vol. 2, appendices.* London, HMSO, 1971 (HC 508, Session 1970/71).

2357 Ward, R. 'Race and housing: issues and policies'. *New Community* vol. 11 no. 3 (Spring 1984) pp. 201–5.

2358 Ward, R. (ed.) *Race and residence in Britain: approaches to differential treatment in housing.* University of Warwick, Research Unit on Ethnic Relations, 1984. (Monographs on ethnic relations 2).

2359 Woods, R. I. 'Ethnic segregation in Birmingham in the 1960s and 1970s'. *Ethnic and Racial Studies* vol. 2 (1979) pp. 455–76.

2360 Woods, R. I. 'Spatiotemporal models of ethnic segregation and their implications for housing policy'. *Environment and Planning A* vol. 13 no. 11 (Nov. 1981) pp. 1415–33.

15.4 North America

2361 Ansley, R. E. *Discrimination in housing.* Chicago, Council of Planning Librarians, 1979. (Bibliography no. 13).

2362 Balakrishnan, T. R. 'Ethnic residential satisfaction in the metropolitan areas of Canada'. *Canadian Journal of Sociology* vol. 1 (1976) pp. 481–98.

2363 Berry, B. J. L. *The open housing question: race and housing in Chicago 1966–1976.* Cambridge, Mass., Ballinger, 1979.

2364 Bianchi, S. M. 'Racial inequalities in housing: an examination of recent trends'. *Demography* vol. 19 (Fall 1982) pp. 37–51.

2365 Bullard, R. D. 'Persistent barriers in housing black Americans'. *Journal of Applied Social Sciences* vol. 7 no. 1 (Fall–Winter 1982–3) pp. 19–31.
Quality of housing among US blacks and restrictions on freedom in the housing market.

2366   Bullard, R. D. and Tryman, D. L. 'Competition for decent housing: a focus on housing discrimination complaints in a sunbelt city'. *Journal of Ethnic Studies* vol. 7 (1980) pp. 51–63.

2367   Cronin, F. 'Racial differences in the search for housing'. In W. Clark (ed.) *Modelling housing market research.* London, Croom Helm, 1982.

2368   Dahmann, D. C. *Housing opportunities for black and white households: three decades of change in the supply of housing.* Washington, DC, Department of Commerce, Bureau of the Census, 1982.

2369   Daniels, C. 'The influence of racial segregation on housing prices'. *Journal of Urban Economics* vol. 2 (1975) pp. 105–22.

2370   Danielson, M. N. *The politics of exclusion.* New York, Columbia University Press, 1976.
Residential segregation in US cities.

2371   Davis, L. G. *Housing in the black community: a selected bibliography of published works on housing laws, problems, planning and covenants in the black community.* Monticello, Council of Planning Librarians, 1975. (Exchange bibliography no. 925).

2372   Farley, J. E. 'Metropolitan housing segregation in 1980: the St. Louis case'. *Urban Affairs Quarterly* vol. 18 (1983) pp. 347–59.

2373   Farley, R. and Colasanto, D. 'Racial residential segregation: is it caused by misinformation about housing costs?' *Social Science Quarterly* vol. 61 (Dec. 1980) pp. 623–37.
Data from Detroit.

2374   Ford, L. and Griffin, E. 'The ghettoization of paradise'. *Geographical Review* vol. 60 no. 2 (Apr. 1979) pp. 140–58.
Detailed examination of factors leading to concentrations of black people in urban areas: study of San Diego.

2375   Forman, E. M. S. 'Ethnic and income housing-occupancy patterns of federal moderate income housing and federal public housing in low and moderate income neighbourhoods of New York City'. *Environment and Planning* vol. 8 no. 6 (1976) pp. 707–14.

2376   Frey, W. H. 'Central city white flight: racial and non-racial causes'. *American Sociological Review* vol. 44 (June 1979) pp. 425–48.
Movement of blacks from US cities to the suburbs.

2377   Galster, G. C. 'A bid-rent analysis of housing market discrimination'. *American Economic Review* vol. 67 no. 2 (Mar. 1977) pp. 144–55.
Survey of housing price discrimination in the US and how it affects non-whites.

2378   Grier, E. and Grier, G. *Privately developed inter-racial housing: an analysis of experience.* Berkeley, University of California Press, 1960.

2379   Haney, R. L. 'Race and housing value: a review of their inter relationship'. *Appraisal Journal* vol. 45 no. 3 (July 1977) pp. 356–64.
Race has significant, but variable, effect on house prices in the US.

2380   Hershkovitz, S. *Spatial segregation trends in cities.* Monticello, Vance Bibliographies, 1981. (Public administration series bibliography P-812).

2381   Hirsch, A. R. *Making the second ghetto: race and housing in Chicago 1940–1960.* Cambridge University Press, 1983.

2382   'Housing discrimination must be dealt with by HUD'. *Journal of Housing* vol. 37 no. 6 (June 1980) pp. 315–22.
How racial discrimination in housing in Chicago should be solved by HUD.

2383   Kain, J. F. and Quigley, J. *Housing markets and racial discrimination.* New York, National Bureau of Economic Research, 1975.

2384   Kantrowitz, N. *Ethnic and racial segregation patterns in the New York City metropolis: residential patterns among white ethnic groups, blacks and Puerto Ricans.* New York, Praeger, 1973. (Special studies in US economic, social and political issues).

2385   King, A. T. and Mieskowski, P. 'Racial discrimination, segregation and price of housing'. *Journal of Political Economy* vol. 81 (1973) pp. 590–606.

2386   Krivo, L. J. 'Housing price inequalities: a comparison of Anglos, blacks and Spanish-origin populations'. *Urban Affairs Quarterly* vol. 17 no. 4 (June 1982) pp. 445–64.
Enquires whether minorities pay more than Anglos for comparable housing in US metropolitan areas.

2387   Kushner, J. A. 'Apartheid in America: an historical and legal analysis of contemporary racial residential segregation in the United States'. *Howard Law Journal* vol. 22 no. 4 (1979) pp. 547–685.

2388   Lake, R. W. 'Changing symptoms, constant causes: recent evolution of fair housing in the United States'. *New Community* vol. 11 no. 3 (Spring 1984) pp. 206–13.

2389   Lake, R. W. 'The Fair Housing Act in a discriminatory market: the persisting dilemma'. *Journal of the American Planning Association* vol. 47 no. 1 (Jan. 1981) pp. 48–58.
The fair housing provisions of the US Civil Rights Act 1968 are insufficient to prevent housing market discrimination against blacks.

2390   Lake, R. W. *The new suburbanites: race and housing in the suburbs.* New Brunswick, Rutgers University, Center for Urban Policy Research, 1981.

2391   Lake, R. W. 'Racial transition and black homeownership in American suburbs'. *Annals of the American Academy of Political and Social Science* vol. 441 (Jan. 1979) pp. 142–56.

2392   Listokin, D. and Casey, S. *Mortgage lending and race: conceptual and analytical perspectives of the urban financing problem.*

New Brunswick, Rutgers University, Center for Urban Policy Research, 1980.

2393 Lopez, M. M. 'Patterns of interethnic residential segregation in the urban Southwest 1960 and 1970'. *Social Science Quarterly* vol. 62 (Mar. 1981) pp. 50–63.

2394 Mann, M. S. *The right to housing: constitutional issues and remedies in exclusionary zoning*. New York, Praeger, 1976. (Praeger special studies in US economic, social and political issues).
Traces the evolution of zoning and the use of law in redress of those discriminated against in housing.

2395 Onderdonk, D. *Interracial housing since 1970: from activism to affirmative marketing*. Chicago, Council of Planning Librarians, 1979. (Bibliography no. 15).

2396 Philpott, T. *The slum and the ghetto*. New York, Oxford University Press, 1978.
Historical study of the formation of ghettoes in US cities.

2397 Polikoff, A. *Housing the poor: the case for heroism*. Chichester, Wiley, 1978.
Background to housing discrimination and ethnic segregation in the US.

2398 Rainwater, L. *Behind ghetto walls: black family life in a federal slum*. Chicago, Aldine Publishing, 1970.

2399 Rich, J. M. 'Municipal boundaries in a discriminatory housing market: an example of racial leapfrogging'. *Urban Studies* vol. 21 part 1 (Feb. 1984) pp. 31–40.
Black settlement away from the central core in Newark, New Jersey.

2400 Ryker, R. E. et al. 'Racial discrimination as a determinant of home improvement loans'. *Urban Studies* vol. 21 no. 2 (May 1984) pp. 177–82.
Racial discrimination in home improvement lending in Memphis, Tennessee.

2401   St. John, C. and Clark, F. 'Racial differences in dimensions of neighborhood satisfaction'. *Social Indicators Research* vol. 15 no. 1 (1984) pp. 43–60.

2402   Saltman, J. 'Housing discrimination: policy research, methods and results'. *Annals of the American Academy of Political and Social Science* vol. 441 (Jan. 1979) pp. 186–96.
Examination of the findings of HUD's housing market practices survey.

2403   Schafer, R. 'Racial discrimination in the Boston housing market'. *Journal of Urban Economics* vol. 6 (Apr. 1979) pp. 176–96.
Differing housing prices in black and white areas.

2404   Schnare, A. *The persistence of racial segregation in housing.* Washington, DC, Urban Institute, 1978.

2405   Schnare, A. *Residential segregation by race in US metropolitan areas.* Washington, DC, Urban Institute, 1977.

2406   Schnare, A. and Struyk, R. 'Segmentation in urban housing markets'. *Journal of Urban Economics* vol. 3 (1976) pp. 146–66.

2407   Schwemm, R. G. 'Compensatory damages in federal fair housing cases'. *Harvard Civil Rights–Civil Liberties Law Review* vol. 16 (Summer 1981) pp. 87–127.
Racial discrimination in US housing.

2408   Schwemm, R. G. *Housing discrimination law.* Washington, DC, BNA Books, 1983.

2409   Siegel, J. A. *Racial discrimination in housing.* Monticello, Council of Planning Librarians, 1977. (Exchange bibliography no. 1201).

2410   Spain, D. 'Black to white successions in central-city housing: limited evidence of urban revitalization'. *Urban Affairs Quarterly* vol. 15 no. 4 (June 1980) pp. 381–96.

2411   Spain, D. et al. *Housing succession among blacks and whites in cities and suburbs*. Washington, DC, Bureau of the Census, 1980. (Current population reports series P-23, special studies no. 101).

2412   Spencer, R. K. 'Enforcement of federal fair housing law'. *Urban Lawyer* vol. 9 no. 3 (Summer 1977) pp. 514–58.
Federal enforcement facilities of title VIII of the US Civil Rights Act 1968 against discriminatory housing decisions.

2413   Sutker, S. *Racial transition in the inner suburb: studies of the St. Louis area.* New York, Praeger, 1974. (Praeger special studies in US economic, social and political studies).

2414   United States, Commission on Civil Rights. *The federal fair housing enforcement effort: a report.* Washington, DC, The Commission, 1979.

2415   United States, Commission on Civil Rights. *Twenty years after Brown: equal opportunity in housing.* Washington, DC, The Commission, 1975.
Progress made since the Supreme Court decision in 1954 in *Brown v. Board of Education.*

2416   United States, Department of Housing and Urban Development. *Affirmative fair housing marketing techniques: final project report.* Washington, DC, The Department, 1976.
Anti-discrimination measures in housing.

2417   United States, Department of Housing and Urban Development. *Fair housing and funding a local strategy.* Washington, DC, The Department, 1976.
Prepared by the Davon Management Company.

2418   United States, Department of Housing and Urban Development. *Guide to fair housing law enforcement: by metro fair housing centers and other local fair housing groups.* Washington, DC, The Department, 1979.

2419   United States, Department of Housing and Urban Development. *How well are we housed: blacks.* Washington, DC, Government Printing Office, 1979.

2420   Van Valley, T. L. et al. 'Trends in residential segregation 1960–1970. *American Journal of Sociology* vol. 82 (1977) pp. 826–44.

2421   Weaver, R. C. *The negro ghetto*. New York, Harcourt Brace Jovanovich, 1948.
Beginnings of anti-discrimination in housing literature.

2422   Wienk, R. E. et al. *Measuring racial discrimination in American housing markets: the housing market practices survey*. Washington, DC, Department of Housing and Urban Development, 1979.

2423   Williams, J. A. 'The effects of urban renewal upon a black community: evaluation and recommendations'. *Social Science Quarterly* vol. 50 (Dec. 1969) pp. 703–12.

2424   Wilson, F. D. *Residential consumption, economic opportunity, and race*. New York, Academic Press, 1979. (Studies in population).
Racial discrimination in US housing.

2425   Yinger, J. et al. 'The status of research into racial discrimination and segregation in American housing markets'. *HUD Occasional Papers* 6 (Dec. 1979) pp. 55–175.

16

Low cost housing

The provision of housing at a price within the budgets of poorer members of society is an increasingly important area of housing policy both in the industrialized world and in developing countries. This section features references on issues such as the construction of working class housing in 19th and 20th century cities, the planning and construction in modern times of starter homes for newly emerging households, and the planning and development of low cost housing and sites and services projects in Third World cities. Reference should be made also to sections 5 'Rebates and allowances', 8 'Home ownership', 12 'Social aspects', 18 'Improvement and urban renewal' and 23 'Mobile homes'.

16.1   International and comparative

2426   Bauer, C. *Modern housing*. New York, Houghton Mifflin, 1934.
   Housing supply for low income families. Mainly US but other countries also examined.

2427   Goodchild, B. *The application of self-help to housing: a critique of self-build and urban homesteading*. Sheffield City Polytechnic, Department of Urban and Regional Studies, 1981.
   Self-help in housing is an unsatisfactory alternative to conventional methods of provision. Study of US and UK.

2428   Hull, J. H. 'Related to low-income housing'. *International Journal for Housing Science and its Applications* vol. 3 no. 2 (1979)

pp. 143–51.
Failure of many low cost housing schemes due to sociological, cultural and psychological factors as well as physical.

2429 Razani, R. et al. *Low cost housing technology: an East–West perspective*. Oxford, Pergamon, 1979.

2430 United Nations, Centre for Human Settlements. *Land for housing the poor: report of the UN Seminar of Experts on Land for Housing the Poor*. Stockholm, Swedish Council for Building Research, 1983.
Organized by Habitat in conjunction with the Finnish Ministry of the Interior and the Swedish Council for Building Research.

16.2 Europe

2431 Bates, A. A. 'Low cost housing in the Soviet Union'. In *Industrialized housing*. Washington, DC, Government Printing Office, 1969. pp. 1–21.

2432 Shapiro, A. L. *Housing the poor of Paris 1850–1902*. Madison, University of Wisconsin Press, 1984.

16.3 United Kingdom

2433 Bentham, C. G. 'The changing distribution of low income households in the British urban system'. *Area* vol. 15 no. 1 (1983) pp. 15–20.
Analysis of information on household incomes from FES data.

2434 Butt, J. 'Working class housing in the Scottish cities 1900–1950'. In G. Gordon and T. R. B. Dicks (eds.) *Scottish urban history*. Aberdeen University Press, 1983. pp. 233–67.

2435 Chapman, S. D. (ed.) *The history of working class housing*. Newton Abbot, David and Charles, 1971.
Case studies of industrial cities (Leeds, Nottingham) and sub-Pennine villages.

2436 Daunton, M. J. *House and home in the Victorian city: working class housing 1850–1914*. London, Edward Arnold, 1983. (Studies in urban history).

2437 Gauldie, E. *Cruel habitations: a history of working class housing 1780–1918*. London, Allen and Unwin, 1974.

2438 Gordon, G. 'Working class housing in Edinburgh 1837–1974'. *Wirtschafts — Geographische Studien, Vienna* vol. 3 (1979) pp. 68–86.

2439 Hardy, D. and Ward, C. *Arcadia for all: the legacy of a makeshift landscape*. London, Mansell, 1984. (Studies in history, planning and the environment).
History of cheap plots and squatter settlements in the early twentieth century.

2440 Hill, O. *Homes of the London poor*. 1883. Reprinted London, Cass, 1970.
Shows her particular ideology in relation to housing and managing the poor.

2441 Jones, C. S. *Outcast London*. Oxford University Press, 1971.
Chs. 8–11 contain information on mid to late nineteenth century demolition and rebuilding in poorer parts of London, including sanitary measures, the impact of industry on housing, and overcrowding.

2442 Karn, V. A. 'Low income occupation in the inner city'. In C. Jones (ed.) *Urban deprivation and the inner city*. London, Croom Helm, 1979.

2443 Tarn, J. N. *Working class housing in 19th century Britain*. London, Lund Humphries, 1971.

16.4 North America

2444 Abbott, S. B. 'Housing policy, housing codes and tenant remedies: an integration'. *Boston University Law Review* vol. 56 (Jan. 1976) pp. 1–146.

Low income housing in the US.

2445   Burchell, R. W. et al. *Mount Laurel II: challenge and delivery of low-cost housing*. New Brunswick, Rutgers University, Center for Urban Policy Research, 1983.

Evaluation of low income housing policy in New Jersey following the Mount Laurel II legal decision in which municipalities were given obligations to solve local housing need.

2446   Clark, T. A. 'Federal initiatives promoting the dispersal of low-income housing in suburbs'. *Professional Geographer* vol. 34 no. 2 (May 1982) pp. 136–46.

2447   Dennis, M. and Fish, S. *Programs in search of a policy: low income housing in Canada*. Toronto, Hakkert, 1972.

2448   Gruen, N. J. *Low and moderate income housing in the suburbs*. New York, Praeger, 1972.

2449   Haar, C. M. and Iatridis, D. S. *Housing the poor in suburbia: public policy at the grassroots*. Chichester, Wiley, 1974.

Case studies of attempts to introduce low income housing into suburban areas in Boston.

2450   Hagman, D. G. 'Taking care of one's own through inclusionary zoning: bootstrapping low- and moderate-income housing by local government'. *Urban Law and Policy* vol. 5 no. 2 (June 1982) pp. 169–87.

Legality and equity of inclusionary zoning by which low and moderate income groups are included in housing developments.

2451   Heumann, L. F. 'Low income housing planning: state of the art'. *ASCE Journal of the Urban Planning and Development Division* vol. 105 no. UP2 (Nov. 1979) pp. 137–49.

US federal government initiatives to improve the housing conditions of low income households.

2452   Jackson, A. *A place called home: a history of low-cost housing in Manhattan*. Cambridge, Mass., MIT Press, 1977.

2453 Jakubs, J. F. 'Low-cost housing: spatial deconcentration and community change'. *Professional Geographer* vol. 34 no. 2 (May 1982) pp. 156–66.

2454 Kaufman, M. *Housing of the working classes and the poor.* 1907. Reprinted Totowa, Rowman and Littlefield, 1975.

2455 Kolodny, R. 'Self-help can be an effective tool in housing the urban poor'. *Journal of Housing* vol. 38 (Mar. 1981) pp. 135–42.
Revised from an earlier article in *Habitat International.*

2456 Levine, M. D. *The long-term costs of lower income housing assistance programs.* Washington, DC, Congress Budget Office, 1979.
Budget issue paper for fiscal year 1980.

2457 Listokin, D. *Fair share housing allocation.* New Brunswick, Rutgers University, Center for Urban Policy Research, 1976.
Plans to construct new lost cost housing in the US where it is most needed.

2458 National Housing Law Project. *The subsidized housing handbook: how to provide, preserve and manage housing for low income people.* London, The Project, 1982.

2459 Reagin, J. R. et al. *Subsidising the poor: a Boston housing experiment.* Lexington, Mass., Lexington Books, 1972.

2460 Schwartz, S. and Johnston, R. A. 'Inclusionary housing: the housing affordability problem is outlined'. *American Planning Association Journal* vol. 49 no. 1 (1983) pp. 3–21.
Reviews previous research, early inclusionary programmes in California, and zoning as used in US cities.

2461 Sidor, J. 'Affordable housing: the state's role'. *Journal of Housing* vol. 39 no. 3 (May–June 1982) pp. 80–3.
Growing state interest in interceding on behalf of lowering housing costs.

2462 Silver, I. R. *Housing and the poor.* Ottawa, Canada Ministry of State for Urban Affairs, 1971.

Housing in Canada, with a good discussion of housing need.

2463   Strauss, B. and Stegman, D. 'Moderate-cost housing after Lafayette: a proposal'. *Urban Lawyer* vol. 11 no. 2 (Spring 1979) pp. 209–46.
Restrictions on resale prices of houses constructed for low to moderate income purchasers in US cities.

2464   Taggart, R. *Low income housing: a critique of federal aid.* Baltimore, Johns Hopkins University Press, 1970.

2465   Taylor, B. 'Inclusionary zoning: a workable option for affordable housing'. *Urban Land* vol. 40 (Mar. 1981) pp. 6–12.
Example from California of requiring a housing developer to reserve units for low and moderate income households.

2466   Welfeld, I. and Carmel, J. 'A new wave housing program: respecting the intelligence of the poor'. *Urban Law and Policy* vol. 6 no. 3 (June 1984) pp. 293–302.
An alternative subsidy programme to respect the wishes of the poor should replace the US Experimental Housing Allowance Program.

2467   White, A. G. *'Lifeline' utility rates: a selected bibliography.* Monticello, Vance Bibliographies, 1980. (Public administration series bibliography no. P. 629).
Cheaper housing and services costs to those in need.

2468   Zaitevsky, C. 'Housing Boston's poor: the first philanthropic experiments'. *Society of Architectural Historians Journal* vol. 42 no. 2 (May 1983) pp. 157–67.

16.5   Africa, Asia and Latin America

2469   Angel, S. et al. 'The low income housing system in Bangkok'. *Ekistics* vol. 44 (Aug. 1977) pp. 78–84.

2470   Bachmayer, P. et al. *Infrastructure programmes for lower income housing areas in developing countries.* Bonn, German Foundation for International Development, 1975.

2471   Bamberger, M. et al. *Evaluation of sites and services projects: the experience from El Salvador.* Washington, DC, World Bank, 1983. (Staff working paper 549).

2472   Bamberger, M. et al. *Evaluation of sites and services projects: the experience from Lusaka, Zambia.* Washington, DC, World Bank, 1983. (Staff working paper 548).

2473   Bendet, S. O. 'Low income housing development in Bogotá'. *Rice University Studies* vol. 61 (Fall 1975) pp. 97–111.
Squatter settlements and government housing in Colombia.

2474   Bhaskara Rao, B. 'Housing the deprived and underprivileged: India's experience'. *Long Range Planning* vol. 12 (Feb. 1979) pp. 75–82.

2475   Brett, S. 'Low income settlements in Latin America: the Turner model'. In E. de Kadt and E. Williams (eds.) *Sociology and development.* London, Tavistock, 1974. pp. 171–96.

2476   Chana, T. and Morrison, H. 'Housing systems in the low income sector of Nairobi, Kenya'. *Ekistics* vol. 36 (1973) pp. 214–21.

2477   England, R. and Alnwick, D. 'What can low-income families afford for housing? The costs of basic nutrition in urban Kenya'. *Habitat International* vol. 6 no. 4 (1982) pp. 441–57.

2478   Gilbert, A. and Ward, P. 'Low income housing and the state'. In A. Gilbert (ed.) *Urbanization in contemporary Latin America.* Chichester, Wiley, 1982. pp. 79–128.

2479   Hasnath, S. A. 'Sites and services schemes in Dacca: a critique'. *Public Administration and Development* vol. 2 (Jan.–Mar. 1982) pp. 15–30.
Development of urban land for low income housing in Bangladesh.

2480   International Development Research Centre. *Low cost housing in Indonesia.* Ottawa, The Centre, 1972.

2481 Jaspan, S. C. 'Low cost housing problems and possible solutions'. *Planning and Building Developments* no. 40 (Sept.–Oct. 1979) pp. 27–39.

2482 Kabagambe, D. and Moughtin, C. 'Housing the poor: a case study in Nairobi'. *Third World Planning Review* vol. 5 no. 3 (Aug. 1983) pp. 227–48.

2483 Kaburu, S. M. 'Low income housing. An analysis of some problems concerning urban housing for low income groups in Kenya'. *Build Kenya* vol. 2 no. 16 (July 1977) pp. 35–43.

2484 Keyes, W. J. and Burcroff, M. C. R. *Housing the urban poor: non-conventional approaches to a national problem.* Manila University, Institute of Philippine Culture, 1975.

2485 Lozano, E. E. 'Housing the urban poor in Chile: contrasting experiences under "Christian democracy" and Unidad Popular'. *Latin American Urban Research* vol. 5 (1975) pp. 177–94.

2486 Madavo, C. E. 'The serviced site approach to urban shelter'. *Ekistics* vol. 38 (1974) pp. 287–90.

2487 Marshall, A. J. 'Roof over our heads'. *Build Kenya* vol. 5 no. 59 (Feb. 1981) pp. 27–34.
Low cost housing policies in Kenya.

2488 Monahan, J. P. 'The economic realities of site and service schemes: two case studies: Malawi and Seychelles'. *Habitat International* vol. 4 no. 3 (1979) pp. 301–13.

2489 Onibokun, A. 'Low cost housing: an appraisal of an experiment in Nigeria'. *Journal of Administration Overseas* vol. 16 no. 2 (Apr. 1977) pp. 114–20.

2490 Oosthuizen, A. J. G. 'Urbanisation in South Africa, and the provision of low cost housing'. *ITCC Review* vol. 11 no. 1 (Jan. 1982) pp. 80–107.

2491 Stepick, A. and Murphy, A. 'Housing and government intervention among the urban poor: a comparison between a squatter settlement (Benito Juarez) and a government sponsored self-help project (Riberas de Atoyac)'. *Ekistics* vol. 46 no. 279 (Nov.–Dec. 1979) pp. 374–8. Low cost housing in Mexico.

2492   Stone, C. and Sutherland, M. *Experiment in low-income housing in Jamaica: an evaluation.* Kingston, University of the West Indies, Institute of Social and Economic Research, 1978.

2493   Swan, P. J. et al. *Management of sites and services schemes: the Asian experience.* Chichester, Wiley, 1983. Asian experience with low income, self-help housing schemes which involve community participation. Examples of 14 projects from 5 countries.

2494   Tipple, A. G. 'A radical approach to low-cost housing in Zambia'. *Openhouse* no. 2 (1976) pp. 6–17.

2495   Turner, G. 'Low cost housing in developing countries: public health issues which need to effect the cost limits of mass programmes'. *International Journal for Housing Science and its Applications* vol. 4 no. 3 (1980) pp. 193–201.

2496   United Nations, Department of Economic and Social Affairs. *Community programmes for low-income populations in urban settlements of developing countries.* New York, United Nations, 1976.

2497   Van Huyck, A. P. 'An approach to mass housing in India with special reference to Calcutta'. In H. W. Eldredge (ed.) *Taming megalopolis vol. 2.* New York, Praeger, 1967. pp. 1018–30.

2498   Van Huyck, A. P. 'The housing threshold for lowest income groups: the case of India'. In J. D. Herbert and A. P. Van Huyck (eds.) *Urban planning in the developing countries.* New York, Praeger, 1968.

2499   Ward, P. M. 'Financing land acquisition for self-build housing schemes'. *Third World Planning Review* vol. 3 no. 1 (Feb. 1981) pp. 7–20.

2500   Wegelin, E. A. *Urban low income housing and development: a case study in peninsular Malaysia.* Leiden, Nijhoff, 1977. (Studies in development and planning no. 6).

2501   World Bank. *Sites and services projects.* Washington, DC, The Bank, 1974.

2502   Yeh, S. 'Urban low-income housing in South-East Asia'. In P. J. Richards and A. M. Thomson (eds.) *Basic needs and the urban poor: the provision of communal services.* London, Croom Helm, 1984.
How public policies and programmes can provide basic amenities.

2503   Yeung, J. M. (ed.) *A place to live: more effective low cost housing in Asia.* Ottawa, International Development Research Centre, 1983.

17

Housing conditions and standards

In an age where investment in the production of new housing cannot be taken for granted, the maintenance of the existing stock has assumed a greater importance. The quality of the housing stock, particularly older housing, and the standards which have been introduced to measure and control it, are an increasingly important aspect of housing policy. This section deals with references on the development of housing standards, the measurement of housing conditions, the various house condition surveys, the problems of overcrowding and the public health aspects of poor housing. Sections 3 'Construction and energy conservation' and 18 'Improvement and urban renewal' should also be consulted.

17.1 International and comparative

2504 Andrzejewski, A. et al. *Housing programmes: the role of public health agencies.* Geneva, World Health Organization, 1964. (Public health papers series no. 25).

2505 Gove, W. R. et al. 'Overcrowding in the home: an empirical investigation of its possible pathological consequences'. *American Sociological Review* vol. 44 (1979) pp. 59–80.

2506 Karn, V. A. *Housing standards and costs: a comparison of British standards and costs with those in the USA, Canada and Europe.*

University of Birmingham, Centre for Urban and Regional Studies, 1973. (Occasional paper 25).

2507   McWhinnie, J. R. et al. 'Measuring housing conditions'. In *Measuring disability.* Paris, Organisation for Economic Co-operation and Development, 1982. (OECD social indicator development programme special studies 5–8).

2508   Martin, A. E. *Health aspects of human settlements.* Geneva, World Health Organization, 1977.
A review based on technical discussions held during the 29th World Health Assembly, 1976.

2509   Martin, A. E. et al. *Housing, the housing environment and health: an annotated bibliography.* Geneva, World Health Organization, 1976. (WHO offset publication no. 27).

2510   United Nations, Department of Economic and Social Affairs. *Human settlements performance standards.* New York, United Nations, 1977.
Report of the ad hoc expert group meeting in human settlements performance standards, New York, 15–19 Dec. 1975.

17.2   Europe

2511   Lonn, B. 'National maintenance planning preserves Sweden's housing stock'. *Journal of Property Management* vol. 49 no. 6 (Nov.–Dec. 1984) pp.10–13.

2512   Nechemias, C. 'The impact of Soviet housing policy on housing conditions in Soviet cities: the uneven push from Moscow'. *Urban Studies* vol. 18 no. 1 (Feb. 1981) pp. 1–8.
Causes of variations in housing conditions between Soviet cities, including literature review.

2513   Thomas, M. and Stott, M. 'The bleak housing standards that help to bring the Poles together'. *Town and Country Planning* vol. 53 no. 5 (May 1984) pp. 143–5.
Housing problems in Poland.

2514   United Nations, Economic Commission for Europe. *Proceedings of the seminar on management, maintenance and modernisation of housing.* 2 vols. New York, United Nations, 1969. Proceedings of a seminar held in Warsaw, Sept. 1968.

17.3   United Kingdom

2515   Brown, C. L. 'Better housing, healthier homes?' *Royal Society of Health Journal* vol. 103 no. 3 (June 1983) pp. 93–6. Classification of effects of housing conditions on physical and mental health.

2516   Doling, J. and Thomas, A. 'Disrepair in the national housing stock'. *Town Planning Review* vol. 53 no. 3 (July 1982) pp. 241–56. Various house condition surveys not directly compatible.

2517   Duncan, T. L. C. *Measuring housing quality: a study of methods.* University of Birmingham, Centre for Urban and Regional Studies, 1971. (Occasional paper 20).

2518   Fairbairns, Z. and Wintour, J. *No place to grow up: a Shelter report on the effect of bad housing on children.* London, Shelter, 1977.

2519   Fletcher, P. 'The control of housing standards in a rural district: a case study'. *Social and Economic Administration* vol. 3 no. 2 (Apr. 1969) pp. 106–20.

2520   Greater London Council. *The Greater London house condition survey.* London, The Council, 1981. (Reviews and studies series no. 7).

2521   Hughes, D. 'Housing repairs: a suitable case for reform'. *Journal of Social Welfare Law* May 1984 pp. 137–61. Sets out basic principles for a new code of housing standards.

2522   Institute of Housing and Royal Institute of British Architects. *Homes for the future: standards for new housing development.* London, The Institutes, 1983.

Updates Parker Morris (*see* no. 2545) and introduces new standards to meet future housing needs.

2523   Institution of Environmental Health Officers. *The future of the housing stock.* London, The Institution, 1983.

2524   Institution of Environmental Health Officers. *Houses in multiple occupation.* London, The Institution, 1985.
Calls for changes in the law to require licensing by local authorities of all houses in multiple occupation.

2525   Keithley, J. et al. 'Health and housing conditions in public sector housing estates'. *Public Health* vol. 98 (Nov. 1984) pp. 344–53.
Findings of a study of health and housing conditions from a sample of eight different types of council housing areas in Gateshead.

2526   Lane, P. *Health and housing.* London, Batsford, 1975.
Links between poor housing and ill health.

2527   Lawrence, R. J. 'The sanitary house: an architectural interpretation of health and housing reforms in England c. 1840–1920'. *Architectural Science Review* vol. 26 no. 2 (June 1983) pp. 39–49.

2528   Matthews, R. 'Conditions suspicious'. *Roof* vol. 8 no. 2 (Mar.–Apr. 1982) pp. 22–4.
Difficulties in comparing the English house condition surveys.

2529   O'Dell, A. 'An assessment of the errors in a housing survey'. *Urban Studies* vol. 17 no. 2 (June 1980) pp. 217–22.
The English house condition survey was studied to show the effects of non-sampling errors.

2530   Ormandy, D. 'Housing standards'. *Roof* vol. 7 no. 1 (Jan.–Feb. 1982) pp. 12–18.

2531   Ormandy, D. 'Overcrowding'. *Roof* vol. 6 no. 2 (Mar.–Apr. 1981) pp. 11–12.

Examines the legislation concerning overcrowding, particularly to accommodation let separately under the standards of the Housing Act 1957.

2532 Quayle, V. J. *Houses in multiple occupation*. London, Shaw, 1980.
Legal text.

2533 Reidy, A. 'Legal rights and housing policy'. *Social Policy and Administration* vol. 14 no. 1 (Spring 1980) pp. 12–22.
Examines cases brought under section 99 of the Public Health Act 1936.

2534 Riley, K. M. 'An estimate of the age distribution of the dwelling stock in Great Britain'. *Urban Studies* vol. 10 no. 3 (1973) pp. 373–9.

2535 Roberts, D. L. H. 'Dwelling stock estimates from the 1981 Census of Population'. *Statistical News* no. 49 (May1980) pp. 1–5.

2536 Robinson, J. *A report on the 1973 Glasgow house condition survey*. University of Glasgow, Department of Town and Regional Planning, 1976. (Discussion papers in planning no. 9).

2537 Skinner, N. P. 'House condition, standards and maintenance'. *Housing Review* vol. 30 no. 4 (July–Aug. 1981) pp. 106–9.

2538 United Kingdom, Department of the Environment. *English house condition survey 1976. Part 1: report of the physical condition survey*. London, HMSO, 1978. (Housing Survey report no. 10).

2539 United Kingdom, Department of the Environment. *English house condition survey 1976. Part 2: report of the social survey*. London, HMSO, 1979. (Housing Survey report no. 11).

2540 United Kingdom, Department of the Environment. *English house condition survey 1981. Part 1: report of the physical condition survey*. London, HMSO, 1982. (Housing Survey report no. 12).

2541 United Kingdom, Department of the Environment. *English house condition survey 1981. Part 2: report of the interview and local authority survey.* London, HMSO, 1983. (Housing Survey report no. 13).

2542 United Kingdom, Department of the Environment. *Sample house condition survey.* London, HMSO, 1971. (Area improvement note no. 1).
Model for house condition surveys.

2543 United Kingdom, Department of Health and Social Security. *Inequalities in health.* London, 1980.
The Black report, which included the observation that standardized mortality rates were highest among occupants of council housing.

2544 United Kingdom, House of Commons, Committee on Scottish Affairs. *Dampness in housing.* London, HMSO, 1983. (HC 207, Session 1982–83).

2545 United Kingdom, Ministry of Housing and Local Government. *Homes for today and tomorrow.* London, HMSO, 1961.
The Parker Morris report, which set standards for housing development for the following 20 years.

2546 United Kingdom, Ministry of Housing and Local Government, Central Housing Advisory Committee. *Our older homes, a call for action.* London, HMSO, 1966.
The Denington report, which first identified the scale of poor housing in Britain and proposed first house condition surveys.

2547 United Kingdom, Northern Ireland Housing Executive. *Housing condition survey 1974.* Belfast, HMSO, 1975.

2548 United Kingdom, Welsh Office. *Welsh house condition survey 1976.* Cardiff, HMSO, 1978.

2549 United Kingdom, Welsh Office. *Welsh house condition survey 1981.* Cardiff, Welsh Office, 1982.

2550 United Kingdom, Welsh Office. *Welsh housing and dwelling survey 1978–1979.* Cardiff, Welsh Office, 1981.

2551   Webster, C. A. R. *Environmental health law*. London, Sweet and Maxwell, 1981.
   Ch. 8 on housing deals with conditions, overcrowding and clearance.

2552   Woodford, G. et al. *The value of standards for the external residential environment*. London, Department of the Environment, 1976. (Research report 6).

17.4   North America

2553   American Public Health Association. *An appraisal method for measuring the quality of housing*. 3 vols. Chicago, The Association, 1948.

2554   Archer, J. 'A history of housing standards'. *Habitat* vol. 24 no. 4 (1981) pp. 10–16.
   Housing standards in Canada.

2555   Association for the Improvement of the Conditions of the Poor. *Housing conditions in Baltimore: report of a special committee of the Association for the Improvement of the Conditions of the Poor and the Charity Organization Society*. 1907. Reprinted Philadelphia, Ayer, 1974. (Metropolitan America series).

2556   Baer, W. C. 'The evolution of housing indicators and housing standards — some lessons for the future'. *Public Policy* vol. 24 no. 3 (Summer 1976) pp. 361–93.
   Study of public and private housing in the US.

2557   Baer, W. C. 'Housing indicators and standards in the USA'. *Ekistics* vol. 44 no. 261 (Aug. 1977) pp. 71–7.
   Distinction between indicators and standards in US context.

2558   Baldassare, M. *Residential crowding in urban America*. Berkeley, University of California Press, 1979.

2559   Gleeson, M. E. 'Estimating housing mortality'. *Journal of the American Planning Association* vol. 47 no. 2 (Apr. 1981) pp.

185–94.
Techniques for estimating the life of housing.

2560   Goedert, J. E. and Goodman, J. R. *Indicators of the quality of US housing.* Washington, DC, Urban Institute, 1977.

2561   Goetze, R. *Changing housing standards.* Washington, DC, Public Technology Inc., 1983.
Impending changes in housing standards as response to economic pressure and household formation patterns.

2562   Hiscox, G. 'Measuring housing quality'. *Habitat* vol. 22 no. 2 (1979) pp. 2–7.
Approach to measuring housing quality in Canada.

2563   Leven, C. L. *Neighbourhood change: lessons in the dynamics of urban decay.* New York, Praeger, 1976. (Praeger special studies in US economic, social and political issues).
Based on a study of St. Louis showing progressive occupation of housing by lower income levels.

2564   Mikesell, J. J. *Population change and metro–nonmetro housing quality differences.* Washington, DC, Department of Agriculture Economic Research Service, 1977. (Agricultural economics report no. 388).

2565   Myers, D. 'Housing progress in the seventies: new indicators'. *Social Indicators Research* vol. 9 (Mar. 1981) pp. 35–60.
Proposes a model for measuring housing quality in the US.

2566   Nivola, P. S. *The urban service problem: a study of housing inspection.* Lexington, Mass., Lexington Books, 1979.
Studies the operation of the Boston Housing Inspection Department.

2567   Spivey, G. H. and Radford, E. P. 'Inner city housing and respiratory disease in children'. *Archives of Environmental Health* vol. 34 no. 1 (Jan.–Feb. 1979) pp. 23–30.
Methodology of studies on the relationship of housing and health in Baltimore.

17.5 Australasia

2568 Lawrence, R. J. 'The sanitary house remodelled: the import of British health and housing reforms to Australia 1860–1920'. *Architectural Science Review* vol. 27 no. 2 (June 1984) pp. 29–36.
Spread of British ideas about health and housing to Australia and the design of residential areas.

17.6 Africa, Asia and Latin America

2569 Ebong, M. O. 'The perception of residential quality: a case study of Calabar, Nigeria'. *Third World Planning Review* vol. 5 no. 3 (Aug. 1983) pp. 273–85.

2570 Mabogunje, A. L. et al. *Shelter provision in developing countries: the influence of standards and criteria.* Chichester, Wiley on behalf of the International Council of Scientific Unions, 1978. (Scope report 11).

2571 Okpala, D. C. I. 'Housing standards: a constraint on urban housing production in Nigeria'. *Ekistics* vol. 45 no. 270 (June 1978) pp. 249–57.

18

Improvement and urban renewal

Poor housing conditions and the creation of slum areas in many parts of the world have prompted increasing government involvement in housing and area improvement. Policies have ranged from total slum clearance through to the modern emphasis on rehabilitation and improvement. The rationale behind these various policies, the arrangements of the policy in practice and the social impact on the community involved are all examined in references in this section. The situation is as acute in many Third World cities where the influx of vast numbers of people to cities with inadequate infrastructure has created enormous planning and housing problems. Many of the references in the latter part of this section refer to projects from those countries for the improvement or upgrading of many of these spontaneous and often illegal settlements. Reference should also be made to section 17 'Housing conditions and standards'.

18.1 International and comparative

2572 'Approaches to inner city revitalization'. *Urban Affairs Quarterly* vol. 15 no. 4 (June 1980) pp. 373–487.
Special issue on revitalization of cities in western countries.

2573 Boleat, M. 'Neighbourhood housing services: urban revitalisation the American way'. *Housing Review* vol. 31 no. 1 (Jan.–Feb. 1982) pp. 20–1.

Applicability of the US neighbourhood housing services concept to Britain for housing rehabilitation.

2574 Huntley, J. *Neighbourhood revitalisation: American and German involvement in the revitalisation of older housing areas.* University of Reading, School of Planning Studies, 1980. (Occasional paper 4).

2575 International Federation for Housing and Planning. *Revitalisation of inner city areas.* 2 vols. The Hague, The Federation, 1984.
Papers and proceedings of the 37th World Congress, West Berlin, 10–14 Sept.

2576 International Federation for Housing and Planning. *Revitalising moderately old urban areas.* 2 vols. The Hague, The Federation, 1978.
Proceedings of the 34th World Congress, Hamburg, 11–16 Sept. 1978.

2577 Jones, A. C. C. 'Addressing issues on the improvement of housing and its surroundings: the UNECE seminar at The Hague, The Netherlands, 15–19 October 1979'. *Urban Law and Policy* vol. 3 no. 2 (June 1980) pp. 157–70.

2578 Koenigsberger, O. et al. (eds.) *Work of Charles Abrams: housing and urban renewal in the USA and the Third World.* Oxford, Pergamon, 1980.
Collection of essays as tribute to the work of Abrams.

2579 Marris, P. 'The meanings of slums and patterns of change'. *International Journal of Urban and Regional Research* vol. 3 (Sept. 1979) pp. 419–41.

2580 Robinette, G. O. (ed.) *How to make cities liveable: design guidelines for urban homesteading.* New York, Van Nostrand Reinhold, 1984.

2581 Rosenthal, D. B. (ed.) *Urban revitalization.* Beverly Hills, Sage, 1980. (Urban affairs annual reviews vol. 18).

Urban renewal from a variety of perspectives, with findings from US, UK and Latin America.

2582   Rowland, J. 'It's the same the whole world over'. *Architects' Journal* vol. 177 no. 3 (19 Jan. 1983) pp. 43–50.
Improvement of vandalized and run-down estates in Egypt and London.

2583   Silzer, V. J. *Housing rehabilitation and neighbourhood change: Britain, Canada and USA: an annotated bibliography.* University of Toronto, Centre for Urban and Community Studies, 1975. (Bibliographic series no. 5).

2584   Smith, D. M. 'Inner city deprivation: problems and policies in advanced capitalist countries'. *Geoforum* vol. 10 no. 3 (1979) pp. 297–310.
Explanations of inner city deprivation arise from an understanding of the capitalist system.

2585   Smith, R. 'Advocating owner-occupation in the inner city: some lessons from American experience for UK low-cost home ownership programmes'. *Planning Outlook* vol. 26 no. 1 (1983) pp. 40–3.
Comparison of US/UK policy towards improvement of older inner city property, especially US experience of homesteading and improvement for sale.

2586   Stokes, C. J. 'A theory of slums'. *Land Economics* vol. 38 no. 3 (1961) pp. 187–97.

2587   Ward, D. 'The progressives and the urban question: British and American responses to the inner city slums 1880–1920'. *Institute of British Geographers Transactions* vol. 9 no. 3 (1984) pp. 299–314.

18.2   Europe

2588   Brochner, J. *Economic aspects of housing rehabilitation: modernising flats in Sweden 1971–1975.* Stockholm, Swedish Council for Building Research, 1978.

Economic influences on rehabilitation and factors determining take up of rehabilitation finance.

2589 Carrick, R. J. and Wrathall, J. E. 'Urban renewal in the Netherlands'. *Planner* vol. 69 no. 3 (May–June 1983) pp. 88–90.
Urban renewal in the Randstad municipalities including Rotterdam.

2590 Draisen, M. D. 'Fostering effective citizen participation: lessons from three urban renewal neighbourhoods in the Hague'. *Planning and Administration* vol. 8 no. 2 (Autumn 1981) pp. 40–62.

2591 Gosschalk, B. 'Urban renewal: local authority responses in a period of economic restraint'. *Housing Review* vol. 31 no. 1 (Jan.–Feb. 1982) pp. 21–3.
Aims of European Campaign for Urban Renaissance and initiatives taken in UK, the Netherlands, and, especially, area improvement in West Germany.

2592 Hale, R. L. 'In the Netherlands, rehabilitation is a national effort with new ideas for the United States'. *Journal of Housing* vol. 35 no. 10 (Nov. 1978) pp. 521–6.
Change in Dutch housing policy from demolition to rehabilitation.

2593 Hale, R. L. 'Rehab. in the Netherlands: tackling both housing and neighbourhoods'. *Habitat* vol. 22 no. 1 (1979) pp. 26–32.
Development of Woonerven as residential precincts with strong citizen participation.

2594 Hull, A. and Kenny, S. 'New houses for old Amsterdam'. *Geographical Magazine* Nov. 1984 pp. 584–9.
Amsterdam's housing policies and problems now emphasize rehabilitation of inner city housing.

2595 Lemberg, K. 'Urban renewal in Copenhagen'. *Building Research and Practice* vol. 7 no. 2 (Mar.–Apr. 1979) pp. 96–106.
Progress towards rehabilitation of housing and barriers overcome.

2596   Nelissen, N. J. M. *Urban renewal participation experiments: heralds of a new local democracy.* The Hague, Council of European Municipalities, 1982.
Text in English, German and French.

2597   Olives, J. 'The struggle against urban renewal in the Cité d'Aliarte (Paris)'. In C. G. Pickvance (ed.) *Urban sociology: critical essays.* London, Tavistock, 1976. pp. 174–97.

2598   Swedish Council for Building Research. *Housing renewal in Sweden.* Stockholm, The Council, 1983.

2599   *To build and take care of what we have built with limited resources: renewal, rehabilitation and maintenance.* 2 vols. Gavle, National Swedish Institute for Building Research, 1983.
Papers and proceedings of the 9th CIB Congress, Stockholm.

2600   United Nations, Economic Commission for Europe. *The improvement of housing and its immediate surroundings, results of an enquiry.* Geneva, United Nations, 1977.

2601   United Nations, Economic Commission for Europe. *The improvement of housing and its surroundings: synthesis report on the seminar held in The Hague (Netherlands), Oct. 15–19, 1979.* New York, United Nations, 1983.

2602   'Urban renewal in Western Europe'. *Urban Ecology* vol. 5 nos. 3–4 (June 1982) pp. 155–390.
Eight case studies of urban renewal in Aachen, Antwerp, Basle, Dublin, Elsinore, Manchester, Mulhouse, and Rotterdam, and general conclusions.

2603   Webman, J. *Reviving the industrial city: the politics of urban renewal in Lyon and Birmingham.* London, Croom Helm, 1982.

2604   Whysall, P. and Benyon, J. 'Urban renewal policies in central Amsterdam'. *Planning Outlook* vol. 23 no. 2 (1981) pp. 77–82.

2605   Wood, P. 'New style renewal in West Germany'. *Town and Country Planning* vol. 49 no. 2 (Feb. 1980) pp. 55–7.

18.3 United Kingdom

2606 Adamson, S. 'The politics of improvement grants: a survey of local authority procedures for implementing housing improvement policies'. *Town Planning Review* vol. 45 no. 4 (Oct. 1974) pp. 375–86.

2607 Association of Metropolitan Authorities. *Policies for improvement: a report on housing repair and renovation.* London, The Association, 1978.

2608 Association of Metropolitan Authorities. *Ruin or renewal: choices for our ageing housing.* London, The Association, 1981.

2609 Baine, S. *Community action and local government.* London, Bell, 1975. (Occasional papers in social administration no. 59). Activities of private landlords and gentrification in Barnsbury in the London Borough of Islington.

2610 Balchin, P. *Housing improvement and social inequality.* Farnborough, Saxon House, 1979.
Study of improvement grant take up and gentrification in London.

2611 Bassett, K. and Short, J. R. 'Housing improvement in the inner city: a case study of changes before and after the 1974 Housing Act'. *Urban Studies* vol. 15 (1978) pp. 333–42.

2612 Benson, J. et al. *The housing rehabilitation handbook.* London, Architectural Press, 1980.
Reprint of series of articles first published in *Architects' Journal.*

2613 Benwell Community Project. *Slums on the drawing board.* Newcastle upon Tyne, 1978. (Final report series no. 4)
Estate built in the 1950s seen through the experiences of residents, deliberately built to low standards and now demolished.

2614 Birmingham Community Development Project. *From failure to face lift.* Birmingham, The Project, 1980. (Final report no. 6 urban renewal).

Study of improvement policy in Saltley, Birmingham .

2615 Birtill, A. and Taylor, S. *Housing action? The myth of area improvement.* London, CDP Political Economy Collective, 1982.

2616 Brierley, E. S. 'The convergence of planning policies concerned with conservation areas of buildings of architectural merit and of housing action areas'. *International Journal for Housing Science and its Applications* vol. 8 no. 3 (1984) pp. 269–81.
Leicester's housing renewal strategy, enveloping and housing improvement policies.

2617 Brookes, J. A. and Hughes, K. 'Housing redevelopment and rehabilitation'. *Town Planning Review* vol. 46 no. 2 (Apr. 1975) pp. 215–25.
Argues for economic comparisons between strategies of redevelopment and rehabilitation, using Cardiff as a case study.

2618 Building Societies Association. *The rehabilitation of owner occupied homes.* London, The Association, 1983.
Papers and proceedings of a seminar held in Jan. 1983.

2619 Bull, D. G. 'Housing departments and clearance areas'. *Social and Economic Administration* vol. 2 no. 4 (1968) pp. 250–70.

2620 Cartmill, D. *Homesteading in Belfast.* Queen's University of Belfast, Department of Town and Country Planning, 1984. (Occasional paper no. 7).
Examines the homesteading programme of the Northern Ireland Housing Executive in Belfast during 1981–2.

2621 Coates, K. and Silburn, R. *Poverty: the forgotten Englishmen.* London, Pelican, 1970.
Includes an analysis of slum clearance.

2622 Community Development Project. *Gilding the ghetto: the state and the poverty experiments.* London, The Project, 1977.

2623 Community Development Project. *The poverty of the improvement programme: revised Inter-Project report.* London, The Project, 1977.

2624 Community Forum. *Are you being enveloped? A resident's guide to enveloping.* Birmingham, 1983.

2625 Cook, K. 'Housing improvement policy in Britain 1949–1979'. *International Journal for Housing Science and its Applications* vol. 7 no. 1 (1983) pp. 65–83.

2626 Davies, J. G. *The evangelistic bureaucrat.* London, Tavistock, 1972. Revitalization of Rye Hill, Newcastle upon Tyne.

2627 Dennis, N. 'Housing policy areas: criteria and indicators in principle and practice'. *Institute of British Geographers Transactions* new series vol. 3 no. 1 (1978) pp. 2–22. Study of clearance, renewal and housing action areas in Sunderland.

2628 Derrick, E. F. *House and area improvement in Britain: bibliography and abstracts.* University of Birmingham, Centre for Urban and Regional Studies, 1976. (Research memorandum 54). Abstracts of relevant material together with a detailed listing of legislation, circulars and reports.

2629 Dible, J. K. *Residential renewal in Scottish cities.* Edinburgh, HMSO, 1981.

2630 Drakakis-Smith, D. W. 'Slum clearance at the regional level. The establishment of priorities for renewal in the context of Wales'. *Town Planning Review* vol. 42 (1971) pp. 293–306.

2631 Duncan, T. L. C. *Housing improvement policies in England and Wales.* University of Birmingham, Centre for Urban and Regional Studies, 1974. (Research memorandum 28).

2632 Duncan, T. L. C. and Cowan, R. H. *Housing action areas in Scotland.* Glasgow, Planning Exchange, 1976.

2633 Dyos, H. J. and Reeder, D. A. 'Slums and suburbs'. In H. J. Dyos and M. Wolff (eds.) *The Victorian City.* London, Routledge and Kegan Paul, 1973. pp. 359–86.

2634 English, J. et al. *Slum clearance: the social and administrative context in England and Wales.* London, Croom Helm, 1976.
History of policy with case studies in Newcastle upon Tyne, Manchester, London Borough of Tower Hamlets, Leeds and Liverpool.

2635 Garner, J. F. *Slum clearance and compensation.* London, Oyez, 1975.
Legal text.

2636 Gibson, M. S. and Langstaff, M. J. *An introduction to urban renewal.* London, Hutchinson, 1982.

2637 Hadden, T. *Housing: repair and improvements.* London, Sweet and Maxwell, 1979.

2638 Hadden, T. 'Housing action areas: an antiquated set of legal tools'. *Journal of Planning and Environment Law* Nov. 1979 pp. 725–30.

2639 Hamnett, C. and Williams, P. *Gentrification in London 1961–1971: an empirical and theoretical analysis of social change.* University of Birmingham, Centre for Urban and Regional Studies, 1979. (Research memorandum 71).
Uses census data to study the changing occupational characteristics of London boroughs.

2640 Hamnett, C. and Williams, P. 'Social change in London: a study of gentrification'. *Urban Affairs Quarterly* vol. 15 no. 4 (1980) pp. 469–87.

2641 Hawke, J. N. and Taylor, G. A. 'The compulsory repair of individual physically substandard housing: the law in practice'. *Journal of Social Welfare Law* May 1984 pp. 129–36.
Ways in which local authorities and individuals use statutory powers in the Housing Act 1957 and the Public Health Act 1936 to deal with disrepair.

2642 Hawkins, N. *Housing grants: a guide to improvement and other grants and subsidies.* 2nd ed. London, Kogan Page, 1982.

2643   Hendry, J. 'Gradual renewal'. *International Journal for Housing Science and its Applications* vol. 7 no. 1 (1983) pp. 1–12. Effectiveness of renewal policy in Britain in combatting problems of housing decay.

2644   Hetzel, O. J. 'Area improvement programmes for housing rehabilitation — some observations on the English and Welsh experiences'. *Journal of Planning and Environment Law* Oct. 1979 pp. 646–60 and Nov. 1979 pp. 735–51.

2645   Institution of Environmental Health Officers. *Area improvement: the report of the Area Improvement Working Party.* London, The Institution, 1981.

2646   Kirby, D. A. *Slum housing and residential renewal: the case in urban Britain.* Harlow, Longman, 1979.

2647   Leather, P. et al. *Review of home improvement agencies.* London, Department of the Environment, 1985.

2648   Mason, T. *Inner city housing and urban renewal policy: a housing profile of Cheetham Hill, Manchester and Salford.* London, Centre for Environmental Studies, 1977. (Research series no. 23).

2649   Mason, T. 'Intention and implication in housing policy'. *Journal of Social Policy* vol. 6 part 1 (1977) pp. 17–30.

2650   Mason, T. 'Politics and planning of urban renewal in the private housing sector'. In C. Jones (ed.) *Urban deprivation and the inner city.* London, Croom Helm, 1979.

2651   Mellor, R. 'Structure and processes in the twilight areas'. *Town Planning Review* vol. 44 no. 1 (Jan. 1977) pp. 54–70.

2652   Monck, E. and Lomas, G. *Housing action areas: success and failure.* London, Centre for Environmental Studies, 1980. (Policy series 10).

2653   Moore, R. *Reconditioning the slums: the development and role of housing rehabilitation.* Polytechnic of Central London, School of Environment, Planning Unit, 1980. (Planning studies no. 7).

2654 Muchnick, D. M. *Urban renewal in Liverpool.* London, Bell, 1970. (Occasional papers on social administration no. 33).

2655 National Home Improvement Council. *Improving our homes: NHIC discussion document with proposals for a better use of resources.* London, The Council, 1985.

2656 Needleman, L. 'The comparative economics of improvement and new building'. *Urban Studies* vol. 6 no. 2 (June 1969) pp. 196–209.

2657 Niner, P. and Forrest, R. *Housing action area policy and progress: the resident's perspective.* University of Birmingham, Centre for Urban and Regional Studies, 1982. (Research memorandum 91).

2658 Nutt, B. et al. *Obsolescence in housing: theory and application.* Farnborough, Saxon House, 1976.

2659 Paris, C. 'Birmingham: a study in urban renewal'. *CES Review* no. 1 (1977) pp. 54–61.

2660 Paris, C. 'Policy change: ideological conflict and consensus — the development of housing improvement in Birmingham'. In M. Harloe (ed.) *Urban change and conflict.* London, Centre for Environmental Studies, 1978. (Conference series 19).

2661 Paris, C. and Blackaby, B. *Not much improvement: urban renewal policy in Birmingham.* London, Heinemann Educational, 1979.

2662 Parson, D. 'Urban renewal and housing action areas in Belfast: legitimation and the incorporation of protest'. *International Journal of Urban and Regional Research* vol. 5 no. 2 (1981) pp. 218–30.

2663 Pepper, S. *House improvement: goals and strategy.* London, Lund Humphries, 1971.

2664 Phillips, M. 'Area improvement: a housing policy which has yet to succeed'. *Environmental Education and Information* vol. 2 no. 3 (July–Sept. 1982) pp. 183–92.

Recommends abandonment of area improvement schemes in favour of a single housing renewal area.

2665 Quayle, V. J. *Compulsory improvement to housing.* London, Shaw, 1980.
Urban renewal in the private sector.

2666 Roberts, J. T. *General improvement areas.* Farnborough, Saxon House, 1976.

2667 Roberts, T. A. *Clementhorpe, York: a study of urban renewal 1976–1982.* University of York, Institute of Advanced Architectural Studies, 1983. (Research paper 21).

2668 Rose, D. 'Rethinking gentrification: beyond the uneven development of Marxist urban theory'. *Environment and Planning D* vol. 2 no. 1 (1984) pp. 47–75.

2669 Royal Town Planning Institute. *Renewal of older housing areas in the 1980s.* London, The Institute, 1981.

2670 SHAC. *Good housekeeping: an examination of housing repair and improvement.* London, SHAC, 1981. (Policy paper 4).

2671 Shankland–Cox Partnership. *The four-day package: a study of the GLC's experience in the rapid modernisation of inter-war flats with tenants in residence: a report for the DOE.* London, Department of the Environment, 1979.

2672 Shankland–Cox Partnership. *Phased improvement with tenants in residence: a study of the repair and improvement of older houses.* London, Department of the Environment, 1981.

2673 Shelter Neighbourhood Action Project. *Another chance for cities: SNAP 69/72.* Liverpool, The Project, 1972.
Final report of an area improvement project in Liverpool.

2674 Short, J. R. 'Housing action areas: an evaluation'. *Area* vol. 10 no. 2 (1978) pp. 153–7.

2675 Sigsworth, E. M. and Wilkinson, R. K. 'Rebuilding or renovation'. *Urban Studies* vol. 4 (1967) pp. 109–21.

2676   Sim, D. *Change in the city centre.* Aldershot, Gower, 1982. Includes a detailed analysis of slum clearance and house-building policy in Glasgow.

2677   Thomas, A. D. 'Area based house improvement: the role of local authorities in England'. *Local Government Studies* vol. 5 no. 6 (Nov.–Dec. 1979) pp. 53–68.

2678   Thomas, A. D. *Area based renewal: three years in the life of a housing action area.* University of Birmingham, Centre for Urban and Regional Studies, 1979. (Research memorandum 72).

2679   Thomas, A. D. *Local authority agency services: their role in house improvement.* University of Birmingham, Centre for Urban and Regional Studies, 1981. (Research memorandum 88).

2680   Thomas, A. D. *Planning in residential conservation areas.* Oxford, Pergamon, 1983. (Progress in planning vol. 20 part 3).

2681   Thomas, A. et al. *Research on urban renewal.* London, Economic and Social Research Council, 1984. (Environment and Planning Committee paper no. 2).

2682   Tinker, A. and White, J. 'How can the elderly owner-occupiers be helped to improve and repair their homes?' *Housing Review* vol. 28 no. 3 (May–June 1979) pp. 74–7.

2683   Tremlett, G. *Living cities.* London, Temple Smith, 1979. Includes support for homesteading, which was pioneered by the Conservative GLC of which Tremlett was Chairman.

2684   United Kingdom, Department of the Environment. *Better homes: the next priorities.* London, HMSO, 1973. (Cmnd. 5339).

2685   United Kingdom, Department of the Environment. *Good practice in area improvement.* London, HMSO, 1984.

2686   United Kingdom, Department of the Environment. *Home improvement — a new approach: government proposals for encouraging the repair and improvement of private sector housing in England and Wales.* London, HMSO, 1985. (Cmnd. 9513).

Long awaited green paper on the reform of home improvement policy.

2687 United Kingdom, Department of the Environment. *Homesteading: the three in one housing gain.* London, The Department, 1982.

2688 United Kingdom, Department of the Environment. *Housing Act 1974.* London, HMSO, 1975. (Circular 14/75). Covers housing action areas, general improvement areas.

2689 United Kingdom, Department of the Environment. *Housing Act 1974: improvement of older housing.* London, HMSO, 1974. (Circular 160/74).

2690 United Kingdom, Department of the Environment. *Housing Act 1974: renewal strategies.* London, HMSO, 1975. (Circular 13/75).

2691 United Kingdom, Department of the Environment. *Networks for house and area improvement.* London, HMSO, 1977. (Area improvement note no. 11).

2692 United Kingdom, Department of the Environment. *New life in old towns.* London, HMSO, 1971.
Report by Robert Matthew, Johnson-Marshall and Partners on two pilot studies in Nelson and Rawtenstall, Lancashire.

2693 United Kingdom, Department of the Environment. *Use of indicators for area action.* London, HMSO, 1975. (Area improvement note no. 10).

2694 United Kingdom, Department of the Environment, Housing Development Directorate. *The economic assessment of housing renewal schemes.* London, The Department, 1979. (Improvement research note 4/78).

2695 United Kingdom, House of Commons, Committee of Public Accounts. *The Department of the Environment's oversight of home improvement grants.* London, HMSO, 1984. (23rd report, HC

482, Session 1983–84).

2696 United Kingdom, House of Commons, Expenditure Committee. *Improvement grants.* London, HMSO, 1973. (Tenth Report, HC 349, Session 1972–73).

2697 United Kingdom, Ministry of Housing and Local Government. *The Deeplish study.* London, HMSO, 1966.
Feasibility study of housing improvement in Rochdale.

2698 United Kingdom, Ministry of Housing and Local Government. *Living in a slum.* London, HMSO, 1970. (Design bulletin 19).
Study of St. Mary's, Oldham.

2699 United Kingdom, Ministry of Housing and Local Government. *Moving from the slums.* London, HMSO, 1956.

2700 United Kingdom, Ministry of Housing and Local Government. *Moving out of a slum.* London, HMSO, 1970. (Design bulletin 20).
Moving out of St. Mary's, Oldham.

2701 United Kingdom, Ministry of Housing and Local Government. *Older houses into new homes.* London, HMSO, 1968. (Cmnd. 3602).

2702 United Kingdom, Ministry of Housing and Local Government. *Slum clearance.* London, HMSO, 1955. (Cmd. 9593).

2703 United Kingdom, National Building Agency. *Case studies of new approaches to urban renewal.* London, The Agency, 1981.

2704 United Kingdom, National Building Agency. *Organisation and staff resources for area improvement: part I, general approach; part II, case studies.* London, The Agency, 1977.

2705 United Kingdom, National Economic Development Office. *New homes in the cities: the role of the private developer in urban renewal in England and Wales.* London, HMSO, 1971.

2706 United Kingdom, Northern Ireland Assembly, Environment Committee. *Northern Ireland Housing Executive. Belfast — housing renewal strategy . Vol. 1: report together with the proceedings of the Environment Committee and the minutes of oral evidence.* Belfast, HMSO, 1983.

2707 United Kingdom, Scottish Development Department. *Area based policies approach to urban deprivation.* Edinburgh, The Department, 1978.

2708 United Kingdom, Scottish Development Department. *Housing action areas: first report.* Edinburgh, HMSO, 1980.

2709 United Kingdom, Scottish Development Department. *The older houses in Scotland: a plan for action.* Edinburgh, HMSO, 1968. (Cmnd. 3598).

2710 United Kingdom, Scottish Development Department. *Towards better homes: proposals for dealing with Scotland's older housing.* Edinburgh, HMSO, 1973. (Cmnd. 5338).

2711 United Kingdom, Scottish Housing Advisory Committee. *Scotland's older houses.* Edinburgh, HMSO, 1967.
Report of the SDD Subcommittee on Unfit Housing. (The Cullingworth report).

2712 Williamson, A. and Wrigley, E. *General improvement areas 1969–1976.* London, Department of the Environment, 1978. (Improvement research note 3/77).
Report of a comprehensive study of progress achieved in the rehabilitation of older housing in general improvement areas.

2713 Willson, K. *Housing improvement policies in England and Wales: a historical and comparative view.* University of Toronto, Centre for Urban and Community Studies, 1981. (Major report 18).

2714 Yelling, J. A. 'LCC slum clearance policies 1889–1907'. *Institute of British Geographers Transactions* vol. 7 no. 3 (1982) pp. 292–303.

18.4 North America

2715 Ahlbrandt, R. *Flexible code enforcement: a key ingredient in neighborhood preservation programming*. Washington DC, National Association of Housing and Redevelopment Officials, 1976.
Role of US local governments in community redevelopment.

2716 Ahlbrandt, R. S. and Brophy, P. C. *Neighborhood revitalization: theory and practice*. Lexington, Mass., Heath, 1975.
Neighbourhood improvement in Pittsburgh.

2717 Ahlbrandt, R. S. and Cunningham, J. V. *A new policy for neighborhood preservation*. New York, Praeger, 1979.

2718 Anderson, M. *The federal bulldozer: a critical analysis of urban renewal 1949–1962*. Cambridge, Mass., MIT Press, 1964.
History and failure of the US urban renewal programme.

2719 Archer, J. 'Planning for infill housing'. *Habitat* vol. 25 no. 2 (1982) pp. 14–19.
Implications of increasing housing development in the older residential areas of Canadian cities.

2720 Bellush, J. and Hausknecht, M. (eds.) *Urban renewal: people, politics and planning*. Garden City, NY, Doubleday, 1967.

2721 Benitez, A. W. *Housing rehabilitation: a guidebook for municipal programs*. Washington, DC, National Association for Housing and Redevelopment Officials, 1976.

2722 Bingham, R. D. *Public housing and urban renewal: an analysis of federal–local relations*. New York, Praeger, 1975. (Praeger special studies in US economic, social and political issues).
Take up and effects of federal housing grants to US local governments.

2723 Black, J. T. et al. *Private-market housing renovation in older urban areas*. Washington, DC, Urban Land Institute, 1977.

2724 Burchell, R. W. and Listokin, D. *Adaptive reuse handbook:*

procedures to inventory, control, manage and re-employ surplus municipal properties. New Brunswick, Rutgers University, Center for Urban Policy Research, 1981.

2725 Buren, A.V. 'Homesteads on the urban frontier'. *Architectural Design* vol. 47 no. 3 (1977) pp. 183–5.
Homesteading in poorer areas of New York and government aid.

2726 'Canadian housing programs: a different approach'. *Journal of Housing* vol. 39 no. 5 (Sept.–Oct. 1982) pp. 136–40.
Canadian programmes for low and moderate income housing rehabilitation and comparisons with the US.

2727 Carlson, D. *Revitalizing North American neighborhoods: a comparison of Canadian and US programs for neighborhood preservation and housing rehabilitation.* Washington, DC, Urban Institute, 1978.

2728 Clark, A. and Rivin, Z. *Homesteading in urban USA.* New York, Praeger, 1977. (Praeger special studies in US economic, social and political issues).

2729 Clay, P. L. *Neighborhood renewal: middle class resettlement and incumbent upgrading in American neighborhoods.* Lexington, Mass., Lexington Books, 1979.

2730 De Giovanni, F. F. 'An examination of selected consequences of revitalization in six US cities'. *Urban Studies* vol. 21 no. 3 (Aug. 1984) pp. 245–59.
Private sector rehabilitation of US inner city housing areas.

2731 Dodge, R. I. 'Rental properties can be rehabilitated using private investment, subsidy techniques'. *Journal of Housing* vol. 37 no. 9 (Oct. 1980) pp. 497–503.

2732 Eisman, E. R. 'Leveraging maximizes the effectiveness of state and federal housing program funds'. *Journal of Housing* vol. 37 (Nov. 1980) pp. 552–6.
Use of limited public funds to lever private money for housing rehabilitation.

2733   Fosler, R. S. and Berger, R. A. *Public private partnerships in American cities.* Lexington, Mass., Lexington Books, 1982.
Case studies of public–private partnerships in urban regeneration in the US.

2734   Friedman, L. M. *Government and slum housing: a century of frustration.* Chicago, Rand McNally, 1968.

2735   Gale, D. E. 'Middle class resettlement in older urban neighborhoods: the evidence and implications'. *Journal of the American Planning Association* vol. 45 (1979) pp. 293–304.

2736   Gale, D. E. *Neighborhood revitalization and the postindustrial city.* Lexington, Mass., Lexington Books, 1984.

2737   Garvin, A. 'Recycling New York. The changing philosophies of community renewal over the last fifty years'. *Perspecta* no. 16 (1980) pp 73–85.

2738   Goodman, A. C. and Shain, R. *Displacement: a selected bibliography.* Monticello, Vance Bibliographies, 1980. (Public administration series bibliography no. P.490).
Residential displacement by urban renewal and gentrification.

2739   Haar, C. *Between the idea and the reality: a study in the origin, fate and legacy of the model cities programs.* Boston, Little, Brown and Co., 1975.
Assessment of the model cities programme to co-ordinate assistance measures, including housing, to lower income slum areas.

2740   Helfeld, E. and Maguire, J. R. '"Stormy controversial" Bunker Hill: Los Angeles' oldest renewal project heads for completion in 1986'. *Journal of Housing* vol. 35 no. 3 (Mar. 1978) pp. 127–30.
The controversial total clearance project at Bunker Hill.

2741   Henig, J. R. 'Gentrification and displacement within cities: a comparative analysis'. *Social Science Quarterly* vol. 61 (1980) pp. 638–52.

2742   Henig, J. R. 'Neighborhood response to gentrification: conditions of mobilization'. *Urban Affairs Quarterly* vol. 17 no. 3 (Mar. 1982) pp. 343–58.
Neighbourhood identity more unlikely with private sector emphasis on gentrification.

2743   Hodge, D. C. 'Inner city revitalization and residential displacement in a growth region'. *Geographical Review* vol. 71 (1981) pp. 188–200.

2744   Hughes, J. W. and Bleakly, K. D. *Urban homesteading.* New Brunswick, Rutgers University, Center for Urban Policy Research, 1975.

2745   Jacobs, J. *The death and life of great American cities.* New York, Random House, 1961.
Need for conservation of housing and neighbourhoods in urban renewal in US cities.

2746   James, F. J. *Back to the city: case studies of private neighborhood revitalization in eight major metropolitan areas.* Washington, DC, Urban Institute, 1977. (Working paper 0241-02).

2747   James, F. 'The revitalization of older urban housing and neighborhoods'. In A. P. Solomon (ed.) *The prospective city: economic, population, energy and environmental developments.* Cambridge, Mass., MIT Press, 1981. pp. 130–60.

2748   Kaiser, S. E. 'Recent developments in urban redevelopment'. *Urban Law Annual* vol. 21 (1981) pp. 317–77.
Includes material on housing rehabilitation in US cities.

2749   Kern, C. R. 'Upper income renaissance in the city: its sources and implications for the city's future'. *Journal of Urban Economics* vol. 9 (1981) pp. 106–24.

2750   Lang, M. H. *Gentrification amid urban decline: strategies for America's older cities.* Cambridge, Mass., Ballinger, 1982.

2751   Laska, S. and Spain, D. (eds.) *Back to the city — issues in neighborhood renovation.* New York, Pergamon Press, 1980.

Contains several articles on rehabilitation, gentrification and displacement.

2752 Lee, B. A. and Hodge, D. C. 'Spatial differentials in residential displacement'. *Urban Studies* vol. 21 no. 3 (Aug. 1984) pp. 219–31.
US housing survey data analysed to discover the areas where displacement occurs most.

2753 Listokin, D. (ed.) *Housing rehabilitation: economic, social and policy perspectives*. New Brunswick, Rutgers University, Center for Urban Policy Research, 1983.
Reprints of material from period 1967–82.

2754 Listokin, D. and Beaton, W. P. *Revitalizing the older suburb*. New Brunswick, Rutgers University, Center for Urban Policy Research, 1984.

2755 London, B. *The revitalization of inner city neighborhoods: an updated bibliography*. Monticello, Vance Bibliographies, 1979. (Public administration series bibliography no. P. 365).

2756 Lubove, R. *The progressives and the slums: tenement house reform in New York City 1890–1917*. University of Pittsburgh Press, 1962.

2757 McConney, M. E. 'An empirical look at housing rehabilitation as a spatial process'. *Urban Studies* vol. 22 no. 1 (Feb. 1985) pp. 39–48.
Study from two US cities to determine whether the repair behaviour of owner occupiers depends on standards of neighbouring houses.

2758 Mayer, N. S. 'Rehabilitation decisions in rental housing: an empirical analysis'. *Journal of Urban Economics* vol. 10 no. 1 (July 1981) pp. 76–94.

2759 Mayer, N. S. and Marshall, S. A. *Neighborhood organization and community development*. Washington, DC, Urban Institute, 1983.

2760   Meadows, G. R. and Call, S. T. 'Combining housing market trends and resident attitudes in planning urban revitalization'. *American Institute of Planners Journal* vol. 44 no. 3 (July 1978) pp. 297–305.
Role of neighbourhood transition and property values in the revitalization of urban areas in the US.

2761   Mendelsohn, R. 'Empirical evidence on home improvements'. *Journal of Urban Economics* vol. 4 no. 4 (Oct. 1977) pp. 459–68.

2762   Mendelson, R. E. and Quinn, M. A. (eds.) *The politics of housing in older urban areas.* New York, Praeger, 1976. (Praeger special studies in US economic, social and political issues).
Based on a seminar held at Southern Illinois University, June 1974, and containing material on urban regions of the East and Midwest of the US.

2763   Miller, Z. L. and Jenkins, T. H. (eds.) *The planning partnership: participant's views of urban renewal.* Beverly Hills, Sage, 1982.

2764   National Urban Coalition. *Displacement: city neighborhoods in transition.* Washington, DC, The Coalition, 1978.

2765   'Neighborhood revitalization'. *Journal of the American Planning Association* vol. 45 no. 4 (Oct. 1979) pp. 460–556.
Several articles from research funded by the US federal government on its neighbourhood based urban policy.

2766   Nolon, J. R. 'Effective strategy is needed for moderate rehabilitation of multifamily housing'. *Journal of Housing* vol. 37 no. 2 (Feb. 1980) pp. 71–80.

2767   O'Loughlin, J. and Munski, D. C. 'Housing rehabilitation in the inner city: a comparison of two neighborhoods in New Orleans'. *Economic Geography* vol. 55 no. 1 (Jan. 1979) pp. 52–70.

2768   Palen, J. J. and London, B. (eds.) *Gentrification, displacement and neighborhood revitalization.* Albany, State University of New York Press, 1984.

2769   Parson, D. 'The development of redevelopment: public housing and urban renewal in Los Angeles'. *International Journal of Urban and Regional Research* vol. 6 (1982) pp. 393–413.

2770   Parson, D. 'Organized labor and the housing question: public housing, suburbanization and urban renewal'. *Environment and Planning D* vol. 2 no. 1 (Mar. 1984) pp. 75–86.
Public housing and urban renewal policies in the US which have developed from class struggle.

2771   Peterson, G. et al. *Property taxes, housing and cities.* Lexington, Mass., Lexington Books, 1973.
Local government's role in community redevelopment in US cities.

2772   Phillips, K. F. and Teitz, M. B. *Housing conservation in older urban areas: a mortgage insurance approach.* Berkeley, University of California, Institute of Governmental Studies, 1978. (Research report 78-2).
Based on a study prepared for the US Housing and Urban Development Department.

2773   Roddewig, R. and Young, M. S 'Neighborhood revitalization and the historic preservation incentives of the Tax Reform Act of 1976: lessons from the bottom line of a Chicago red brick three-flat'. *Urban Lawyer* vol. 11 no. 1 (Winter 1979) pp. 35–74.

2774   Rogg, N. H. 'Urban housing rehabilitation in the United States'. *Urban Land* vol. 37 no. 1 (Jan. 1978) pp. 10–18.

2775   Rose, D. 'Rethinking gentrification: beyond the uneven development of Marxist urban theory'. *Environment and Planning D* vol. 2 (1984) pp. 47–74.
Concepts of gentrification in North American cities.

2776   Rothenberg, J. *Economic evaluation of urban renewal.* Washington, DC, Brookings Institution, 1967.

2777   Schill, M. H. and Nathan, R. P. *Revitalizing America's cities: neighborhood reinvestment and displacement.* Albany, State University of New York Press, 1983.

Investment and human costs in urban revitalization in five US cities.

2778   Smith, N. 'Gentrification and uneven development'. *Economic Geography* vol. 58 no. 2 (Apr. 1982) pp. 139–55.
Process of gentrification in US cities is only a small part of a restructuring of urban space.

2779   Smith, N. 'Toward a theory of gentrification: a back to the city movement by capital not people'. *Journal of the American Planning Association* vol. 45 (1979) pp. 538–48.

2780   Sternlieb, G. and Hughes, J. W. *Neighborhood decline in urban areas.* New Brunswick, Rutgers University, Center for Urban Policy Research, 1973.

2781   Stokes, B. 'Recycled housing'. *Environment* (US) vol. 21 no. 1 (Jan.–Feb. 1979) pp. 6–14.
Rehabilitation of urban housing, mainly in the US.

2782   Strickland, D. 'National urban policy and the shifting priorities of inner-city revitalization'. *Urban Analysis* vol. 7 no. 2 (Feb. 1983) pp. 155–68.
Shift from low income housing policies to private investment.

2783   Struever, C. W. 'Public/private partnerships: the federal withdrawal'. *Journal of Housing* vol. 39 no. 3 (May–June 1982) pp. 72–5.
Reagan administration's withdrawal from urban revitalization activities.

2784   Sumka, H. J. and Blackburn, A. J. 'Multifamily urban homesteading: a key approach to low-income housing'. *Journal of Housing* vol. 39 no. 4 (July–Aug. 1982) pp. 104–7.
Residents' co-operatives in the US renovating, owning and managing derelict blocks of flats.

2785   United States, Department of Housing and Urban Development. *Action grants: revitalizing and conserving cities.* Washington, DC, The Department, 1980.

2786   United States, Department of Housing and Urban Development. *Additions to the housing supply by means other than new construction.* Washington, DC, The Department, 1982.

2787   United States, Department of Housing and Urban Development. *Displacement report.* Washington, DC, The Department, 1979.
   Report on families displaced by urban redevelopment in US cities.

2788   United States, Department of Housing and Urban Development. *Home improvement financing.* Washington, DC, The Department, 1977.

2789   United States, Department of Housing and Urban Development. *Neighborhood conservation and property rehabilitation: a bibliography.* Washington, DC, The Department, 1979.
   Updates a similar bibliography produced in 1969; mainly of US interest.

2790   United States, House, Committee on Banking, Currency and Housing, Subcommittee on Historic Preservation and Coinage. *Preservation programs of the federal government in the area of housing and community development: staff report.* Washington, DC, Government Printing Office, 1976.

2791   United States, National Commission on Urban Problems. *Building the American city.* Washington, DC, Government Printing Office, 1969. (91st Congress, 1st session, House document no. 91-34).
   Final report of the Douglas Commission into urban renewal.

2792   Urban Systems Research and Engineering. *Evaluation of the urban homesteading demonstration program: final report.* Washington, DC, Department of Housing and Urban Development, 1983.
   Final report of the US homesteading programme providing rehabilitated housing for low and moderate income families.

2793   Vaughn, S. J. *Private reinvestment, gentrification, and dis-*

320

placement: selected references with annotations. Chicago, Council of Planning Librarians, 1980. (CPL Bibliography no. 33).
Movement of relatively affluent home owners to poorer urban areas, and effects.

2794   Weir, M. *House recycling: the best real estate opportunity for the 1980s.* Chicago, Contemporary Books, 1982.

2795   Weiss, M. 'The origins and legacy of urban renewal'. In P. Claval et al. (eds.) *Urban and regional planning in an age of austerity.* New York, Pergamon, 1980. pp. 53–80.

2796   Welfeld, I. W. et al. *Perspectives on housing and urban renewal.* New York, Praeger, 1974.
Post-war experience of public housing and urban renewal in the US.

2797   Weston, J. 'Gentrification and displacement'. *Habitat* vol. 25 no. 1 (1982) pp. 10–19.
Problems posed by gentrification in Canada and the displacement of lower income people from the inner city.

2798   Wiley, T. M. 'Financing redevelopment projects'. *Journal of Housing* vol. 3 no. 4 (July–Aug. 1982) pp. 108–11.
Private/public partnerships for financing urban renewal projects in the US.

2799   Woodbury, C. (ed.) *The future of cities and urban redevelopment: problems and practices.* University of Chicago Press, 1953.
Collection of essays which have become a seminal work on the origins of urban renewal policy.

2800   Zeitz, E. *Private urban renewal: a different residential trend.* Lexington, Mass., Lexington Books, 1979.

18.5   Australasia

2801   Australia, Department of Environment, Housing and Community Development. *Urban renewal.* Canberra, Australian Government Publishing Service, 1978.

2802 Badcock, B. A. and Cloher, D. U. U. 'Neighbourhood change in inner Adelaide 1966–76'. *Urban Studies* vol. 18 no. 1 (Feb. 1981) pp. 41–55.
Urban renewal in Adelaide.

2803 Johnson, J. J. *Urban renewal, urban rehabilitation: a selective, annotated bibliography.* Adelaide, South Australian Housing Trust, 1978. (Library bibliography no. 23).
Contains 125 entries on urban renewal issues mainly in Australia, but also including the US and Britain.

2804 Kendig, H. *New life for old suburbs.* Sydney, Allen and Unwin, 1979.
Urban renewal in Australia.

2805 Loomis, T. M. 'Housing rehabilitation as a catalyst for social change: an Auckland case study'. *New Zealand Architect* no. 2 (Apr. 1979) pp. 16–25.

2806 Pugh, C. 'Older residential areas and the development of economic analysis'. In J. C. McMaster and G. R. Webb (eds.) *Australian urban and regional economics: a reader.* Sydney, Australian and New Zealand Book Co., 1976.

2807 Seek, N. H. 'Adjusting housing consumption: improve or move'. *Urban Studies* vol. 20 no. 4 (Nov. 1983) pp. 455–69.
Home improvement decisions and activity in Australia.

18.6 Africa, Asia and Latin America

2808 Angel, S. 'Upgrading slum infrastructure: divergent objectives in search of a concensus'. *Third World Planning Review* vol. 5 no. 1 (Feb. 1983) pp. 5–22.

2809 Atman, R. 'Kampong improvements in Indonesia'. *Ekistics* vol. 40 no. 238 (Sept. 1975) pp. 216–20.

2810 Baross, P. (ed.) *Experiences with settlement improvement policies in Asia: four case studies.* Rotterdam, Bouwcentrum International Education, 1981.

2811   Batley, R. 'Urban renewal and expulsion in Sao Paulo'. In A. Gilbert (ed.) *Urbanization in Latin America*. Chichester, Wiley, 1982. pp. 231–62.

2812   Blunt, A. 'Ismailia sites and services and upgrading projects: a preliminary evaluation'. *Habitat International* vol. 6 nos. 5–6 (1982) pp. 587–97.

2813   Burns, L. 'Cost-benefit analysis of improved housing: a case study'. *Ekistics* vol. 21 (1966) pp. 304–12.

2814   Carmon, N. and Hill, M. 'Neighbourhood deterioration and rehabilitation — the Israeli experience'. *ITCC Review* vol. 10 no. 1 (Jan. 1981) pp. 40–9.

2815   Cheung, S. N. S. 'Rent control and housing reconstruction: the post war experience of prewar premises in Hong Kong'. *Journal of Law and Economics* vol. 22 no. 1 (Apr. 1979) pp. 27–53.
Ingenious approach of Hong Kong to the problem of urban renewal under rent control.

2816   Choe, A. F. C. 'Urban renewal'. In O. Jin-Bee and H. D. Chiang (eds.) *Modern Singapore*. Singapore University Press, 1969. pp. 33–58.

2817   Cousins, W. J. and Goyder, C. *Changing slum communities*. Delhi, Manohar, 1979.
Study of Hyderabad.

2818   Davidson, F. and Payne, G. (eds.) *Urban projects manual: a guide to the preparation of projects for new development and upgrading relevant to low income groups based on the approach used for the Ismailia Demonstration Projects, Egypt*. Liverpool University Press, 1983. (Liverpool planning manual 1).

2819   Devas, N. *Indonesia's Kampung improvement programme: an evaluative case-study*. University of Birmingham, Institute of Local Government Studies, Development Administration Group, 1980. (Occasional paper 10).

2820   Drakakis-Smith, D. W. 'Urban renewal in an Asian

context: a case study in Hong Kong'. *Urban Studies* vol. 13 no. 3 (Oct. 1976) pp. 295–305.

2821 Indian Institute of Public Administration. *Seminar on slum clearance and improvement.* New Delhi, The Institute, 1979.
Papers from a seminar held in Feb. 1974.

2822 Jere, H. E. 'Squatter up-grading: a policy put into practice'. *International Journal for Housing Science and its Applications* vol. 3 no. 3 (1979) pp. 227–32.
Implementation of squatter upgrading in Zambia.

2823 Martin, R. 'Housing options, Lusaka, Zambia'. *Ekistics* vol. 44 (Aug. 1977) pp. 88–95.
Squatter settlement upgrading.

2824 Martinez, E. and Baross, P. 'Upgrading low income residential areas in developing countries: the social organisation of decision-making'. *Openhouse* vol. 3 no. 4 (1978) pp. 41–52.

2825 Masembejo, L. M. and Tumsiph, N. J. W. *Upgrading in Dar es Salaam.* Gavle, National Swedish Institute for Building Research, 1981. (Meddelande M81:22).

2826 Mathey, K. 'The rehabilitation program of Alagados squatter settlement, Brazil'. *Ekistics* vol. 45 no. 270 (June 1978) pp. 257–61.

2827 Nientied, P. *Karachi squatter settlement upgrading.* Amsterdam, Vrei University, 1982.

2828 Okoye, T. O. 'Urban planning in Nigeria and the problem of slums'. *Third World Planning Review* vol. 1 no. 1 (Spring 1979) pp. 71–85.

2829 Pasteur, D. *The management of squatter upgrading: a case study of organisation procedures and participation.* Farnborough, Saxon House, 1979.
Study of Lusaka, Zambia.

2830 Pasteur, D. *The management of squatter upgrading in Lusaka:*

phase 2: the transition to maintenance and further development. University of Birmingham, Institute of Local Government Studies, Development Administration Group, 1982. (Occasional paper 15).

2831   Payne, G. K. (ed.) *Low income housing in the developing world: the role of sites and services and settlement upgrading.* Chichester, Wiley, 1984. (Public administration in developing countries). Manual and reference work for students and teachers of development administration, urban studies and architecture in developing countries.

2832   Pfister, F. 'Housing improvement and popular participation in the Upper Volta'. *Habitat International* vol. 6 nos. 1–2 (1982) pp. 209–14.

2833   Phillips, D. R. and Yeh, A. G. O. 'Changing attitudes to housing provision: BLISS in the Philippines'. *Geography* vol. 68 part 1 no. 298 (Jan. 1983) pp. 37–40.
The Bagong Lipunan improvement of sites and services policy of providing housing for poorer people in the Philippines .

2834   Rakodi, C. and Schlyter, A. *Upgrading in Lusaka: participation and physical changes.* Gavle, National Swedish Institute for Building Research, 1981.

2835   Saini, B. 'Practical slum housing'. *Architecture Australia* vol. 68 no. 1 (Mar. 1979) pp. 30–7.
Urban slum problem in Third World cities and the need for services.

2836   Schlyter, A. *Upgrading reconsidered: the George studies in retrospect.* Gavle, National Swedish Institute for Building Research, 1984.
Squatter upgrading in Lusaka, Zambia.

2837   Schoorl, J. W. et al. (eds.) *Between Basti dwellers and bureaucrats: lessons in squatter settlement upgrading in Karachi.* Oxford, Pergamon, 1983.

2838   Sen, M. K. 'The rehousing and rehabilitation of squatters in Kuala Lumpur'. *Ekistics* vol. 40 no. 238 (Sept. 1975) pp. 207–10.

2839   Steinberg, F. 'Slum and shanty upgrading in Colombo: a help for the urban poor?' *International Journal of Urban and Regional Research* vol. 6 (1982) pp. 372–91.

2840   Strassmann, W. *The transformation of urban housing: the experience of upgrading in Cartagena.* Baltimore, Johns Hopkins University Press, 1982. (A World Bank research publication).

2841   Taylor, J. L. and Williams, D. G. 'Upgrading of low-income residential areas in Jakarta and Manila'. In J. L. Taylor and D. G. Williams (eds.) *Urban planning practice in developing countries.* Oxford, Pergamon, 1982. pp. 239–58.

2842   United Nations, Centre for Housing, Building and Planning. 'A sites and services and area upgrading project in the Upper Volta, Africa'. *Ekistics* vol. 45 no. 270 (June 1978) pp. 262–7.

2843   United Nations, Department of Economic and Social Affairs. *Improvement of slums and uncontrolled settlements.* New York, United Nations, 1971.
   Studies of squatters in Bandung, Caracas, Ibadan, Istanbul, Kuala Lumpur, Lima, Manila and Seoul.

2844   Van der Linden, J. 'Actors in squatter settlement upgrading: their interests and roles'. *Openhouse* vol. 6 no. 1 (1981) pp. 36–43.
   Squatter settlement upgrading in Pakistan.

2845   Van der Linden, J. J. 'The Bastis of Karachi: the functioning of an informal housing system'. In J. W. Schoorl et al (eds.) *Between Basti dwellers and bureaucrats: lessons in squatter settlement upgrading in Karachi.* Oxford, Pergamon, 1983. pp. 43–60.

19

New communities

Since the origins of the new town idea in the writings of Ebenezer
Howard and other early 20th century visionaries and its expression in the early garden cities, town planners have seen new
towns, built with low density, landscaped housing, as the answer
to overcrowded and insanitary conditions of inner city and
metropolitan areas. The period since the Second World War has
seen the establishment and growth of new towns in virtually all
parts of the world. Housing development in the new towns has
been extremely well documented, and, while the new town
concept has met with mixed success in different countries, its
adoption by many governments in both the industrialized and
developing worlds justifies its inclusion as a separate section in
this bibliography.

19.1   International and comparative

2846   Fishman, R. *Urban utopias in the twentieth century.* New York,
Harper and Row, 1978.
> Examines the ideal cities planned by Ebenezer Howard, Frank
> Lloyd Wright and Le Corbusier, and assesses the relevance of
> their ideas and the persistence of the Utopian vision.

2847   Galantay, E. Y. 'New towns in national development:
goals, policies and strategies'. *Ekistics* vol. 46 no. 277 (July–Aug.
1979) pp. 200–5.
> Summary of the final report of the International Federation
> for Housing and Planning Working Party on 'New Towns in

National Development'.

2848 Golany, G. (ed.) *International urban growth policies: new town contributions.* Chichester, Wiley, 1978.
Review of new town policies from European countries, developing countries, Canada, Australia, Japan, India, Israel, making a total of 18 countries.

2849 Golany, G. *New towns planning and development: a world-wide bibliography.* Washington, DC, Urban Land Institute, 1973. (Research report 20).

2850 Johnston, M. 'Public policies, private choices: new town planning and lifestyles in three nations'. *Urban Affairs Quarterly* vol. 13 no. 1 (Sept. 1977) pp. 3–32.
Policies towards new towns and social consequences in UK, USSR and US.

2851 *New towns in national development.* The Hague, International Federation for Housing and Planning, 1980.

2852 United States, Department of Housing and Urban Development. *Planning new towns: national reports of the US and the USSR.* Washington, DC, The Department, 1981.
'Joint report of the US/USSR New Towns Working Group under the Agreement on Co-operation in the Field of Housing and other construction'.

19.2 Europe

2853 Bullock, N. 'Housing reform and the garden city in Germany 1890–1915'. *Martin Centre for Architectural and Urban Studies Transactions* vol. 1 no. 1 (1976) pp. 203–23.

2854 Cooke, C. 'Activities in the garden city movement in Russia'. *Martin Centre for Architectural and Urban Studies Transactions* vol. 1 no. 1 (1976) pp. 225–49.

2855 Cooke, C. 'Russian responses to the garden city idea'. *Architectural Review* vol. 163 no. 976 (June 1978) pp. 354–63.

2856 'Garden city housing'. *Architectural Review* (Aug. 1979) pp. 315–77.
Special issue on garden city housing in Britain, USSR, France and West Germany.

2857 Hamilton, I. 'New towns in planned economies'. *Town and Country Planning* vol. 49 no. 10 (Nov. 1980) pp. 353–6.
New towns in Eastern Europe and USSR.

2858 Perczel, K. 'Planning new towns in Hungary'. *Ekistics* vol. 46 no. 277 (July–Aug. 1979) pp. 210–14.

2859 Read, J. 'The garden city and the growth of Paris'. *Architectural Review* vol. 163 no. 976 (June 1978) pp. 345–52.
French interpretation of the garden city idea and the design of large housing developments.

2860 Rubenstein, J. M. *The French new towns.* Baltimore, Johns Hopkins University Press, 1978. (Johns Hopkins studies in urban affairs).

2861 Tuppen, J. N. 'The development of French new towns'. *Urban Studies* vol. 20 no. 1 (Feb. 1983) pp. 11–30.

2862 Underhill, J. A. *French national urban policy and the Paris region new towns: the search for community.* Washington, DC, Department of Housing and Urban Development, 1980.

2863 Zimmerman, J. F. 'New town development in the Dublin area'. *Planning and Administration* vol. 5 no. 1 (Spring 1978) pp. 68–80.

19.3 United Kingdom

2864 Aldridge, M. *The British new towns: a programme without a policy.* London, Routledge and Kegan Paul, 1979.

2865 Cherry, G. E. 'New towns and inner-city blight'. *New Society* 8 Feb. 1979 pp. 296–9.

Examines immediate post-war housing.

2866 Cullingworth, J. B. *Environmental planning 1939–1969, vol. 3, new towns policy.* London, HMSO, 1979.
See in particular the chapter entitled 'housing issues' (pp. 385–447).

2867 Cullingworth, J. B. *Housing needs and planning policy: a restatement of the problems of housing need and overspill in England and Wales.* London, Routledge and Kegan Paul, 1960.

2868 Farmer, E. and Smith, R. 'Overspill theory'. *Urban Studies* vol. 12 (1975) pp. 151–68.
How overspill policy emerged as a way of clearing Glasgow's slums.

2869 Gee, F. A. *Homes and jobs for Londoners in new and expanding towns.* London, HMSO, 1972. (Social survey 452).
Through the Industrial Selection Scheme people gaining employment in new towns were eligible to rent a home.

2870 Hall, P. 'Ebenezer Howard'. *New Society* vol. 62 no. 1043 (11 Nov. 1982) pp. 252–4.
Social visions of Howard, and how they have been abused in the new towns programme in the UK.

2871 Heraud, B. J. 'The new towns and London's housing problem'. *Urban Studies* vol. 3 (1966) pp. 8–21.
Discusses London's new towns, especially Crawley, in the context of their role as relief to London's housing problems.

2872 Horrocks, M. *Social development work in the new communities.* University of Birmingham, Centre for Urban and Regional Studies, 1974. (Occasional paper no. 27).
Report of a three-year research project on the work of social development staff in the new towns.

2873 Howard, E. *Garden cities of tomorrow.* 1898. Reprinted London, Faber and Faber, 1965.
By the father of the new town and garden city movement.

2874   Joseph Rowntree Village Trust. *One man's vision: the story of the Joseph Rowntree Village Trust.* London, Allen and Unwin, 1954.
Traces the development of the Trust and the estate at New Earswick near York, emphasising Rowntree's determination to construct new communities as well as improved housing.

2875   Miller, M. 'Garden city influence on the evolution of housing policy'. *Local Government Studies* vol. 5 no. 6 (Nov.–Dec. 1979) pp. 5–22.

2876   Ogilvy, A. A. *Bracknell and its migrants: twenty-one years of new town growth.* London, HMSO, 1975.
Detailed examination of the development of one of London's new towns. Housing is shown to be the main motive encouraging migration; however, it is difficult to assess Bracknell's contribution to London's housing problems.

2877   Potter, S. 'The alternative new towns'. *Town and Country Planning* (Nov. 1984) pp. 306–11.
Performance of the expanded towns programme.

2878   Thomas R. 'The 1972 Housing Finance Act and the demise of the new town and local authority housing programmes'. *Urban Law and Policy* vol. 5 (June 1982) pp. 107–26.

2879   United Kingdom, House of Commons. *Reports of the Development Corporations.* London, HMSO, annual.
Reports, published since 1947, of the activities of New Town Development Corporations, each with an informative section on housing.

2880   United Kingdom, Ministry of Health. *Garden cities and satellite towns: report of a departmental committee.* London, HMSO, 1935.
The Marley report, which recommended the dispersal of population and the creation of satellite towns. An interesting observation was 'the opportunity to provide individual cottage homes'.

2881   United Kingdom, Ministry of Housing and Local Government. *The ownership and management of housing in the new towns.* London, HMSO, 1968.

Report by J. B. Cullingworth and V. A. Karn, which studied the existing situation with discussion of alternative policies for the future. Based largely on social surveys of Aycliffe, Crawley, East Kilbride and Stevenage, but appendix VI does give facts and figures for several other new towns.

2882 United Kingdom, New Towns Committee. *Final report.* London, HMSO, 1946. (Cmd. 6876).

The Reith report, which recommended building new towns as part of post-war housing policy.

2883 United Kingdom, Royal Commission on the Distribution of the Industrial Population. *Report.* London, HMSO, 1940. (Cmd. 6153).

The Barlow report. See especially chs. 5, 8, 10, 13, 16. Outlined plans for the wartime reconstruction programme and advocated new towns as homes for dispersed people and industry.

2884 Veal, A. J. *New communities in the UK: a select bibliography.* University of Birmingham, Centre for Urban and Regional Studies, 1973. (Research memorandum 21).

Supplementary bibliography published in 1975.

19.4 North America

2885 Brown, R. *Housing policy and development within the planned communities in South-west USA.* Brisbane, University of Queensland, Department of Regional and Town Planning, 1983. (Queensland planning papers 26).

2886 Budgen, M. 'Tumbler Ridge: planning the physical and social development of a new community'. *Habitat* vol. 26 no. 1 (1983) pp. 8–12.

Emphasis on home ownership in a new town in Canada.

2887 Burby, R. and Weiss, S. *New communities, USA.* Lexington, Mass., Lexington Books, 1976.

Includes sections on housing.

2888   Evans, H. and Rodwin, L. 'The new towns program and why it failed'. *Public Interest* no. 56 (Summer 1979) pp. 90–107.
History of the US new communities programme and why it failed.

2889   Golany, G. and Walden, D. *The contemporary new communities movement in the United States.* Urbana, University of Illinois Press, 1974.
New towns in the US.

2890   Kaiser, E. J. *Residential mobility in new communities.* Cambridge, Mass., Ballinger, 1976.

2891   Perloff, H. S. and Sandberg, N. C. *New towns: why and for whom?* New York, Pall Mall, 1973.
New communities in the US planned by the federal government from 1968.

2892   Schaffer, D. *Garden cities for America: the Radburn experience.* Philadelphia, Temple University Press, 1982.

19.5   Australasia

2893   Freestone, R. 'Australia and the garden city tradition'. *Town and Country Planning* vol. 52 no. 6 (June 1983) pp. 180–3.

19.6   Africa, Asia and Latin America

2894   Berger, A. *New towns in Israel.* New Brunswick, Transaction Books, 1980.

2895   Cockburn, R. 'Dummar new town: a formula for tackling Syria's housing problems'. *Middle East Construction* vol. 5 no. 4 (Apr. 1980) pp. 61–4.
Planning, financing and construction of a new town near Damascus.

2896 Fook, T. L. T. 'Housing through new towns: the case of Petaling Jaya'. In S. H. Tan and H. Sendut (eds.) *Public and private housing in Malaysia*. Kuala Lumpur, Heinemann, 1979. pp. 267–88.

2897 Okpala, D. C. I. 'A critique of the application of new town concepts in Nigeria: the case of Ajoda New Town'. *Third World Planning Review* vol. 1 no. 1 (Spring 1979) pp. 57–70.

2898 Pressman, N. 'Israel's new towns: urban development by design'. *Habitat* vol. 23 no. 1 (1980) pp. 48–53.

2899 Weiner, H. R. 'Israel's new towns: a Mediterranean perspective'. *Ekistics* vol. 48 no. 290 (Sept.–Oct. 1981) pp. 393–9.
New town programmes in Israel, Italy, Libya, Spain and Algeria.

20

High rise housing

The now largely discredited policy of high rise housing construction was widely considered during the post Second World War period to be an answer to the problems of the shortage of land for new housing and the need for quickly built mass housing. The technical deficiencies and sociological disadvantages of high rise housing very soon became evident, however, and gave rise to widespread concern in the housing literature. That the problem is world-wide can be seen from references to problems with high rise housing from many parts of the world, including developing countries, although there appears to be a conspicuous lack of material from North America. Users should also refer to sections 1 'Housing policy: general works', 3 'Construction and energy conservation' and 18 'Improvement and urban renewal' for further reading on high rise and associated issues.

20.1   International and comparative

2900   Beedle, L. S. 'High-rise Habitat'. *Habitat* vol. 2 nos. 1–2 (1977) pp. 101–31.

2901   Carlson, E. 'Community integration and community development in high rise housing'. In *The social environment and its effect on the design of the dwelling and its immediate surroundings.* Stockholm, National Swedish Institute for Building Research, 1968. pp. 171–93.

2902   Conway, D. J. (ed.) *Human response to tall buildings.*

Stroudsburg, Dowden, Hutchinson and Ross, 1977. (Community development series vol. 34)

Proceedings of a conference sponsored by the American Institute of Architects and the Joint Committee on Tall Buildings and held at Sears Tower, Chicago, July 1975.

2903   Marmot, A. F. 'The legacy of Le Corbusier and high-rise housing'. *Built Environment* vol. 7 no. 2 (1981) pp. 82–95.

2904   Mitchell, R. E. 'Some social implications of high density housing'. *American Sociological Review* vol. 36 (Feb. 1971) pp. 18–29.

2905   Williamson, R. C. 'Socialisation of the high rise'. *Ekistics* vol. 45 no. 268 (Mar.–Apr. 1978) pp. 122–9.

High rise intolerable for people who need neighbourliness.

2906   Young, S. *Social and psychological effects of living in high rise buildings.* University of Sydney, 1976. (Ian Buchan Fell research project on housing no. 16).

20.2   Europe

2907   Enders, M. J. 'Pruitt-Igoe abroad: public housing problems in France'. *Journal of Housing* vol. 40 no. 2 (Mar.–Apr. 1983) pp. 47, 50.

Reassessment of multi-storey housing schemes in France.

2908   Michelson, W. *Reversing the 'inevitable' trend: high-rise housing in Sweden and Denmark.* University of Toronto, Centre for Urban and Community Studies, 1976. (Research paper no. 79).

2909   Williamson, R. C. 'Adjustment to the highrise: variables in a German sample'. *Environment and Behavior* vol. 13 no. 3 (May 1981) pp. 289–310.

Interviews with residents of high rise housing in West Germany. Satisfaction was conditioned by a number of variables, including social networks.

2910   Wynn, M. 'The residential development process in Spain: a case study'. *Planning Outlook* vol. 24 no. 1 (1981) pp. 20–9.

High rise housing development in a Barcelona suburb.

20.3   United Kingdom

2911   Anderson, R. et al. *Tower blocks*. London, Institute of Housing, 1984.
Alternative uses for high rise flats.

2912   Ash, J. 'The rise and fall of high rise housing in England'. In C. Ungerson and V. Karn (eds.) *The consumer experience of housing: cross-national perspectives*. Farnborough, Gower, 1980. pp. 93–123.

2913   Blake, J. 'High living'. *Built Environment* vol. 4 no. 3 (1978) pp. 189–94.

2914   Coleman, A. 'Design influences in blocks of flats'. *Geographical Journal* vol. 150 no. 3 (Nov. 1984) pp. 351–8.
Develops work of Oscar Newman in assessing social problems of high rise flats. Published as the first article in a double feature entitled 'Trouble in Utopia'.

2915   Dunleavy, P. *The politics of mass-housing in Britain 1945–1975: a study of corporate power and professional influence in the welfare state*. Oxford, Clarendon Press, 1981.
Origins of, and justification for, the post-war boom in high rise housing.

2916   Gillis, A. R. 'High-rise housing and psychological strain'. *Journal of Health and Social Behaviour* vol. 18 no. 4 (1977) pp. 418–31.
Women more affected by high rise living than men.

2917   Gittus, E. *Flats, families and the under fives*. London, Routledge and Kegan Paul, 1976.
Study of the problems of bringing up young children in local authority housing on Tyneside in the 1960s.

2918   Hole, V. 'The origin and development of high density housing policies in the UK 1945–1970'. *Planning History Bulletin* vol. 3 no. 3 (1981) pp. 2–6.

2919   Jephcott, P. *Homes in high flats.* Edinburgh, Oliver and Boyd, 1971.
Study of high rise building in Glasgow.

2920   Littlewood, J. and Tinker, A. *Families in flats.* London, HMSO, 1981.

2921   McCutcheon, R. 'High flats in Britain 1945 to 1971'. In Conference of Socialist Economists, *Political economy and the housing question.* London, The Conference, 1975.

2922   Pepper, S. 'Ossulston Street: early LCC experiences in high rise housing 1925–29'. *London Journal* vol. 7 no. 1 (Summer 1981) pp. 45–64.

2923   Randall, B. (ed.) *Trends in high places: how six housing authorities are making the most of tower blocks.* London, Institute of Housing, 1983.

2924   Sutcliffe, A. (ed.) *Multi-storey living: the British working class experience.* London, Croom, Helm, 1974.
Historical study of the unpopularity of flats in Britain.

2925   United Kingdom, Department of the Environment, Housing Development Directorate. *The social effects of living off the ground.* London, The Department, 1975.
Good review of problems of high rise housing. Success depends on households and the family life cycle.

2926   United Kingdom, Ministry of Housing and Local Government. *Collapse of flats at Ronan Point, Canning Town.* London, HMSO, 1968.
The Griffiths report on the collapse of a high rise tower block in East London.

2927   United Kingdom, Ministry of Housing and Local Government. *Families living in high density.* London, HMSO, 1970.
Studies of Leeds, Liverpool and London.

2928   United Kingdom, Ministry of Housing and Local Government. *Living in flats.* London, HMSO, 1952.

2929   Vint, J. and Bintliff, J. 'Tower blocks: the economics of high-rise housing'. *Social Policy and Administration* vol. 17 no. 2 (Summer 1983) pp. 118–29.

20.4   Africa, Asia and Latin America

2930   Brandt, D. P. 'Optimum residential building heights. The case of the Min Sheng new community, Taiwan'. *Third World Planning Review* vol. 3 no. 4 (Nov. 1981) pp. 432–8.

2931   Hassan, R. 'Social and psychological implications of high density housing in Hong Kong and Singapore'. *Ekistics* vol. 39 no. 235 (June 1975) pp. 382–6.

2932   Walter, M. A. H. B. 'The territorial and the social: perspectives on the lack of community in high rise/high density living in Singapore'. *Ekistics* vol. 45 no. 270 (June 1978) pp. 236–42.

21
Rural housing

Whereas the issues created by urban housing provision have been relatively well covered in the housing literature, the rural housing sector has suffered from a lack of attention, almost becoming in some cases the forgotten arm of housing. Increasing disillusionment with city life and a gradual resurgence of interest in the rural sector have, however, led to an increasing awareness of the issues facing rural housing in recent years. This section includes references to works where the rural nature of the housing issue raised overrides other considerations, such as tenure, finance or housing market. Attention should therefore also be paid to sections 2 'Housing market', 4 'Housing finance' and 7 'Housing tenure' as well as sections 10 'Private rental sector', which includes some references to tied accommodation, and 22 'Second homes', since second homes are almost exclusively to be found in rural areas.

21.1 International and comparative

2933 Marantz, J. K. *Discrimination in rural housing: economic and social analysis of six selected markets.* Lexington, Mass., Lexington Books, 1976.

2934 United Nations, Department of Economic and Social Affairs. *Rural housing: a review of world conditions.* New York, United Nations, 1969.

21.2 Europe

2935 Doxiadis, C. A. and Vafeiadis, V. I. 'Housing: the key to Greece's rural reconstruction'. *Ekistics* vol. 44 no. 263 (Oct. 1977) pp. 208–13.

2936 Pratschke, J. L. 'Rural and farm dwellings in the European community'. *Irish Journal of Agricultural Economics and Rural Sociology* vol. 8 no. 2 (1981) pp. 191–211.

2937 Pudikov, D. S. 'Regulating the financing and crediting of co-operative and individual housing construction'. *Problems of Economics* vol. 22 (Feb. 1980) pp. 93–103.
Rural housing in the USSR.

2938 United Nations, Economic Commission for Europe. 'Rural housing in selected European countries'. In United Nations, Department of Economic and Social Affairs. *Rural housing: a review of world conditions.* New York, United Nations, 1969. pp. 38–67.

21.3 United Kingdom

2939 Clark, D. *Rural housing initiatives.* London, National Council for Voluntary Organisations, 1981.

2940 Clark, G. *Housing and planning in the countryside.* Chichester, Wiley, 1982. (Geography and public policy research series vol. 2).

2941 Dunn, M. et al. *Rural housing: competition and choice.* London, Allen and Unwin, 1981. (Urban and regional studies series no. 9).

2942 Fletcher, P. 'The agricultural housing problem'. *Social and Economic Administration* vol. 3 no. 3 (1969) pp. 155–66.
Problems of tied accommodation in agricultural areas.

2943 Giles, A. K. and Cowie, W. J. G. 'Some social and economic aspects of agricultural workers' accommodation'. *Journal of Agricultural Economics* vol. 14 no. 2 (1961) pp. 147–69.

2944   Jones, A. K. *Rural housing — the agricultural tied cottage.* London, Bell, 1975. (Occasional papers on social administration no. 56).

2945   Larkin, A. 'Rural housing and housing needs'. In J. M. Shaw *Rural deprivation and planning.* Norwich, Geo Books, 1979. pp. 71–80.

2946   National Federation of Housing Associations. *Rural housing: hidden problems and possible solutions: report of a NFHA Working Party.* London, The Federation, 1981.

2947   Neate, S. *Rural deprivation: an annotated bibliography of economic and social problems in rural Britain.* Norwich, Geo Books, 1981. (Bibliography no. 8).

2948   Newby, H. *The deferential worker.* London, Allen Lane, 1977.
Study of rural workers, including their housing conditions.

2949   Penfold, S. F. 'Housing problems of local people in rural pressure areas'. In G. Williams (ed.) *Community development in countryside planning.* University of Manchester, 1974.

2950   Phillips, D. R. and Williams, A. M. *Rural housing and the public sector.* Aldershot, Gower, 1982.

2951   Phillips, D. and Williams, A. 'The social implications of rural housing policy: a review of developments in the past decade'. In A. Gilg (ed.) *Countryside planning yearbook vol. 4.* Norwich, Geo Books, 1983. pp. 77–102.

2952   Rogers, A. W. 'Housing'. In M. Pacione (ed.) *Progress in rural geography.* London, Croom Helm, 1983. pp. 106–29.

2953   Rogers, A. W. 'Rural housing'. In G. E. Cherry (ed.) *Rural planning problems.* London, Leonard Hill, 1976. pp. 85–121.

2954   *Rural resettlement handbook.* 3rd ed. Sherborne, Prism Alpha, 1984.

Practical advice on choosing a house, shared housing, planning and building regulations, and information sources on rural housing issues.

2955 Shucksmith, D. M. *No homes for locals?* Aldershot, Gower, 1981.
Study of rural housing with special emphasis on the Lake District.

2956 United Kingdom, Ministry of Works and Planning. *Report of the committee on land utilisation in rural areas.* London, HMSO, 1942. (Cmd. 6378).
The Scott report. Policies for building and development in rural areas.

21.4 North America

2957 Bird, R. and Kampe, R. *25 years of housing progress in rural America.* Washington, DC, Department of Agriculture Economic Research Service, 1977. (Agriculture economics report no. 373).
Covers period 1950–75.

2958 Croutch, A. *Housing migratory agricultural workers in California 1913–1948.* Palo Alto, R+E Publications, 1975.

2959 Nelson, B. F. 'Rural housing: a new possibility for local housing authorities'. *Journal of Housing* vol. 32 (May 1975) pp. 227–32.
Rural housing programmes of the Farmers Home Administration, an agency of the US Department of Agriculture.

2960 *Quality housing environment for rural low-income families.* Muscle Shoals, Tennessee Valley Authority, 1976.
Proceedings of a workshop held in Atlanta, Sept. 1975.

2961 United States, Department of Housing and Urban Development. *Report of the Task Force on Rural and Non-Metropolitan Areas.* Washington, DC, The Department, 1978.
Role of the Task Force and HUD in aiding the problems of rural areas in the US.

2962   United States, General Accounting Office. *Long-term cost implications of Farmers Home Administration subsidized and guaranteed loan program: report by the Comptroller General of the United States.* Washington, DC, The Office, 1979.
Loans for rural housing.

2963   United States, General Accounting Office. *Ways of providing a fairer share of federal housing support to rural areas: report to Congress.* Washington, DC, The Office, 1980.

2964   United States, Senate, Select Committee on Nutrition and Human Needs. *Promises to keep: housing need and federal failure in rural America.* Washington, DC, Government Printing Office, 1972.

2965   Wright, M. 'Rehabilitation of dwellings in rural areas'. *Housing and People* vol. 8 (Summer 1977) pp. 23–7.
Canadian situation.

21.5   Africa, Asia and Latin America

2966   Andersen, K. B. *African traditional architecture — a study of the housing and settlement patterns of rural Kenya.* Oxford University Press, 1977.

2967   Baldwin, K. D. S. 'The significance of rural housing'. *Ekistics* vol. 43 no. 257 (Apr. 1977) pp. 206–10.
Rural housing in developing countries.

2968   Brammah, M. 'Planning new rural settlements in Indonesia'. *Ekistics* vol. 43 no. 257 (Apr. 1977) pp. 199–203.

2969   Brebner, P. and Briggs, J. 'Rural settlement planning in Algeria and Tanzania: a comparative study'. *Habitat International* vol. 6 nos. 5–6 (1982) pp. 621–8.

2970   Ghaswala, S. K. 'Rural housing in India'. *Indian Institute of Architects Journal* vol. 44 no. 1 (Jan.–Mar. 1978) pp. 10–12.

2971   Kulaba, S. M. 'Rural settlement policies in Tanzania'. *Habitat International* vol. 6 nos. 1–2 (1982) pp. 15–29.

2972   United Nations, Department of Economic and Social Affairs. *Financing rural housing: selected policies and techniques for developing countries.* New York, United Nations, 1974.

2973   United Nations, Department of Economic and Social Affairs. *The significance of rural housing in integrated rural development.* New York, United Nations, 1978. Report of the ad hoc group of experts on the significance of rural housing and community facilities in integrated rural development held at the United Nations, New York, May 1976.

2974   United Nations, Inter-Agency Committee on Housing and Urban Development for Latin America. *Evaluation of the binational rural housing demonstration project in Colombia and Ecuador.* New York, United Nations, 1977.

2975   Yagi, K. 'Rural housing for future development'. *International Journal for Housing Science and its Applications* vol. 3 no. 5 (1979) pp. 345–58.

22

Second homes

A small body of literature has appeared in recent years on the subject of second home ownership and its effects on the communities in which such housing is located. References to these topics may be found in this section, while the planning issues raised by the expansion of second home ownership are also considered in many of the references in the previous section on rural housing.

22.1 International and comparative

2976 Coppock, J. T. (ed.) *Second homes: curse or blessing.* Oxford, Pergamon, 1977.

22.2 Europe

2977 Bielckus, C. L. 'Second homes in Scandinavia'. In J. T. Coppock (ed.) *Second homes: curse or blessing.* Oxford, Pergamon, 1977. pp. 35–46.

2978 Clout, H. D. '"Résidences secondaires" in France'. In J. T. Coppock (ed.) *Second homes: curse or blessing.* Oxford, Pergamon, 1977. pp. 47–62.

2979 Gardavsky, V. 'Second homes in Czechoslovakia'. In J. T. Coppock (ed.) *Second homes: curse or blessing.* Oxford, Pergamon, 1977. pp. 63–74.

22.3 United Kingdom

2980 Ashby, P. et al. 'Second homes in North Wales'. *Town Planning Review* vol. 46 (July 1975) pp. 323–33.

2981 Bollom, C. 'Attitudes towards second homes in rural Wales'. In G. Williams (ed.) *Social and cultural change in contemporary Wales*. London, Routledge and Kegan Paul, 1978.

2982 Clout, H. D. 'The growth of second-home ownership: an example of seasonal suburbanization'. In J. H. Johnson (ed.) *Suburban growth: geographical processes at the edge of the western city*. Chichester, Wiley, 1974.

2983 Coleman, R. 'Second homes in Norfolk'. In M. J. Moseley (ed.) *Power, planning and people in rural East Anglia*. Norwich, University of East Anglia, Centre for East Anglian Studies, 1982.

2984 Dartington Amenity Research Trust. *Second homes in Scotland*. Totnes, The Trust, 1977.

2985 Downing, P. and Dower, M. *Second homes in England and Wales*. Cheltenham, Countryside Commission, 1972. (Dartington Amenity Research Trust publication no. 7).

2986 Haines, G. H. 'The problem of second homes'. *Housing and Planning Review* vol. 29 (May–July 1973) pp. 5–8.
Discusses the adverse effects of second homes on the economy and social life of villages.

2987 Rogers, A. W. 'Secondary homes in England and Wales: a spatial view'. In J. T. Coppock (ed.) *Second homes: curse or blessing*. Oxford, Pergamon, 1977. pp. 85–102.

2988 Shucksmith, D. M. 'Second homes: a framework for policy'. *Town Planning Review* vol. 54 no. 2 (Apr. 1983) pp. 174–93.

22.4 North America

2989 Clout, H. D. 'Second homes in the United States'. *Tijdschrift voor Economische en Sociale Geografie* vol. 63 (1972) pp. 393–401.

2990 Ragatz, R. L. 'Vacation homes in rural areas: towards a model for predicting their distribution and occupancy pattern'.

In J. T. Coppock (ed.) *Second homes: curse or blessing.* Oxford, Pergamon, 1977. pp. 181–94.
Second homes in the US.

2991　Ragatz, R. L. 'Vacation housing: a missing component in urban and regional theory'. *Land Economics* vol. 46 (1970) pp. 118–26.

2992　United States, Bureau of the Census. *Second homes in the USA.* Washington, DC, Government Printing Office, 1969. (Current housing reports series H-121).

2993　Wolfe, R. I. 'Summer cottages in Ontario: purpose-built for an inessential purpose'. In J. T. Coppock (ed.) *Second homes: curse or blessing.* Oxford, Pergamon, 1977. pp. 17–34.

22.5　Australasia

2994　Robertson, R. W. 'Second home decisions: the Australian context'. In J. T. Coppock (ed.) *Second homes: curse or blessing.* Oxford, Pergamon, 1977. pp. 119–38.

22.6　Africa, Asia and Latin America

2995　Henshall, J. D. 'Second homes in the Caribbean'. In J. T. Coppock (ed.) *Second homes: curse or blessing.* Oxford, Pergamon, 1977. pp. 75–84.

23

Mobile homes

For those people unable or unwilling to be housed in conventional housing, or for travelling people, mobile homes have become an accepted form of housing provision. Policies for the control and regulation of these dwellings are referenced in this section. Related topics may also be found in sections 13 'Homelessness and squatting' and 16 'Low cost housing'.

23.1 United Kingdom

2996 Constable, M. *Factory built houses*. London, Shelter, 1975.
Examines the present and future use of mobile homes.

2997 Cripps, J. *Accommodation for gypsies: a report on the working of the Caravan Sites Act 1968*. London, HMSO, 1977.
Study made on behalf of the Department of the Environment to consider the effectiveness of the Caravan Sites Act 1968 in providing accommodation for gypsies.

2998 Home, R. K. 'The Caravan Sites Act 1968: progress and problems with designation'. *Journal of Planning and Environment Law* Apr. 1984 pp. 226–34.

2999 Kenny, P. H. and Wilson, S. 'A caravan by any other name'. *Journal of Planning and Environment Law* Dec. 1984 pp. 853–8.
Considers the definition of mobile home and finds that it can apply to reasonably substantial developments.

3000 Thomas, R. 'Mobile Homes Act 1983'. *New Law Journal* vol. 133 no. 6110 (1 July 1983) pp. 599–602.
Outlines the main provisions of the Act.

3001 United Kingdom, Department of the Environment. *Report of the Mobile Homes Review.* London, HMSO, 1977.

3002 United Kingdom, Ministry of Housing and Local Government. *Caravans as homes.* London, HMSO, 1959. (Cmnd. 872). The Wilson report.

23.2 North America

3003 Bernhardt, A. D. *Building tomorrow: the mobile/manufactured housing industry.* Cambridge, Mass., MIT Press, 1980.

3004 Buchanan J. and Burkert, F. *Mobile homes and mobile home living: a bibliography.* Monticello, Vance Bibliographies, 1979. (Public administration series bibliography no. P-363).

3005 Canada, Mortgage and Housing Corporation. *Planning for the mobile home: advisory document.* Ottawa, The Corporation, 1982.

3006 Center for Auto Safety. *Mobile homes: the low cost housing hoax: a report.* Toronto, Macmillan, 1975.

3007 Drury, M. J. *Mobile homes: the unrecognized revolution in American housing.* Rev. ed. New York, Praeger, 1972.

3008 Drury, M. J. 'Mobile homes: who lives in them and why?' *Habitat* vol. 2 nos. 3–4 (1977) pp. 303–10.

3009 Fessenden, A. 'An investigation of subsidized mobile homes for low income families'. *Tennessee Planner* vol. 33 no. 2 (1976) pp. 3–20.
Reasons why mobile homes neglected as a form of housing in the US, and characteristics of current mobile home owners.

3010 'Mobile homes'. *Popular Government* (Summer 1975).

Special issue, including regulation, taxation, and other aspects of mobile home ownership in the US.

3011   Swanick, E. L. *Mobile homes in Canada: a revised bibliography.* Monticello, Vance Bibliographies, 1979. (Public administration series bibliography no. P-301).

3012   Vasché, J. D. 'Structural change and mobile home housing'. *Business Economics* vol. 15 (Jan. 1980) pp. 35–40. Current state of the market and reasons for its growth during the 1970s.

3013   Weitzman, P. 'Mobile homes: high cost housing in the low income market'. *Journal of Economic Issues* vol. 10 (Sept. 1976) pp. 576–97.

24

Housing training and research

The growth of housing as a legitimate area of study in institutions of higher education in many parts of the world has led to increasing opportunities for academic research on housing policy issues. The parallel professionalization of the housing profession, particularly in the development of housing management, has created the need for formal training procedures for new recruits to the housing profession. The need for both education and training was emphasized in the recommendations of the United Nations Conference on Human Settlements (Habitat) in 1976. This section contains references to housing training and research as issues in their own right. Other sections may be referred to for applications of training and research to particular housing issues.

24.1 International and comparative

3014 Harloe, M. and Martens, M. 'Comparative housing research'. *Journal of Social Policy* vol. 13 no. 3 (July 1984) pp. 255–77.
  Review of 20 years of comparative housing research, discussion of problems, and ideas for the future.

3015 Hellstern, G. M. et al. (eds.) *Applied urban research: towards an internationalization of research and learning, vol. 3, housing policies and research.* Bonn, Bundesforschungsanstalt für Landeskunde

und Raumordnung, 1982.
Proceedings of the European Meeting on Applied Urban Research, Essen, Oct. 1981.

24.2 Europe

3016 European Communities Commission. *ENREP. Directory of Environmental Research Projects in the European Communities*. Stevenage, Peter Peregrinus, latest ed. 1982.
Part 1: Research projects. Part 2: Indexes.

24.3 United Kingdom

3017 British Library. *Research in British universities, polytechnics and colleges, vol. 3, social sciences*. London, The Library, annual.
National register of research undertaken in academic institutions, replacing since 1978 the *Scientific research in British universities and colleges*.

3018 City University. *Housing training: findings and recommendations: the final report*. London, The University, 1977. (Education and training for housing work project paper no. 31).

3019 City University. *Key issues in housing training: final report of the housing training project*. London, The University, 1981.

3020 City University. *Training in three housing organisations 1978–1979*. London, The University, 1980.

3021 Davies, E. M. (ed.) *INLOGOV register of local government research projects*. University of Birmingham, Institute of Local Government Studies, annual.
Housing included as separate category in listing of research currently undertaken in local government. Published material included.

3022 Economic and Social Research Council. *Research supported by the Economic and Social Research Council*. Merstham, School Government Publishing Co., annual.
List of research, including housing, supported by the ESRC

(formerly the Social Science Research Council).

3023   Groves, R. and Niner, P. *A register of housing research in England and Wales since 1980*. University of Birmingham, Centre for Urban and Regional Studies, 1983. (Research memorandum 95).

3024   Groves, R. and Niner, P. *A review of recent housing research in England and Wales*. University of Birmingham, Centre for Urban and Regional Studies, 1984. (Research memorandum 100).
Updates no. 3023.

3025   Hole, V. 'Social research in housing: a review of progress in Britain since World War II'. *Local Government Studies* vol. 5 no. 6 (Nov.–Dec. 1979) pp. 23–40.

3026   Institute of Housing. *'Where next?' A housing training policy statement*. London, The Institute, 1982.

3027   Local Government Training Board. *Identifying training needs in housing departments: a practical guide*. Luton, The Board, 1983.

3028   Merrett, S. 'University-based research into the British housing system'. *Habitat International* vol. 8 no. 2 (1984) pp. 11–30.

3029   Newson, T. *A second list of UK student theses and dissertations in planning and urban and regional studies*. University of Birmingham, Centre for Urban and Regional Studies, 1983. (Research memorandum 94).
Includes many housing theses and dissertations. Updates no. 3033.

3030   Tinker, A. and Brion, M. 'The dissemination of research findings with particular reference to housing'. *Journal of Social Policy* vol. 8 no. 1 (1979) pp. 61–82.

3031   United Kingdom, Department of the Environment. *Housing requirements: a guide to information and techniques*. London, HMSO, 1980.
Manual of information sources and research techniques for

local authority housing.

3032 United Kingdom, Department of the Environment. *Report on research and development.* London, HMSO, biennial. Reviews in-house and contracted research, including housing. Published annually since 1977, biennially since 1982.

3033 Veal, A. J. and Duesbury, W. K. *First list of UK student theses and dissertations in planning and urban and regional studies.* University of Birmingham, Centre for Urban and Regional Studies, 1976. (Research memorandum 55)
Comprehensive list of material from most institutions in the UK. Supported by author and subject indexes. Updated by no. 3029.

24.4 North America

3034 Cullingworth, J. B. *Canadian housing policy research — some initial impressions.* University of Toronto, Centre for Urban and Community Studies, 1980. (Research paper no. 117).

3035 Goering, J. 'Housing and public policies: a strategy for social science research'. *Urban Affairs Quarterly* vol. 17 no. 4 (June 1982) pp. 463–90.
Methodological strategy for policy research on housing issues.

3036 Goodrich, S. 'Training for housing work in Canada and the USA'. *Housing Review* vol. 26 no. 3 (May–June 1977) pp. 60–2.

3037 Wexler, H. J. and Peck, R. *Housing and local government: a research guide for policy makers and planners.* Lexington, Mass., Lexington Boks, 1975.
Study of policy related research on local housing services in the US.

24.5 Australasia

3038 Smith, B. N. and Thorns, D. C. 'Housing research: problems and possibilities'. *New Zealand Journal of Public Administration* vol. 40 (Mar. 1978) pp. 61–71.

24.6 Africa, Asia and Latin America

3039 Blair, T. 'Education for habitat'. *Architectural Association Quarterly* vol. 12 no. 1 (1980) pp. 8–21.
Housing training for developing countries.

3040 Boapeah, S. N. and Tipple, G. 'Estimating housing stock in a Third World city. A method used in Kumasi'. *Third World Planning Review* vol. 5 no. 2 (May 1983) pp. 177–88.
Study of Ghana.

3041 Childers, V. E. 'Housing in Latin America: a research agenda'. *International Journal for Housing Science and its Applications* vol. 3 no. 6 (1979) pp. 469–75.
Future research needed to explore consequences of US involvement in Latin American housing in the 1950s and 1960s.

3042 *Education and training: based partially on the UN Centre for Housing, Building and Planning meeting, Enschede, August 1978.* Oxford, Pergamon, 1979.
Special issue of *Habitat International* (vol. 4 nos. 1–2 (1979)) devoted to the training of planners, designers, builders and managers of human settlements.

3043 Haider, G. 'Design education and housing in the developing nations'. *Industrialization Forum* vol. 6 no. 2 (1975) pp. 35–46.

3044 Juppenlatz, M. 'A comprehensive approach to training for human settlements: a response to Habitat 1976'. *Third World Planning Review* vol. 1 no. 1 (Spring 1979) pp. 86–99.

3045 United Nations, Centre for Human Settlements. *Directory.*
Published in five parts, a directory of organizations in developing countries undertaking research and training in human settlements.

3046 United Nations, Centre for Human Settlements. *Training for improving human settlements.* Nairobi, United Nations, 1978.
Report of the ad hoc meetings of experts, Enschede, Aug. 1978.

3047   United Nations, Department of International Economic and Social Affairs. *Principles and recommendations for population and housing censuses.* New York, United Nations, 1981. (Statistical paper series M no. 67).

3048   Wakely, P. I. et al. *Urban housing strategies: education and realization.* London, Pitman, 1976.

The case for training of professionals in housing development, and training techniques and exercises, compiled by the Development Planning Unit, University College, London.

25

Statistics

This section makes reference to general works on housing statistics and the more significant statistical publications which cover a variety of housing issues. Statistics on specific aspects of housing policy such as housing market, construction and energy conservation, housing finance, and improvement and urban renewal are included with other references on these topics in sections 2, 3, 4 and 18 respectively.

25.1 International and comparative

3049   United Nations, Department of International Economic and Social Affairs. *Demographic yearbook*. New York, United Nations, annual.
   Includes statistics of population, cities and household formation.

3050   United Nations, Economic Commission for Europe. *Annual bulletin of housing and building statistics for Europe*. Geneva, United Nations, annual.
   Trends in housing and construction in Europe and North America.

3051   United Nations, Economic Commission for Europe. *A statistical survey of the housing situation in the ECE countries around 1970*. New York, United Nations, 1978.
   Housing conditions in Europe and North America.

25.2 Europe

3052 European Community. *Economic and social features of households in member states of the European Community.* Luxemburg, occasional.
Deals with statistical data on the family and household in the EC.

3053 European Community. *Eurostat review.* Luxemburg, annual.
Since 1981 has published the most significant EC statistics over a ten-year period and compared them with other areas.

3054 European Community. *Social indicators for the European Community 1960–1978.* Luxemburg, 1980.
See ch. 8 on housing.

3055 European Community. *Yearbook of regional statistics.* Luxemburg, annual.
Includes disaggregated statistics on a number of housing variables.

25.3 United Kingdom

3056 Farthing, S. M. *Housing in Great Britain.* London, Heinemann Educational, 1974. (Reviews of UK statistical sources vol. 3).
Bound with no. 3057. Seminal work on sources of statistics on UK housing policy.

3057 Fleming, M. C. *Housing in Northern Ireland.* London, Heinemann Educational, 1974. (Reviews of UK statistical sources vol. 4).
Bound with no. 3056.

3058 O'Dell, A. and Parker, J. *The use of census data to identify and describe housing stress.* Watford, Building Research Establishment, 1977. (Current paper 6/77).

3059 Penrice, G. 'Recent developments in housing statistics'. *Economic Trends* no. 181 (Nov. 1968) pp. xii–xxvii.

3060 Rayner, D. *Review of government statistical services: report by Sir Derek Rayner to the Prime Minister.* London, 1980.

Main recommendations reproduced in *Government statistical services* (London, HMSO, 1981, Cmnd. 8236), and interesting observations on the workings of the Department of the Environment in *The report of the study officer for the Departments of the Environment and Transport.*

3061 Schifferes, S. 'The use or misuse of housing statistics'. *Roof* vol. 5 no. 4 (July–Aug. 1980) pp. 106–8.

3062 Thomas, R. and Peacock, R. *Housing.* Milton Keynes, Open University, 1975.

Introduction to housing statistics measurements, definitions and methods employed in official data collection.

3063 United Kingdom, Central Statistical Office. *Annual abstract of statistics.* London, HMSO, annual.

Data on, for example, housing completions by tenure, public expenditure on housing, and council housing.

3064 United Kingdom, Central Statistical Office. *Guide to official statistics.* London, HMSO, 1982.

Essential guide to whole range of British official statistics, including section on housing.

3065 United Kingdom, Central Statistical Office. *Social trends.* London, HMSO, annual.

Annual review of social indicators in the UK, including comprehensive section on housing.

3066 United Kingdom, Central Statistical Office. *United Kingdom national accounts.* London, HMSO, annual.

Contains statistics on housing accounts, rents and subsidies, and loans for house purchase. Formerly known as *National income and expenditure* (The Blue Book).

3067 United Kingdom, Department of the Environment. *Housing and construction statistics.* London, HMSO.

Quarterly issued in two parts, and annual cumulation covering ten-year period, of main UK housing statistics.

3068   United Kingdom, Department of the Environment. *Local housing statistics*. London, HMSO, quarterly.
  Variety of housing statistics for each local authority area in England and Wales.

3069   United Kingdom, Department of the Environment. *National dwelling and housing survey*. London, HMSO, 1979.

3070   United Kingdom, Department of the Environment. *National dwelling and housing survey. Phases 2 and 3*. London, HMSO, 1980.

3071   United Kingdom, Office of Population Censuses and Surveys. *Census 1981: housing and households England and Wales*. London, HMSO, 1983.
  Housing results from the last national decennial census.

3072   United Kingdom, Office of Population Censuses and Surveys. *Recently moving households: a follow up to the 1978 national dwelling and housing survey*. London, HMSO, 1984. (SS 1126).

3073   United Kingdom, Registrar General, Scotland. *Census 1981: Scotland: housing and household report*. Edinburgh, HMSO, 1984.

3074   United Kingdom, Scottish Development Department. *Scottish housing statistics*. Edinburgh, HMSO, annual.
  Quarterly to 1982, annual from 1983.

3075   United Kingdom, Scottish Office. *Scottish abstract of statistics*. Edinburgh, HMSO, annual.

3076   United Kingdom, Welsh Office. *Digest of Welsh statistics*. Cardiff, HMSO, annual.

3077   United Kingdom, Welsh Office. *Welsh housing statistics*. Cardiff, HMSO, annual.

25.4 North America

3078   Beveridge, A. *Reliability in large scale household surveys: the case of the annual housing survey*. City University of New York,

Queens College, Department of Sociology, 1982.

3079   Canada Mortgage and Housing Corporation. *Canadian housing statistics*. Ottawa, The Corporation, annual.

3080   Fuller, P. 'Canadian housing statistics: CMHC's unique statistical service'. *Habitat* vol. 24 no. 2 (1981) pp. 26–8.
Discusses the range of valuable statistics on Canadian housing collected and published by the Canada Mortgage and Housing Corporation.

3081   Goering, J. *Housing in America: the characteristics and uses of the annual housing survey*. Washington, DC, Department of Housing and Urban Development, Office of Policy Development and Research, 1979. (Annual housing survey studies no. 6).

3082   United States, Bureau of the Census. *Annual housing survey*. Washington, DC, The Bureau, annual.
Statistics published in various parts for the US and its regions:
A General housing characteristics
B Indicators of housing and neighborhood quality by financial characteristics
C Financial characteristics of the housing inventory
D Housing characteristics
E Urban and rural housing characteristics
F Financial characteristics by indicators of housing and neighborhood quality.

3083   United States, Bureau of the Census. *Statistical abstract of the United States: national data book and guide to sources*. Washington, DC, The Bureau, annual.
Includes sections on construction and housing and comparative international statistics.

3084   United States, Bureau of the Census. *Vacancy rates and characteristics of housing in the United States: annual statistics*. Washington, DC, The Bureau, annual.

3085   United States, Department of Housing and Urban Development. *Statistical yearbook*. Washington, DC, The Department, annual.

Detailed data on operations of the Department and statistical information on housing.

25.5   Australasia

3086   New Zealand, Department of Statistics. *The census of population and dwellings.* Wellington, The Department, five-yearly.

3087   New Zealand, Department of Statistics. *Report of the review committee on housing statistics.* Wellington, The Department, 1979.

3088   Walker, P. A. and Davis, J. R. 'Reconciling dwelling stock estimates with census data'. *Review of Public Data Use* vol. 9 no. 3 (Nov. 1981) pp. 167–74.
Difficulties of estimating private dwelling stock between censuses in Australia. Use of electricity meter records is discussed.

Author index

This index contains an entry for the author or editor of each work included in the bibliography. The names of joint authors and editors are also included, but as in the main text, where three or more authors are responsible for a work, only the first-named appears in the index. A work by a corporate body appears under the name of that body, and a work by a government agency for which there is no clearly defined personal author is indexed under the **name of** the country followed by the agency, e.g. UK, Department of the **Environ**ment. Numbers refer to items rather than pages.

AUTHOR INDEX

Subject index

This index contains entries for each of the major subjects covered in the bibliography. The numbers against each heading refer to the first and last entries of the section in which that subject appears. A *see* reference refers to a preferred heading used in the main text and a *see under* reference refers to a larger section in which that subject appears.